FROM *BIOGRAPHY* TO *HISTORY*

THE HISTORICAL IMAGINATION AND
AMERICAN FICTION, 1880–1940

FROM

Biography

TO

History

The Historical Imagination and
AMERICAN FICTION, 1880–1940

Lois Hughson

University Press of Virginia

Again, for Howard

THE UNIVERSITY PRESS OF VIRGINIA
Copyright © 1988 by the Rector and Visitors
of the University of Virginia
First published 1988

Library of Congress Cataloging-in-Publication Data
Hughson, Lois.
    From biography to history : the historical imagination and
American fiction, 1880–1940 / Lois Hughson.
      p.   cm.
    Includes index.
    ISBN 0-8139-1157-5
    1. American fiction—20th century—History and criticism.
2. Literature and history. 3. American fiction—19th century—
History and criticism. 4. Biography (as a literary form)
5. Historical fiction, American—History and criticism. I. Title.
PS374.H5H84 1988
813'.4'09358—dc 19   87-25272
                                                                              CIP

Printed in the United States of America

Contents

ACKNOWLEDGMENTS

I wish to thank Studies in the Novel *for the use of material that first appeared there in my articles* "Dreiser's Cowperwood and the Dynamics of Naturalism," *16 (Spring 1984), and* "Dos Passos's World War: Narrative Technique and History," *121 (Spring 1980). I also thank* Dickens Studies Annual: Essays on Victorian Fiction *for the use of my article* "History and Biography as Models for Narrative: James's The Bostonians, The Princess Casamassima, and The Tragic Muse," *13 (1984). Chapter 2, "Biography as an Education of Consciousness," first appeared as "Power and Self in Henry Adams's Art of Biography," in* Biography: An Interdisciplinary Quarterly, *7:4 (1984), © 1984 by the Biographical Research Center. Some material from my conference paper "From Biography to History: Competing Models for Fiction in James, Howells and Dos Passos" is reprinted from* CUNY English Forum, I *by permission of AMS Press, Inc.*

I wish also to thank my colleagues at Queens College, especially Frederick Buell, William P. Kelly III, and Fred Kaplan for their faith and intellectual encouragement. And I thank Ellen Zimmerman and Howard Hughson for their exemplary patience and generosity.

FROM *BIOGRAPHY* TO *HISTORY*

THE HISTORICAL IMAGINATION AND

AMERICAN FICTION, 1880–1940

Introduction

In *The Education of Henry Adams,* one of the great summary texts of nineteenth-century American intellectual life, Henry Adams wrote a history of his period in the form of a biography, and in it expressed the bankruptcy of history as biography. Adams's rejection spoke for an important rethinking of the individual's relation to his experience that was common in America during the period from 1880 to 1940. His rejection and consequent search for new versions of historical narrative are my starting point for a study of history and biography as models for the American novel at a time when historical narrative itself was changing.

Much of the comment on what Adams is supposed to have failed to tell us about his life hinges on a conception of his book as an autobiography. Yet in treating his life as if it were another's and in finding its point and shape in the historical events in which it is embedded rather than in the personal events he so egregiously omitted, he self-consciously placed the book in the company of the biographies of his earlier career, and for the purposes of this study I will leave it there, not pursuing here the interesting but distracting question of the relationship between biography and autobiography, another book in itself. The importance of the *Education* for this study lies in its pursuit of the relationship of the biographical to the historical. Indeed, Adams's book moves toward a theory of history as the culmination of its narrative, thereby emphasizing its central importance in his long meditation on biography and history as narrative modes.

Ralph Waldo Emerson had written: "The world exists for the education of man."[1] He believed that everything in history corresponded to something in a man's own life. "All history becomes subjective; in other words there is properly no history, only biography," he concluded. In the *Education,* Adams both denied and affirmed the idea that the world existed for the education of man. He sought a moral education that would teach him the relative value and the meaning of things. What he wanted to learn was not only the source of his coherence and continuity as an individual but the source of the coherence and continuity of his culture. What he found, in the Civil War, in the Italian fight for independence, in the Grant administration, in aesthetic taste, in personal relations, in geology, in biology, in chemistry, and in physics, was incoherence and discontinuity. What he did not find was any reason to suppose that what had happened could be taken for a guide to what would happen or to how he should act.

For Adams the history of the Western world was an intolerable acceleration of events concluding in what he calls the "supersensual chaos" of 1900.[2] At that point, the recognizable world of people and actions yielded to a world of atoms and energy. The revelation of the inexhaustible power of radium was the climax of Western history and created a crisis for Adams in the writing of history. The historical world he had so masterfully created earlier in the *Education,* full of contradictory motives, competing goals, social roles, institutions, the arts, appetite, and love, did not and could not yield the principles of its own existence. Occupied only with it, the historian would never be able to establish sequence or show cause and effect, let alone distribute praise and blame. After 1900, Adams turned instead to a world abstracted to forces, orbits, and calculations, hoping to bring to fruition a theory of history that would make it possible "to plot the past and future orbit of the human race as accurately as that of the November meteorides" (501). The picture of man in the *Education* confronting multiplicity and humbled by his failure to understand or dominate his experience is moving. The image of power restored through the new theory of history is chilling in its abstraction and inhumanity.

Yet the theory was an attempt to reenter history which for a time appeared threateningly to be a process which went on outside of man—impenetrable—in which he had no active part. If man's reason was not what his grandfather's eighteenth-century world told him it was and his will was not the instrument of moral judgment that Emerson's generation believed it to be, then the grounds for participation in a history conceived in these terms seemed to him exhausted. However, if the energy of radium was the energy of history, then man, who he feared initially had only the power to react to force that was outside him, could come to know and to manage its energy so that his will would be energized anew and he would no longer be alienated from his history and his own life. In the sixty years from 1880 to 1940, historical writing came repeatedly to grapple with the problem of overcoming man's alienation from historical change and with the need to understand the principles which governed it in such a way that men and women would regain a measure of power. And not historians alone, but novelists also sought in history an alternative to the growing sense of disorder and loss of power apparent from the perspective of the individual life.

I

Adams's *Education* marks a turning point in the conception of history in an American culture particularly aware just then of history as a way of explaining itself. The period from the 1880s to the 1930s in America is marked by realism, a movement especially concerned with the dynamics of society and with the attempt in its literary form, as Erich Auerbach characterized it, to embed the individual in the course of history.[3] But what does it mean to embed the individual in the course of history? Such an enterprise means more than invoking the manners and public events of the period of the novel. Costume dramas, whether set in the past or the present, do not in themselves embed the individual in the course of history. The novelist himself must have a particular view of experience marked by a sense of history. In rejecting Emerson's conception of history as biography, that is, the account of man's birth, childhood, and maturation, Adams was essentially branding that conception ahistorical. Adams could not agree with Emerson that experience educated us for more experience, nor could he imagine history to be like our personal experience, an education of consciousness that prepares us to know ourselves and to master our world. This was to imagine continuity, not disjunction, as the fundamental characteristic of history, to see a coherence in experience that mirrors the coherence of the self.

For Emerson the mysterious reaches of the past were lit and peopled by man's insight into his own nature. Distant lands and cultures otherwise mute spoke their meanings and took reasonable shapes as our own intellectual and spiritual lives deepened and expanded. Only "when a thought of Plato becomes a thought to me will the history of the Greeks come alive," he wrote. History, then, was essentially a study of the individual, whose capacities "predict the world he is to inhabit as the fins of fish foreshadow that water exists." These conceptions combine to abolish the sense of forward moving time and real change essential to the historical sense that developed in the later nineteenth century. These two elements were central to the writers who are the subjects of this study when they thought of history.

Emerson's view relegated history to a category of moral philosophy or to a storehouse of texts for spiritual meditation, exhortation, and instruction. Whatever the individual changes in their view of history, these later writers all thought of it as the appearance and transformation of concrete forms through time. They would all have agreed with Leopold von Ranke, who midway in the nineteenth century denied to his own historical narrative the possibility of judging the past or instructing the present for the benefit of the future. His purpose, in the famous phrase that echoed through American history and fiction from Adams to John Dos Passos, was "to show only what really happened."[4] What the English philosopher R. G. Collingwood wrote in the 1930s would have been understood by these writers of the preceding fifty years. Historical thinking, he argued, was a fundamental activity of the mind. In seeking to understand what really happened, historical thinking takes a position that is not allowed for by the traditional dichotomy in philosophy between "perception which is of the here and now" and "abstract thought which is of the everywhere and always." Historical thought is exclusively neither. It is abstract thought—or what Collingwood calls "reasoned knowledge"—of the "transient and concrete."[5]

The surrender of moral judgment and instruction was one characteristic of the history Adams strove to write, and the faith in historical thinking as a distinct mode of knowledge, dominated by a vision of particular events occurring through time, was another. An important third characteristic was the surrender of Emerson's view of the individual's relation to the past. All these writers inverted the Emersonian dependence of history's form and purpose on the individual. Rejecting the great strain of romantic optimism that fuels Emerson's celebration of the individual's capacity to master and reshape his world, denying a view that makes the past man's childhood, they rejected also the Jeffersonian faith in a human reason that can mold society according to a

human nature that transcends time and place. The European historian
Wilhelm Dilthey spoke for an important strain in the two generations
that spanned the turn of the century in America when he called for the
surrender of the individual to the forces of history as a way of liberation
"from the pain of the moment and egotistical joy."[6] Like Adams responding to the exhaustion of romantic individualism, the immobiliza-
tion of individual power, and the elusiveness of personal gratification,
he argued that "neither subjective caprice nor egotistic pleasure can
reconcile man with life. Only surrender of his sovereign personality to
the course of the world can effect this reconciliation."

The Education of Henry Adams shows an American consciousness
coming to this conclusion. The failure that Adams writes of, whatever
its connection to his own psychological dynamics, is not merely personal failure. He means to expose the inadequacy of inherited views of
historical events. The evolutionary theories, the psychologies of individual effort and will, the unexamined assumptions about the centrality of political action and the power of institutions, all these failed to
provide adequate explanations, let alone predictions, of events. The
dense chapters in which he wrestles with imperfectly understood laws
of science and mathematics in an attempt to transform historical studies are his response to his dissatisfaction with the explanatory force of
individual action. His efforts to see history in a new way entailed "the
surrender of his sovereign personality."

While Carlyle, who believed with Emerson that history was the
sum of many biographies, sought in his philosophy of clothes finally to
uncover the authentic self, Adams begins his *Education* by telling us
that the object of his study is the garment, not the figure. And more
inportantly, that once the garment—the education that will teach the
economy of forces—is achieved, the manikin, only a tool like a geo-
metrical figure used for the study of relation, may be discarded. He
speaks of his particular self but means at the same time any self—the
individual becomes mere convenience for the measure of the human
condition and the forces that act on it making history. His reasons for
willingly dispensing with the concept of the self are bitterly recounted
at the end of the *Education* in his fable of the mind:

> *Every fabulist has told how the human mind has always struggled like*
> *a frightened bird to escape the chaos which caged it; how—appearing*
> *suddenly and inexplicably out of some unknown and unimaginable*
> *void; passing half its known life in the mental chaos of sleep; victim*

even when awake, to its own ill-adjustment, to disease, to age, to external suggestion, to nature's compulsion; doubting its sensations, and in the last resort, trusting only to instruments and averages—after sixty or seventy years of growing astonishment, the mind wakes to find itself looking blankly into the void of death. That it should profess itself pleased by this performance was all that the highest rules of good breeding could ask; but that it should actually be satisfied would prove that it existed only as idiocy. (460)

It was just Adams's growing view of history as science rather than literature, that is, as a more privileged discourse and as the narrative of group movements rather than individual action, that made it a powerful alternative to the beseiged biographical principal, both for Adams in the *Education* and for Henry James, William Dean Howells, and John Dos Passos in their novels.

II

It has been impossible thus far to speak of the changing concepts of history without references to ideas about biography. Nor is it possible to speak of the way the novel uses history as a model without reference to ideas about biography. When Auerbach speaks of embedding the individual in history we recognize an implicit distinction between the biographical and the historical that reflects a desire to transcend the "sovereign personality." In *The Theory of the Novel*, Georg Lukács argues that the novel overcomes what he calls "its 'bad' infinity" by "recourse to the biographical form." The hero's experiences limit the scope of the world while its multiplicity—to use Adams's word—can be organized "by his development towards finding the meaning of life in self-recognition."[7]

The use of biography as a model in the novel must always, however, be at variance with the simultaneous effort to embed the individual in the course of history. The tension is least when the idea of history emphasizes the rise of a society which follows the biographical model, a rise marked by a concern with coherence, identity, self-recognition, and definition of will. For the historian who sees history as coming to an end in the present, history itself is close to biography. If like Ranke, the historian sees the past as the process by which the nation states of his age come into being and the future as the continuity of the forms they have achieved, then the process of history is analogous to the process of the maturation of the individual.[8]

Nor is the tension between history and biography great when, as Carlyle and Emerson believed, "the whole purport" of history is biographical. For Carlyle the biographer and historian alike should satisfy "the hope to see how other men, now gone, took part in moral contests and triumphed over or were defeated by 'the Devil.'"[9] While some scholars, because man cannot be separated from social cultural and economic forces, consider biography as history in microcosm,[10] other theorists wish to secure their distinction on the grounds that history is not the accumulation of biographies but "generalized narrative."[11] Indeed most biographers would agree that their aim is not merely to tell the story of a self but to make a self live.[12] In American biography the question is particularly complicated by the fact that lives and events were inextricable in early American writing. John Norton, in his life of John Cotton (1657), spoke of biography as the history of particular men's lives. And in the histories of John Winthrop and William Bradford, the public event is providential, and individuals are agents of Providence, whose special concern in early American experience is the life of the community. Furthermore, not only was the private experience of conversion a public act for the Puritan, but the individual action was also inseparable from the purposes and ends of the community. So from the outset in American letters, biography and history were very close.[13]

The familiar distinction between the two that was early made by Dryden in his preface to Plutarch's *Lives* (1686) is also instructive. He writes: "There you are conducted only into the rooms of state, here you are led into the private lodgings of the hero: you see him in his undress, and are made familiar with his most private actions and conversations." Such a distinction leaves important identities untouched. It merely changes the locus of action, retaining the individual at the center of the public as of the private, without illuminating the issue of whether political actions must be understood in different terms from personal. The same blurring of senses can be seen in another early example, the work of John Aubrey, who is regarded by a present-day critic as more historian than biographer because he recorded the social and intellectual movements of his time rather than the character of individuals, a distinction Aubrey apparently did not make.

Similarly, an opposition between biography and history may

seem to disappear if the individual is seen as a locus of historical forces. As when Henry Adams tried out this concept in his biographies and early history, such a view may seek to explain our sense of the importance of individual action without ascribing to it a power whose real source is elsewhere. In his work, this view also devalues the interest and importance of the personal and distinctive as opposed to the shared or public and rejects the centrality of the biological. However, one of the most interesting contemporary theorists dealing with the intersection of biography and history, Cushing Strout, recasts the relationship by seeing that part of the biographical subject of the development of the self as the "emergence of the person into the role of a historical agent."[14] But this emergence was just what was most doubtful to the subjects of this study. The disappearance of the opposition between biography and history, then, depends, as in all these explanations of their relationship, not only on what writers take these terms to mean but on how much power the individual as an agent is seen to have.

In the later nineteenth century, when the individual plays a less central role in historians' understanding, the biographical becomes more sharply differentiated from the historical than it had been in the eighteenth century. The new distinction comes through with great clarity in the little controversy between William James and the historian John Fiske in the 1880s.

Trying to maintain the individual's commanding position in the face of historians' growing valuations of transpersonal elements in events, James demanded to know whether anyone else could have written Shakespeare's plays. The question in itself suggests how hard put James was; pushed into the realm of art where few historians ventured, where mystery and fable reigned uncontested, and individual psychology still seemed absolute, he thought at least there he could elicit but one answer. The popular historian John Fiske, however, took the debate back to an arena familiar to historians, an arena that had once been witness to the triumph of individual intention and power, when he replied: "one might learn all of Plutarch's lives by heart and still have made very little progress towards comprehending the reasons why the Greek states were never able to form a coherent political aggregate."[15]

The distinction between biography and history also emerges in the discussion among its practitioners that revolves around the question of how truthful a biography should be. What right has the public to the most private incidents of a subject's life, incidents sometimes painful, even shaming, and frequently, at the least, deflating in their effects? The question may arise from a desire to affirm the public hero as a reflection of the private man. But the very framing of the question expresses the pressure against such an identity, the new willingness to see the true biography as private and revealingly intimate with personality and ego.[16] While the biographers' debate over the fullness of truth is a part of a process which distinguishes biography from history, it also shows the newly felt pressures on the idea of the coherent self that Adams so vividly expressed. Not respectability alone, as Carlyle had complained, argued against the whole truth in biography. The desire was not merely to cling to a heroic view of the subject but to a consistent view. Unpleasant truths were assaults on the coherent self that were ill-tolerated in a period when it was besieged not only in historical narrative but also in the rising psychological sciences.

III

What we mean then by historical or biographical models is itself rooted in the historical context and the assumptions contained within it. Nevertheless, I would argue that, primarily, a biographical model of narrative moves toward coherence and identity, while a historical model seeks to show the way the past explains the present and to uncover the essential forces that make for change. In a biography, as the subject's identity is established, the degree of change the narrative depicts diminishes. Historical narrative, however, has no inherent reason to trace a pattern of change diminishing toward stasis, though it may show such a pattern if it is written on the model of biography, that is, if it intends to show the birth, growth, and maturation of a society on the model of a human life or if it is based on the model of religious narrative, which moves toward a revelation of God's order. Otherwise, in the biological aspect of human experience, there is something foreign, if not inimical, to history. Because of biology, biography is subject to laws of reproduction, aging, and death that are only metaphors in the history written on the model of biography.[17] Furthermore, while some conception of the individual self, whether or not capable of self-recognition or a consciousness adequate to its experience, is the essence of biography, the individual self is not necessary to historical narrative. The "infinity" of the narrative may be limited by recourse to other principles, such as groups, land, money, steampower: in other words, any concept of agency or focus of power. In looking beyond a single consciousness, history's standard of coherence is more capacious, its tolerence of conflict and multiplicity greater, its view of experience potentially broader and fuller.

The tension between the models of history and biography is further complicated by the fact that the self has often been for biographers, as Adams suggests in his *Education,* a frame for hanging views of experience. Underlying Lukács's conception of the novel as biography is the assumption that experience is the education of consciousness to self-awareness and self-definition, and what the *Education* makes clear is that as the idea of history changed, so did the idea of biography. By the end of the century it was no longer possible to take such a view of experience and of biography without radical redefinition. As inclusiveness and transindividual experience become more important in theories about the way things really happen, then the idea that experience educates is hard-pressed. Just as the individual is reduced in power and importance in the historian's explanation of events, so is his consciousness reduced in the novelist's explanation of the character's life. And the narrative model is no longer the progress of the character toward self-recognition; the reader is invited to see and understand many things that the character never perceives. When Adams came to visualize and advocate history as the center of a new curriculum that would prepare men and women for twentieth-century multiplicity, it was as a specific replacement for the long moral tradition that placed the individual self at the center of the world. His own excursions into biography early in the period of this study show both the older tradition and his transformation of it.

And finally, the metahistorical concern over whether history gives us knowledge or opinion is part of the impetus toward changing historical narrative and has a bearing on its attraction for fiction. When the self-described "scientific" historian of the nineteenth century thought he could present all the facts and let them speak for themselves, he thought he was surmounting the moralizing of earlier historians and their nationalistic or sectarian biases as well. Adams's effort to write a new program for scientific history came from a conviction that such a presentation of facts could speak only chaos, never yielding what he sought: sequence, he called it, reliable, true causal linkage. His rejection of the dominant scientific disciplines of his young manhood, paleontology and biology, as models arose from his perception of them as contaminated by desires and expectations which led to a pretense of causal links in the theory of evolution unsupported by evidence. At the beginning of progressive history as it was written by Charles Beard and Frederick Jackson Turner, the historian believed he was uncovering hitherto overlooked or hidden aspects of the past which would, by making events transparent, allow the principles which underlay them to shine through with rational explanations. Even when Beard, in the 1930s, realized the degree to which relativism and subjectivity ruled the historical narrative, he never surrendered the belief, or as he called it, the faith, that the historian brought us true knowledge. The novelist turned to the historical model because he, too, was looking for more reliable, fuller explanations of the way things happen. With the discovery that facts were dumb, however, and that the historian's purpose imposed a meaning, the relation between fiction and history was altered. While awareness of the historian's purpose and presuppositions was offered as insurance for the truth of his history, there was no way to eliminate the personal, and the writing of history reached the end of a vital period in its existence when it could be looked to by other forms of narrative seeking to render human experience more truly.

IV

Henry James and William Dean Howells both turned from biography to history as a model for the novel in the 1880s and 1890s. As a group, their novels of this period are distinguished by a concern with social change, an interest in explaining events in terms of the consequences of the past, and in creating characters whose situations cannot entirely be understood outside of historically determined circumstances and whose destiny cannot be explained without reference to the processes of the public world. The model of biography persists in all of them, and its competition with the historical model is sometimes a source of great richness and sometimes a factor in the novel's failure to be fully realized. But while the biographical model persists, it does so in a way that questions the idea of the self and that proposes through the multiple perspectives of the historical model a self that is less coherent and less differentiated from its circumstances than modern biography had hitherto assumed. A lively biographical theorist, James Clifford, today criticizes biography as "bound to a still-active myth of personal coherence" and wants to redefine it "as a narrative of transindividual occasions" ("Looking Glasses," 52). These late twentieth-century doubts about biography's underlying view of experience and their consequences for the writing of biography have their roots in the period of this study and form an important part of the matrix in which the American novel turned toward history. James and Howells wished not only to show their characters in time and moving through time but to expand the time that is properly the characters' as well as the space that is theirs so that on all sides a proper understanding of experience is seen as transcending the individual and as favoring plenitude over coherence. To multiply the perspectives in which the actions of the novel appear, to place the characters in a moment of social change with roots in a social past and expectations of a social future, to show them as playing multiple roles with varying demands made of them and contradictory responses arising from them, to withhold resolution of the action at the conclusion of the novel and to see it instead as ongoing into a future created in part by the elements of the novel's present is to approach even the reality of our inner lives with greater truth, rendering its discontinuities, rich potentialities, and inconsistencies rather than a mythic single self that once discovers its essence and acts in accordance with it.

However, Theodore Dreiser, coming to much the same conclusions about the falseness of traditional views of action, morality, and power as did Henry Adams, nevertheless rejected history as a way of establishing rational sequence in human affairs. In the tradition of Emerson, reflecting the Emersonian equivocality about the individual's exercise of power, Dreiser sought to understand experience through representative lives, and biography wholly supplants history as a model for his fiction. Nevertheless, his idea of the self is also much less individuated and greatly dependent on transindividual experience for its definition. In contrast, his younger contemporary John Dos Passos made the most thoroughgoing attempt of all these writers to write fiction on the model of history. In *U.S.A.* he entirely subordinates biography to history in an effort to transcend his characters' powerlessness and inability to understand their own lives.

The competition between the historical and biographical models in fiction from James to Dos Passos is inseparable from the changing view of history that can be followed in the historical narratives of Adams and Dos Passos. These changes turn on the same questions about the sources of historical energy, the morality of history, and the place of intention in human action that govern the competition between the historical and biographical models in fiction. The irony of Adams's *History of the United States of America during the Administrations of*

Jefferson and Madison (1889–91) comes from a recognition that history does not support the individual's claim to power, that the gap between intention and achievement is great. Adams makes this recognition while continuing to resist the view of historical change that does not have human agency at its center. Adams's dynamic theory of history is his attempt to transcend that irony and reconstitute the relation of action and intention so that historical development would not be, as he described it early in his career, as unconscious as that of a tree. The attempt to transcend irony is linked always to salvaging the individual's claim to power in some form.

Dos Passos's novels on the model of history, in contrast, transcend irony only through the surrender of this claim to power. For him the gap between experience and history can never be closed; experience remains irrational and the individual impotent. Only in history, that is, in a conceptualization of the relation of the past and present, can the fragmentary nature of experience be completed and made comprehensible. Like Adams he believed that none of us can master experience while we are in its midst but in possessing our history we overcome our alienation.

My study of these fictional and historical narratives moves from Adams's rejection of Emersonian history and his subsequent search for a way for man to take part in the energy of history to James's and Howells's use of historical and biographical models. It then examines Dreiser's decisive rejection of the historical model and his loyalty to biography as the sole model of arriving at the authentic in social as well as personal experience in spite of his denial that experience educates. My study turns finally to Dos Passos's efforts to reorder the relation of biography to history both in fictional and historical narrative.

These writers as a group represent a moment in American cultural life when history promised a great deal as an integrating intellectual mode. But even at its most influential, there were doubts and outright rejections of its significance and value. There were always other writers of this period, like Edith Wharton and Willa Cather, for whom, as for Dreiser, the biographical model for fiction had no competition, or if it did, as for the late James and the rising modernist, it was to be found in myth rather than history. Yet any attempt to lead a rational life must come to grips with the historical as well as the merely individual dimension of our existence, and the writers who are the subject of this study made the most powerful and moving efforts in our literature to understand their connection.

1 Henry Adams and the Irony of Political History

Although it is only in *The Education of Henry Adams* that Adams explicitly rejected a view of history dominated by human motive and achievement and supported by the conviction that our communal past, like our own present experience, constitutes an education that fits us for our lives, the *History of the United States of America during the Administrations of Jefferson and Madison* shows in its pervasive irony that he doubted the validity of such a history from the first. A monument to the realist credo of representing events objectively, it adheres to the realist faith that such an objective representation, in rejecting the dramatic, the artistic, the impressionistic, and the moralistic, not only could show how things really happened but would figure forth the principles of their happening. Yet Adams's *History* carries in it the skepticism that taints in one way or another realism's claim to an unmediated yet coherent vision.[1] While he has no doubts yet about his methodology, the irrationality of what it uncovers gives rise to the irony that dissolves realism's assumptions about the role of men in social change.

The emergence of a stable political identity in the United States is the organizing principle of the *History* as a whole and the touchstone by which all its events are judged. The constitutional questions raised by the Louisiana Purchase and the preeminence of the Supreme Court and the foreign policy questions of embargo and war are all considered in the light of their contribution to the political form that would permit America to survive and grow. The irony with which Adams recounts

Jefferson's political and social aims, however, dissolves not only Jefferson's claim to shaping this political identity but the pretensions of any individual to such a role.

When Henry Steel Commager says in his introduction to the 1930 edition of the *History* that Adams was really just writing a conventional political diplomatic history and cannot be credited with anything new in historical narrative, he is thinking of the dramatic change in historical writing after Adams's day toward cultural history, toward a history that includes events below the sphere of the great public moment.[2] The distinction of Adams's *History* from earlier American history lies rather in its approach to events and in his conception of the kind of narrative that would best reflect the nature and significance of those events. Central to this conception is Adams's view of human agency, of the relation of men to the events which comprise both their lives and our history. It is, therefore, crucially important to determine what constitutes an explanation for events in this history.

I

In the conclusion of the *History,* Adams tells us that the United States, because of its isolation from Europe, gives us the opportunity to trace in its history the evolution of a race, and by race he means a people and a nation both.[3] "Race" seems to promise an epic and what David Levin calls history as romantic art. But Adams's model in that sentence is scientific, not literary. Implicit in the call for "scientific" history, as Adams understood and practiced it in the 1880s, was the presentation of evidence that could speak for itself. The historian was a guide, but not someone privileged by being acquainted with evidence unknown to the reader. Not for him was the role appropriated by a Francis Parkman or a George Bancroft, an omniscient voice offering a synthesis of material not specified or brought before the reader for his judgment.[4] One of the assumptions underlying that kind of synthesis was that the unprejudiced observer could have but one understanding of the meaning and motive of the actions recounted. In the much less stable moral world of the *History,* not only could the evidence speak for itself, but it had to speak for itself. The historian was no longer morally privileged, trusted by the reader for judgments of the moral quality and significance of the actions he recounted. The model for history was neither biography, nor epic, nor tragedy. Readers of history could no longer expect to read the story of a single man whose life provided either a moral example or a spiritually energizing view of human possibility.

Nor was history any longer the account of the actions that formed the people, that made a nation, that legitimized its past and justified its present. Nor was its subject the downfall of former greatness, made inevitable by moral fissures and the worm of time. Nor was it the triumph of reason. Insofar as it was "scientific," history meant the presentation of documents by a historian whose role as moral guide had diminished and the search for the general historical principles underlying the events under review. The colorful, emotional, dramatic, these were the mere picturesque of history, looked down upon by Adams as they would be by the realist novelist William Dean Howells or the realist painter Thomas Eakins. And finally, of utmost importance, the underlying metaphor, the paradigm shaping the historical narrative of the *History,* was to be from evolutionary science: the emergence of a new organism through its adaptation to its environment.[5]

Because of Adams's claim that he presented individuals as types, many scholars see character as central to the *History.* Early in the critical literature, William Jordy found the comparison of Jefferson to Napoleon an organizing principle, and most recently William Dusinberre wrote of the way Adams develops Jefferson's character by contrasting it with the men who surround him.[6] However, Adams's use of character is rather different from what is usually implied by such a term, and the fact that he rarely uses it himself, but speaks of his historical figures as types, is no accident. Strikingly, we learn nothing about these men that does not bear directly on the public event of which they are a part. The scene in which Napoleon shouts at his brother from the bathtub stands out as an almost unique example of the exploitation of colorful private circumstances. The use of character to explain actions is downplayed, and the impetus of the book is to find explanations in the public sphere. When political, economic, diplomatic, or commercial necessity cannot explain an action, only then is character evoked. When character is called on as explanation, it is often shown to be in the service of policy, not the reverse, as when Adams tells us that truth and deceit were equally good policies in Napoleon's eyes. But as Adams explicitly states, character counts for most in diplomacy and battle. Accordingly, the most prominent example of character as explanation is in the account of the treaty commission. Here, Gallatin is shown to be the strongest and most intelligent of the commissioners and thereby becomes the chief architect of the favorable treaty. Similarly, in the burning of Washington and the military campaign in New York State, personal qualities of judgment and courage are shown to count for much. What we must remember, however, is that the battles and diplomatic efforts do not count for much in the outcome of the major action in the *History.*

It is true that the reader often feels that, far from being types, the actors are realized in quite vivid, individual ways. Through their own letters, through the letters of others about them, and through Adams's comments, their personalities as well as their characters unquestionably appear as elements in the events. This, however, is a far cry from calling character the central interest of the *History.* Jordy uses the fact that Adams withholds sympathy for Jefferson's private suffering during his last years as president as evidence of Adams's interest in the statesman only as a participant in significant events. However, Jordy makes a distinction between character—the public figure—and personality—the private man—that allows him to discuss Adams's work in terms of "public morality" (65). The *History,* in his view, is "the greatest moral history ever produced in America" (67). This approach has been highly influential in subsequent studies, and it is part of Richard Vitzthium's formulation that includes Adams with historians like Parkman and Bancroft. Yet such a view makes assumptions about choice, responsibility, and moral judgment that the *History* itself does not make. Jordy's own work shows how such conceptions of character are inseparable from certain kinds of narrative. In his discussion of character, Jordy speaks of the historical moment of which Adams wrote as "a moment when democracy became a nation, when it finally flung aside both foreign domination and its own internal doubts to assert the power of that larger community of interest which posterity has simplified into the 'era of good feelings' "(75). This sentence with its personifications and active verbs, with its inferences of choice and achieved intention, is foreign to the *History.* Physical circumstance, acquisitive instinct, European politics, the interplay of conflicting and failing policies—these fuel the push toward nationalism, not choice, intent, and rationality.

Jordy quotes Adams's review of Hermann Von Holst's *Constitutional and Political History of the United States* in the *North American Review* of 1876 to support his argument that Adams was interested in character—moral behavior in the public sphere—as distinct from personality. In that review, Adams, however, urges the historian to "shut his eyes for a moment to the microscopic analysis of personal motives and idiosyncracies . . . [and] become conscious of a silent pulsation that commands his respect, a steady movement that resembles in its mode of operation the mechanical action of Nature herself" (74). Jordy notwithstanding, when personality goes, it is hardly character that takes its place, but a process empty of man or his character. The force of Adams's rhetoric is aimed at the diminution of the importance of the individual as individual in history. Furthermore, his types illustrate policy, not moral qualities. These men embody the political possibilities of America, and when Adams says he is ascertaining America's character, he means its political form. The process by which this political form is achieved is outside the control of individuals or even groups of individuals. To say as Jordy does, "All but leaderless, the people redeemed the blunders of their statesmen and stumbled through the War of 1812" (95) is to recast events through the eyes of a Bancroft. The people in the *History* blunder and stumble with their leaders. The very point of Adams's types is that they represent the beliefs and attitudes of the various segments of the people. That is what makes them significant to Adams.

To show the interaction of individual desire, circumstance, and principle in such a way as to show them the real forces at work in historical change and to banish the notion of the hero, or the spirit of the age, or destiny, or the hand of God is the aim of the *History,* an aim that puts it at variance with Bancroft. Adams's narrative shows further that the political identity that emerged was neither intended nor inevitable. His ideal of scientific history makes the reader an observer of events as they happen. His metaphor of evolution eschews teleological explanations. British policy is the result of the contempt engendered by Jefferson's "passion for peace," but it is also the result of the economic pressure of the merchant class, the personality of Canning, and, as Adams also reminds us, the public opinion outside the merchant class that saw an injustice in British policy. Tocqueville wrote in this regard: "When the traces of individual action upon nations are lost, it often happens that you see the world move without the impelling force being evident. As it becomes extremely difficult to discern and analyze the reasons that acting separately on the will of each member of the community concur in the end to produce movement in the whole mass, men are led to believe that this movement is involuntary and that societies unconsciously obey some superior force ruling over them."[7]

Adams's ideal of scientific history impelled him to find and bring before the reader those traces of individual action. When he leaves his documents and letters to speak in his own voice, it is not, like Bancroft's, resonant with the great ends toward which he sees events moving. It is a skeptical voice that deepens our sense of the number of often contradictory elements in the events he describes. He says, for example, of Marshall's decision in favor of Burr that "an uneasy doubt could not fail to suggest itself that the chief justice, with an equal effort of ingenuity, might have produced equal conviction in a directly opposite result" (*History*, 3:467–68). By including an incapacity for national government in his summary of American characteristics at the end of the *History*, he provides the climactic irony that the political form which America has assumed as a result of the events of these sixteen years is the one for which its citizens have no natural talent.

Yet Adams's irony does not interfere with the effectiveness of the informing principle for this *History*, a principle as powerful as any underlying Bancroft's works although not as apparent. The nation Adams depicts is moving toward stronger centralized government, not at a uniform rate, not without many detours, and not through policy, but it is moving nevertheless. Indeed that movement is the source of much of the irony of the authorial voice. When Jefferson disposed of the people of Louisiana without their consent, it is irony and not moral outrage that prompts Adams's comparison of Jefferson to Napoleon. It is ironic that the nation should finally go to war with England for the wrong reason—impressment and not the orders in council—and at the wrong time—in 1806 there were funds for the war as well as public support. Neither of these were available in 1812. The British army fresh from victories in Europe was ineffective against insignificant numbers of poorly led American troops. The South, which stood to lose so much in the war as its markets closed and against whose most dearly loved principles the war was fought, supported the war while it suffered. New England, whose manufacturers were protected and so grew both under the embargo and the war, bitterly opposed both.

The closest Adams comes to allowing moral condemnation to supplant irony is in his treatment of the radical Federalists. The activities of this group seem to him simple treason, from the men of the Essex Junto, who saw in the war the crisis that would bring an end to the Union and create an independent New England Confederacy, to the governor of Massachusetts, who would not permit the state militia to be used outside the state, and the Vermont farmers who kept the British army in Canada alive to fight in New York State. Though the treason is clear in these pages as it is in those on Burr, the controlling irony, here, modulates into serious judgment. The difference is, of course, that Burr was never a threat to the Union and the radical

Federalists were. It is clearly not without satisfaction that Adams recounts the economic decline of New England caused at least in part by
the end of the war its citizens so intemperately opposed.

II

A comparison of Adams's treatment of Jefferson and Madison shows
emerging centralization once again used as a touchstone for the value
of actions and as a source of irony. Early in the history of Jefferson's
administration, Adams states that he sees its events as a test showing
whether Jefferson could secure peaceful justice by relying on the commercial interests of foreign countries. The resolution of this issue
would also answer the question of the political form America would
take. As a matter of political principle, the Republicans saw both aristocracy and war as drags on the economy. "[Economic] interest not
violence would rule the world," is how Adams puts Jeffersonian theory,
making armies and the taxation that supported them unnecessary
(1:217). Accordingly, politics shades easily in the first part of the *History*
into political economy: The New England disaffection, the Louisiana
Purchase, the war itself, are all brought before us very largely in
economic terms.

However, Adams's treatment of the Louisiana Purchase shows
the limits of his economic explanations. He is explicit about the South
wanting Louisiana and Florida but refers only scantily to the way such
acquisition would protect the trading interest of the planters and
farmers. The South's position could have been seen as yet another
instance of regional economic interests contributing to a stronger national government, although such strengthening was counter to the
political principle of that region. Yet Adams doesn't stress this approach either. Jefferson, too, comes off badly, at least in part because
the economic basis for acquiring Florida is scanted. Not that economic
advantage would have justified what Adams finds to be deception and
bad faith, but it would have put those unattractive moral qualities in
the service of what might be seen as national good, or at least national
necessity. Instead, Jefferson's claim of West Florida under a Franco-
Spanish treaty commonly held to have transferred only Louisiana from
Spain to France appears the act of an individual who can be held to
moral standards not entirely applicable to a government striving for its
existence. By downplaying economic interests or allowing them to
appear only as acquisitive desires, Adams is also able to diminish the

sense of the Louisiana Purchase as an intentional exercise of national power and to make it appear as an ironic instance of the unintended growth of centralization in the face of the principles of the men who brought it about, who were acting on mean motives.

In Jefferson, Adams shows us a philosophic leader whose principles are at war with circumstance. The instances are complex and not easily reducible to a coherent view of Jefferson because Adams's overriding conception is that circumstances call insistently for exercise of national power and therefore Jefferson must be shown to resist. If he responds he is a hypocrite, and his contribution to the growth of the American political organism accidental, ill-conceived, at most immoral and at best ironic. In the Louisiana Purchase, Jefferson acts as a Federalist might have, loosely interpreting the Constitution in such a way as to make possible the purchase and governance of a large new territory. Insofar as it was admitting that government had the right to govern, Adams supports it. Insofar as it was a despotic disposition of the people of Louisiana without consulting their wishes, Adams deplores it. Insofar as Jefferson wishes to amend the Constitution to make the purchase legal, Adams approves the strength of his commitment to strict constructionist principles. In allowing himself to be overborne by an anxiously acquisitive Congress, Jefferson provokes Adams's irony for what amounts to a Republican contribution to the destruction of Republican constitutional theory and to the strengthening of central government. Yet in the spectacle of Jefferson's handling of Burr, Adams shows a Jefferson who by simply speaking out could have dissipated the danger of conspiracy and whose inexplicable failures are exceeded only by his fumbling in the Chesapeake affair. But his failures are not ultimately placed in a personal perspective; they are not failures of Jefferson's judgment or courage or intelligence. They are failures of political organization, of the absence of the American polity whose emergence the *History* recounts.

Adams writes, "The inefficiency of the Government in doing those duties which governments had hitherto been created to perform, was shown even more strikingly in the story of the 'Chesapeake' than in the conspiracy of Burr" (4:4). This sentence is not merely Adamsian irony. It permits us to see the criteria by which Adams judged American political form. It is certainly typical in its pragmatism; a government defines itself as such by being able to do what governments do. But underlying the pragmatism is the evolutionary metaphor. Like any organism, the American political life must function in the world into which it emerges and by which it is molded. By its adaptation to its environment and its ability to stabilize and assure its own life, we shall know it.

The scholars who find Adams's primary interest the character of his protagonists see the account of Jefferson's role in the Louisiana Purchase as intentionally telling very heavily against Jefferson. Vitzthium, in particular, takes this view, and in the moral similarity of Napoleon and Jefferson implied in the narrative, he would also locate an important characteristic of Adams as a historian. Jefferson, in Vitzthium's interpretation of the *History,* is culpable because he represents an extreme of radical democracy whose opposite pole is Napoleon's tyranny. Both are to be avoided by the path of pragmatic compromise (160–62). But such a pragmatic approach has already been compromised by the polar linking of Jefferson and Napoleon in such a way that makes Jefferson's position morally wrong, and this, as I have been arguing, seems to me foreign to Adams's intention or effect.

At the same time, Adams does not characterize Jefferson's position with the positive term "idealism," as George Hochfield does.[8] Hochfield succinctly expresses Adams's guiding principle as that which is historically possible (83), but he sees Adams opposing the pragmatic to the idealistic. I would prefer to oppose Hochfield's category of the historically possible with the historically impossible. In Adams's vision, Jefferson does not understand the conditions that govern the emergence and growth of the new organism which is the American polity. Nor does he understand the laws of that organism's being and so would destroy it. Early in the *History,* Adams speaks of his hopes for Jefferson as a scientist who could bring to America the technology represented by the steamboat, a technology that would have relieved America's entanglements in European politics. Adams goes so far as to say that the steamboat would have resolved America's problems with England and France. Such a statement would be hard to understand if we did not realize that Adams believed technology would transform the environment, thus making possible the emergence of another kind of organism, one closer to the kind envisioned by Jefferson.

For these reasons also it seems to me a distortion to see in Adams's narrative the sense of conflict between decentralization and individual liberty on the one hand and national sovereignty and union on the other that Melvin Lyon argues for.[9] Nothing could wring from the *History* such an identification of liberty with decentralization. While Napoleon unquestionably appears as a tyrant and America embodies new democratic possibilities, it is hard to see the replacement of Jefferson's embargo with Madison's war either as a defeat for individual liberty or a movement toward a "compromise between the [democratic] dream and European practice," as Lyon characterizes it (72).

Jefferson's embargo, by which he hoped to show that economic interest could control America's adversaries, is represented as ruinous to the country financially and morally, ineffective against England commercially, and worse than ineffective psychologically because it fed aggressive rather than conciliatory impulses in the English. It brings out in Adams one of his highest flights of rhetoric quite untouched by irony and therefore very rare: "England required America to prove by acts what virtue existed in her conduct or character which should exempt her from the common lot of humanity, or should entitle her to escape the tests of manhood,—the trials, miseries, and martyrdoms through which the character of mankind had thus far in human history taken, for good or bad, its vigorous development" (4:74).

Not that Adams glorified war. He saw it as the pursuit of a primitive society and found that "the chief sign that Americans had other qualities than the races from which they sprang, was shown by their dislike for war as a profession, and their obstinate attempts to invent other methods for obtaining their ends" (4:136).

In comparing the embargo to war, Adams relies heavily on the irony that it brought about many of the evils Republicans expressed in their arguments for a policy of peace. They feared that a standing army would endanger liberty at home, yet the first use of the navy in New England and the army in New York was to enforce the embargo. As in so many instances in these volumes on Jefferson, he is represented ironically as following Federalist principles in using government to enforce the embargo, using Federalist judges, and indeed pushing Federalist beliefs to such an extreme that he invited bloodshed. Finally, while war at least could teach certain virtues, "courage, discipline and a stern sense of duty," the embargo "turned every citizen into an enemy of the laws . . . making many smugglers and traitors, but not a single hero" (4:277).

Interestingly, Adams spends many pages showing that except in Virginia, which suffered badly under the embargo, the country could and did manage. Yet in summary afterwards he inexplicably says the embargo "emptied the Treasury, bankrupted the mercantile and agricultural class, and ground the poor beyond endurance" (4:284). This is one of the few places in the history where his argument is not entirely convincing because the evidence seems at variance with the conclusion. Similarly, the ultimate question of how effective the embargo was seems to escape final judgment. It might have been argued on the evidence Adams presents that the orders in council were indeed lifted as a result of the embargo. Certainly the question of why the orders in council were repealed is not entirely satisfied. Adams quotes from the London *Times* the sentiment that England would agree to rescind its orders in council "if America will withdraw her Embargo and Non-importation acts" (5:62–65). This seems to argue that Jefferson's policies were successful. Yet two pages later, Adams writes that it was the "mere shadow" of Madison's war policy that "brought Perceval and Canning almost to their senses." This conclusion is dictated by Adams's view of Jefferson as someone who does not understand the emerging organism whose life he oversees, who contributes to its growth unintentionally, and whose policies are as likely to be dangerous to it as not.

Madison's management of the events that finally lead to the declaration of war, however, is represented in some ways as less admirable than Jefferson's attempts to avoid war. Madison is shown acting against his principles rather than in their service. As the narrative represents it, first he allows himself to be duped by Napoleon in the matter of the embargo on the European coast. Then when it is clear to Madison and to all the world that the French decrees meant American shipping in European ports was to be seized, when indeed, Sweden and Russia were on the verge of fighting with France to protect American ships from this fate, Madison insisted on the Napoleonic fiction that the decrees had been repealed. On that basis he demanded that England repeal its blockade and its orders in council, which it had defined as merely retaliatory against neutral shipping. As Adams describes it, war breaks out at a time when Madison and the country are as angry at Napoleon as at England. Yet plans for war with England seem to carry the day despite the country's inability to prepare for it. Gallatin cannot raise money. The banks will not buy government notes. The secretary of war cannot raise an army nor provision it if he could. The secretary of the navy has no boats. It is Adams's view that legitimate complaints against England had all existed for five years, but war was avoided because it was inexpedient. Although Madison's task was to show that it was now expedient, England was ready for some concession and Napoleon ready for none.

Furthermore, Adams's account makes James Monroe's conditions for an armistice at the beginning of the war, when England repealed the orders in council, seem like a subordination of American to Napoleonic interests for the price of Canada and the Floridas, for which latter territory Adams had already shown American cupidity. He emphasizes this effect not because he believes Madison to be in Napoleon's service. He has explicitly defended Madison against that charge. He might easily have argued, as other historians have, that the desire for Canada and Florida was a primary motive, but he does not. Rather, his purpose is to underline for the reader an outcome which was at variance with the intentions and the values of the men whose actions produced that outcome.

Nor should we suppose that this failure of judgment, this inability to bring about the objects of one's desire, is to be explained by the moral or intellectual defects of Madison or Monroe. It is not merely that there are no heroes in this period of American history; there are no heroes in history, no protagonists with the power to shape their ends. Adams explicitly states that what he shows us here is typical of history: "Only with difficulty could history offer a better example of its processes than when it showed Madison, Gallatin, Macon, Monroe, and Jefferson joining to create a mercenary army and a great national debt, for no other attainable object than that which had guided Alexander Hamilton and the Federalists toward the establishment of a strong government fifteen years before" (6:418).

So much do the events of these years appear to be at odds with the expectations and desire of Jefferson and Madison, that Adams ends his narrative with a barely veiled invitation for his readers to surrender the view of them as makers of the nation: "Readers might judge for themselves what share the individual possessed in creating or shaping the nation; but whether it was small or great, the nation could be understood only by studying the individual. For that reason, in the story of Jefferson and Madison individuals retained their old interest as types of character; if not as sources of power" (9:226).

Here in the great work of Adams's mid-career is the attitude fully formed that dominates the chapters on history in the *Education*. Yet the *Education* retains one image of man as an effective agent in the figure of John Hay, a commanding diplomat. In the *History*, too, the diplomat is seen as a privileged person, and Adams says "in diplomacy as in generalship, the individual commanded success" (9:14). For this reason Adams stresses the superiority of the Americans entrusted to work out the Treaty of Ghent to the English given that mission. Yet even in this instance, the narrative seems to undercut severely the extent to which an individual can place his stamp on events. The commanding individual, in this case, Gallatin, had to be remarkable to make himself felt in very difficult circumstances. His colleagues were so different from each other they were unlikely to work well together. English goals were difficult to fathom at least in part because the English themselves were not clear what their goals were and because the men chosen to carry on the negotiations for England were inferior in tact and understanding.

Adams points out how these circumstances almost destroyed the commission, just as he has shown in the chapters on Erie and Plattsburgh how often good soldiers were sacrificed by circumstances and the stupidity of others. Many times the negotiators believed that their responses to the British would precipitate the breaking off of negotiations. John Quincy Adams's position as the head of the commission is represented as untenable. He would be ruined by any peace achieved by the sacrifice of Massachusetts's interests and equally ruined in his own view by a peace achieved through the rebellion and intrigue of Massachusetts.

Adams identifies two decisive elements that made a peace treaty possible. One is the character of Gallatin, about whom Adams says, "unless Gallatin were one of the loftiest characters and most loyal natures ever seen in American politics, Adams's chance of success in controlling the board [of commissioners] was not within reasonable hope" (9:15). Gallatin brings Henry Clay and Adams at last into a suspension of antagonism. In three patient days of "urging Clay and restraining Adams" on the two linked and significant stumbling blocks to agreement with Britain, he at last brought the matter to the point he wished (9:48). Note, however, that in these two verbs, "urging" and "restraining," we have all the detail of Gallatin's efforts that Adams gives us. In a work distinguished by the wealth of diplomatic and legislative detail, we are given none of the specific elements of Gallatin's argument that would make us feel the decisive action Adams claims for him. And indeed the effect of this elision is to weaken that claim.

The internal dissension that marked the British camp gives us a complementary series of events which further undercut the claim for diplomacy and generalship as areas in which the individual can shape history. In Adams's account, the British surrender their demand for territorial concession because the British army's failure in New York State causes Wellington to advise Castlereagh that the ministry "had no choice but to abandon its claim to territory" (9:42). Adams reminds us here that Wellington played a crucial role in the European hostilities just concluded, but that role is not the subject of Adams's narrative. Indeed, there is nothing in the *History* to assure us that Adams would, if he had written the history of the Napoleonic wars, have shown Wellington to be anything but a subordinate figure to the economic and nationalistic urgencies that ultimately decided the conflict. His voice invoked at this point ironically underscores the failure of the British army, fresh from its triumph in Europe, to decide the conflict in the Americas.

Ultimately Adams presents the treaty as achieving nothing for either side and settling no questions, while the Americans "gained their greatest triumph in referring all their disputes to be settled by time, the final negotiator, whose decision they could safely trust" (9:52–53). This is an extraordinary conclusion to an account that began with the assertion that in diplomacy the individual commanded success. By making the individual's greatest triumph merely the referral of the disputes to the negotiation of time, Adams radically reduces the power of the diplomat at the very moment of his triumph. However, this rhetoric should not surprise the attentive reader. In ascribing to Gallatin the power of shaping the nation, Adams seemed to be going against everything the *History* had shown us about its chief actors.

III

William Dusinberre sees the instances of good generals and good diplomats as much more important in the *History*. He argues from them that Adams's theory, which he understands as asserting that "statesmen were mere grasshoppers carried along by uncontrollable historical forces," was seldom "pursued" in the *History* and that in fact his history was psychological rather than sociological and economic (131). I would argue that this formulation is even more misleading than the argument that Adams's primary interest was character. Certainly, Adams thought it made a great difference that Napoleon, not General Moreau, was head of France, but principally because of Napoleon's policy and his political methods for implementing that policy. Adams found personality the proper material of psychology and of rather a low order of interest. It plays a larger part in the biography of John Randolph, which Adams conceived of as a popular rather than a scientific biography, thus requiring the color of drama and personality whose true domain was fiction. But even there, when he wishes to show his true subject he writes of Randolph: "Whether his opinions were wrong or right, criminal or virtuous, is another matter, which has an interest far deeper than his personality and more lasting than his fame; but at least those opinions were at that time expressed with the utmost clearness and emphasis, not by him but by the legislatures of more than one State: and as he was not their author, so he is not to be judged harshly for accepting or adhering to them."[10] The effect of these lines is to make Randolph only an outlet for opinions both created and expressed more clearly by state legislatures who bear the true responsibility for them.

Here Randolph, like the figures in the *History*, represents political ideas. For all Adams's exploitation of Randolph's eccentricities, his morbidity, his irrationality, Randolph's tragedy is political. His fall is the fall of a region, the perversion of a great political system. His life encompassed the degradation of republicanism until, in its narrowed conception, states' rights was prostituted to slavery.

The entire narrative structure of the *History* bears out the small degree in which statesmen were sources of power. Dusinberre's analysis of Adams's narrative art is excellent on metaphor, sentence structure, and aphorism. However, he gives little time to the overall structure, finding it weakened by the great complexity that resulted from faithfulness to chronology. I have tried to show that the great complexity of the narrative is its most powerful resource and the vehicle by which Adams's ideas are enacted without the didactic passages his concept of scientifc history rejected.

It is just this complex narrative that prevents me from agreeing, however, that Adams implies a society developing "by laws of its own independent of the value and the will of men" (Levenson, 26). Everything happens through the value and will of men, although not with the outcomes the individual actors seek. The clash of political and economic ideas and systems constitute the single great explanation of the *History*. The importance of the type is precisely that it enables Adams to make political principles primary, without making the error of reifying them or ascribing to them the power he denied his actors. Nonetheless, the complexity of the narrative is one of the chief sources for the felt reduction of individual influence in the *History*. Adams's ability to organize immense and detailed quantities of political and diplomatic controversy, both personal and documentary, into a narrative dominated by the large issues of national shape and destiny makes possible a powerful vision of history as a process incalculable in advance, beyond the commanding will of any actors, fostering the emergence of good from unlikely places and bad from promising beginnings. At the same time, because of the detail, events issue from men's desires and interactions, whatever the irony revealed in the outcomes.

The collapse of foresight, intelligence, and expectation in the *History* and the helplessness characteristic of American government that it chronicles do not of course lead to failure. But Adams has no explanation for that. Early in Adams criticism, William Jordy's devastating critique of Adams as a scientific historian advanced the idea that Adams might have made the triumph of nationalism less of a paradox and come closer to true explanation if he had selected his documents more widely. But I don't think it was a question of Adams not finding explanations either in his statesmen or in his documents. He says explicitly that this ironic process, full of reversal, indirection, malice, blunder, accident, honest misjudgment of circumstance, intermittent triumph of good sense or patience, occasional demonstrations of skill and technology—this process is history, and there are no other explanations for events. Ultimately, Adams, like Jordy, felt the insufficiency of this view of history. He could not rest with such limited explanation and came to insist that such history was transitional. But in the desire of his later years to transcend the ironic mode in writing history, he left behind the realm of human action and never again wrote history with the same scope and power.

2 Biography as the Education of Consciousness

enry Adams's biographies of Albert Gallatin and John Randolph provide an unusual opportunity to see in biography the same impingement of the narrative model of history on an account of experience conceived of as the education of consciousness that informs the fiction of James, Howells, and Dos Passos. Written at the same time he was undertaking the monumental *History of the United States of America during the Administrations of Thomas Jefferson and James Madison, The Life of Albert Gallatin* (1879) and *John Randolph* (1882) approach the events of that period from a perspective modified by the biographical aim of achieving coherence and explaining the motivating principles, characters, and significance of the lives studied. The biographies show early in Adams's career his ambivalence about personal power and its relation to accomplishment. They, thus, illuminate his investigation of the real sources of power in human affairs, an investigation that led him first to ironic history and then away from it. In these two works, biography itself is invaded and modified by the beliefs that shaped Adams's later historical narratives. The principle of experience as education persists but in a way that transforms assumptions about character and will.

I

Adams says of both Gallatin and Randolph that they were young men who took "life awry."[1] In Adams's view Gallatin threw away "the advantages of education, social position, and natural intelligence" to seek his destiny on George's Creek in the Monongahela hills of western Pennsylvania. But whereas Gallatin's life was to carry him toward those places and actions that best "suited his true taste and needs" and he was to find the deepest and most fruitful integration into the national life of his adopted country, Randolph is seen as having "sucked poison with his mother's milk." Although he followed her advice to buy land to the point of avarice, this commitment to his native soil did not raise him to the height of leadership he desired. He became a representative of Virginia much as Don Quixote is representative of Spain: "a caricature of Virginia failings" as well as a caricature of "Virginia genius" (25).

In Adams's view, Gallatin's emigration as a young man marked him as a person capable of change. It made possible his transition from Jeffersonian republicanism with its stress on the sovereignty of the states to the nationalism made necessary by America's relations with Europe, which Adams sees as the next step in America's political development. Gallatin was not a Pennsylvanian as Jefferson and Randolph were Virginians. Other American leaders were citizens of their states before they were citizens of America. This was not the case with Gallatin and was an important factor in his ability to survive the wreck of Jeffersonian principles. In contrast, Adams uses Randolph's tainted identification with land and with Virginia to explain Randolph's inability to progress beyond the principles of 1800 and embrace a national perspective. Rather it alienated him from the national life he wished to dominate.

Randolph is not presented simply as a man who clung to principles that did not withstand the test of circumstances. The problem of the biography is to show him as loyal to a set of great political principles, principles that Adams characterizes in *Gallatin* as one of the two great political alternatives possible in this country and at the same time show him as a man destroyed and destructive. He is destroyed not by that loyalty but by a personal perversity that in combination with that loyalty transformed the love of Virginia into the aggression of an aggrandizing slavepower. The poison he took with his mother's milk is both his attachment to the land and his will to power. This combination wrecks Randolph, even as Gallatin's lack of the desire to dominate, shown by his airy surrender of social advantage in the land of his birth, saves him. Yet in both biographies temperament works itself out only through political action. It is only through their public acts that we know these men and understand the unity and therefore the significance of their lives.

Randolph's career is opened for us by a characteristic scene. The promulgation of the Virginia and Kentucky Resolutions threatens the federal government and brings the administration to ask Patrick Henry, a southern representative of every republican principle who is, nonetheless, loyal to the Union, to speak against the use of force. Henry does, calling any such act patricide. Randolph responds with a three-hour speech in favor of force and against Henry and the generation that made the American Revolution. In Adams's account, the scene ends as it does in popular tradition with Henry's response: "Keep justice, keep truth,—and you will live to think differently." Adams notes: "Randolph never did live to think differently but ended as he began, trying to set bounds against the power of the national government and to protect those bounds, if need be by force" (36).

Gallatin's career is launched for us by an account of his part in the Whiskey Rebellion where, unlike Randolph, he stands for peaceful protest against force. Ultimately Gallatin was sent to Congress by a district that had opposed him in the rebellion but elected him because he was the "embodiment of the principle of law and order" (141). His leadership in Congress was based on ability and moral qualities. What Adams says of him in Congress he might have said as well of his career as secretary of the treasury: "His power lay in courage, honesty of purpose, and thoroughness of study" (154). From the first, Gallatin is characterized as someone whose actions were guided by principles that transcended political loyalties. His mind, Adams tells us, was scientific rather than political, capable of grasping the broadest principle or smallest detail, disregarding the emotions and seeing both sides of a political question. Such a scientific perspective was Adams's own ideal. In the *History,* he underscores the potential of Jefferson's interest in science, an interest that might have led him to see the significance of the steamboat. Adams believed that technology promised the young American republic a control of its land and waters. Such control would have put it out of reach of European politics and therefore enabled it to avert the political catastrophes that are so great a part of his subject. In the *History,* however, Jefferson's scientific foresight fails him, and, instead, he devotes his energies to a political theory that in Adams's view takes far too little notice of actual circumstance. In *The Life of Gallatin,* Adams depicts Gallatin as initially following Jefferson in believing America to be on the threshold of a new age, free from the hand of the past. But his resolutely scientific mind distinguishes him from Jefferson, who is swayed by considerations of political theory, and permits him to withstand intact the crash of Jefferson's administration.

Indeed, as we shall see, Gallatin's scientific mind makes possible the transcendence of politics toward which the biography moves. In this, *The Life of Gallatin* is the earliest expression of Adams's view of the relation of politics and history adumbrated in the *History* and developed in *The Education of Henry Adams*. Science and technology eventually put an end to history as it had been understood, and the reign of politics is concluded. Ultimately, Adams sees both government and the writing of history as the domain of scientific minds that recognize and facilitate power without commanding it.

Randolph's thinking, however, is dominated by political ideals and drives. Adams describes him in 1800 as one of a company of young Virginians who see themselves as classical Greeks. "The world's great age had for them begun anew," he writes, "and the golden years returned. They were real Gracchi, Curtii, Casii" (45). For them Jefferson ranked as "a resplendent figure seated by the side of Moses and Solon, of Justinian and Charlemagne" (54). Adams tells us that Randolph came to Congress with the image of the elder Pitt to emulate, hoping to rule there as Pitt did in the House of Commons at the age of twenty-five. But the lesson at the core of both these biographies is the idea that experience is an educative power, and the outcome of that education depends on the nature of the mind—be it scientific or political—that receives it.

The first experience Adams chooses to present after Randolph enters Congress shows Randolph insulted in public for his antimilitary comments, writing rudely to the president for redress, and censured publicly for both of these events in Congress. The effect is salutary, Adams tells us, teaching what he most needs to know, "to curb his temper, to bide his time, and not expose himself to ridicule" (45). Gallatin also requires an education when he comes to national politics. He believes, like Jefferson and Randolph, that "human nature was to show itself in new aspects and that the failures of the past were due to the faults of the past" (266). He writes to his wife after the election of 1801, in which John Adams was defeated and Jefferson was brought in: "Everyman, from John Adams to John Hewitt [a tailor who had spoiled a coat of his], who undertakes to do what he does not understand deserves a whipping." To this Adams comments: "He had yet to pass through his twelve years of struggle and disappointment in order to learn how his own followers and his own President were to answer his ideal, when the same insolence of a recalcitrant party presented to their and to his own lips, the cup of which John Adams was now draining the dregs." (266).

II

The Gallatin biography supplies excellent support for those who believe that a strong motive in Adams's historical writing is the desire to justify his great-grandfather. I do not think, however, that the assuagement of family feelings is his major goal. Rather Adams's historical studies are a means by which a great subject is opened up for him, at least in part because of his privileged access to materials. His sympathy and pride are ruled by a great scrupulousness, and these three qualities working together transform the events of which his family was a part into a vision of history in which the efforts of any single participant are dwarfed by a tangle of opponents, economic necessity, and international circumstances. His own beliefs as a New Englander after the Civil War were consonant with John Adams's on the primacy of the national government. The family piety that initially caused Adams to become engaged with these materials gave way to the broader based belief evident throughout the *History* that the power of statesmen had in general been exaggerated. He would show that it was not John Adams alone who would drink or deserve to drink the cup of defeat were they all to understand the little individual intent counted for.

In 1807 it appeared that Jefferson's administration, with Gallatin as its secretary of the treasury, was on the verge of securing all its aims. The debt was nearly gone, and a great plan for internal improvements and higher education was brought into being. All this had been achieved without a military establishment. "For this result," Adams writes, "Mr. Gallatin in the ripened wisdom of his full manhood, might fairly say his life had been well spent" (355). But the great lesson of his life was yet to come. And here we see how the events of the *History* assume a different aspect under the biographical pressure which put Adams's hero at their center. Here, in contrast to the *History*, the ruin of the aims of Jefferson's administration is seen as

> *neither his fault nor that of Mr. Jefferson; it was the result of forces*
> *which neither he nor any other man or combination of men, neither*
> *his policy nor any other policy or resource of human wisdom could*

control. In the midst of the great crash with which the whole structure of Mr. Jefferson's administration toppled over and broke to pieces in its last days, there is ample room to criticize and condemn the theories on which he acted and the measures which he used, but few critics would now be bold enough to say that any policy or any measure could have prevented that disaster. (355)

In the *History* Adams condemns both the theories and the man who tried to enact them. In one of the few places in the *History* where Adams's rhetoric is not ironic, he blames Jefferson for imagining that America could be free of the common fate of mankind. In the *Gallatin*, he presents Jefferson's ideas as one of the two great political possibilities ever envisioned in America, but in the *History* Adams argues that it was doomed from the beginning because it assumed the world to be a different place than it was. In shaping the Gallatin biography, Adams makes the primacy of circumstances over theory the lesson that experience brings Gallatin, the eminently educable hero. In 1808 Gallatin writes to his wife that between England and France, America's situation is "extremely critical and I believe that poor, limited human wisdom can do and will do but little to extricate us." He leaves the future to a faith in justice and Providence. He is ready now to see America as having been "too happy and too prosperous and we consider as great misfortunes some privations and a share in the general calamities of the world" (374–75).

In 1808 Gallatin, himself, embodies what response to circumstance has done to the Republican party. It has become the antithesis of itself, bringing about through the embargo and what Adams derisively calls repeatedly in the *History* but never once in the biography of Gallatin, "Jefferson's passion for peace," the very centralization and militarism it abhorred. And Gallatin is the agent of this change, for it is he who requests the Enforcement Act necessary to carry out the embargo. The Enforcement Act gave the federal government powers far beyond any Federalist imagination. In a moment without parallel in the *History*, where the actors act and only the reader reflects and understands, Gallatin's education is seen as part of a terrible enlightenment that gripped the entire Republican party: "As a result of eight years experience and painful effort, the situation was calculated to sober and sadden the most sanguine Democrat. The idea was at last impressed with unmistakable emphasis upon every honest and reflecting mind in the Republican party that the failures of the past were not due to the faults of the past only, and that circumstances must by their nature be stronger and more permanent than men" (379).

Rarely does Adams permit himself to point to any significance in events that he cannot justify as a lesson learned by his protagonist. Here the rather general idea that circumstances are stronger than men is part of the education of Gallatin and the Republicans. But in speaking of the period of America's great helplessness in 1809–10, Adams wants to treat an instance of deeper political significance and makes an exception to this policy. Of this period, which he describes as an "inevitable stage in national development," he says, "It was clear, therefore, or rather it is now clear, that until the sentiment of nationality became strong enough to override resistance and to carry the Administration on its shoulders, no effective direction could be given to government" (397). He cannot ascribe this lesson to Gallatin because he cannot find Gallatin drawing such a conclusion in what Adams calls "political philosophy." The unifying theme of Gallatin's life is what Adams calls later "practical statesmanship," in specific contrast to "philosophic and *a priori* principles" (560). In the *History,* the narrative represents events as unfolding while the reader reads with as little intrusion by the narrator as possible. Political philosophy is kept to introductory and summary chapters. The entire thrust of the narration in the *History* emphasizes that it was not clear then what was happening. At this point in *Gallatin,* his conviction that the significance of events is not clear as they occur keeps him from making such an assertion without modification. He cannot ascribe it to Gallatin because it is not until the end of Gallatin's life, long after the events, that Gallatin can be shown to believe that the war secured the permanence of the Union because it aroused the national feeling which had lessened after the Revolution. In the midst of the events of 1809–10, Adams must make a specific excursion into "political philosophy" and must therefore say, "rather it is clear now."

Gallatin survives the debacle of the Jeffersonian administration, and Jefferson does not. Jefferson, although "sanguine and supple," felt "the solid earth reel under him" (379) and retreats into passivity, refusing to rule in the last months of his presidency. Gallatin and Madison take up his duties, and in this difference lies the source of Adams's generosity toward Madison in the *History.* Madison is no more successful than Jefferson in shaping events, has no more useful policy, is no more honest about the necessary surrender of republican theory, is often shown to lack force and to be ridiculous in self-assertion, and finally to enjoy a popularity no more deserved than Adams thought Jefferson's to be. Yet above all else, he grapples with circumstance and by allowing it to direct him avoids being destroyed by it.

Adams tells us that Gallatin survives because he is made of "different stuff" from Jefferson. This is an appeal to temperament as explanation, but Adams also uses the figure of growth, development, and adaptation to environment so central to nineteenth-century biography. Adams says that, as a youth, Gallatin was almost as sanguine as Jefferson, but "he knew better how to accept defeat and adapt himself to circumstances, how to abandon theory and to move with his generation" (379). Gallatin's development is from politician to statesman. In 1816, after Gallatin had spent years as a diplomat, which suited him best of all his activities, John Quincy Adams offered him the post of secretary of the treasury again and the chance to reenter the world of political power. He turned it down. Adams says of him that he had lost what was "to a politician . . . more important than either experience, wisdom, or maturity . . . sublime confidence in human nature. . . . His statesmanship had become, what practical statesmanship always has and must become, a mere struggle to deal with concrete facts at the cost of philosophic and *a priori* principles" (559–60). In one of the few substantial studies of the *Gallatin*, Melvin Lyon sees this summary as a moment when "validity yields to practicality as Adams's principal criterion of value . . . . this idea will become the principal human truth Adams has to teach: that man at his best acts on the basis of ideas which he believes to be true although they are, in fact, illusions."[2]

Certainly, practicality is exalted here and everywhere in Adams, but surely not at the cost of validity or in favor of illusion. The greatest illusion in the biography of Gallatin is the illusion of power. Gallatin reaches his highest development when he realizes how limited power is. Gallatin becomes something greater than a politician through his ability to act without a sense of his own power, and he rises to that height through the failure of his political convictions. He is at his greatest working in the cabinet even while faction destroys his political base. Adams tells us that Gallatin is in his proper sphere, happy and well suited to the life of diplomacy, yet we learn that in seven years his efforts to pursue American claims against the French and the Dutch went nowhere. In England Gallatin achieves a treaty only when Canning dies and a new prime minister is appointed. He is represented as a man without illusions, with magnificent adaptability to circumstance, without a need of power or of popularity, and sensible of the limits of poor human wisdom. He is content to follow justice and await the fruits of time.

Gallatin's growth from theoretical politician to practical states-man also explains Adams's treatment of Gallatin's lifelong desire to live in the wilderness of western Pennsylvania. Melvin Lyon rightly identi-fies this desire as part of the cluster of Rousseauistic beliefs in which the moral superiority of the wilderness accompanies the right of each generation to be free of the past. He thinks Adams missed the chance to posit this as a source of coherence in Gallatin's life. But as we have seen, for Adams it is crucial that Gallatin surrender belief in freedom from the past. He locates Gallatin's coherence precisely in those qualities that enable him to do so. He sees his life not as an enactment of principles clear at the opening of his life but as an education that makes possible change and survival. Adams does not miss the unifying thread in his material, as Lyon suggests. Aware of the connection with Rousseau, he believes the wilderness home should have gone the way of belief in freedom from the past. Adams calls Gallatin's preference for the Monongahela hills mere "youthful prejudice," something he retained only in theory while his true needs were met by urban society. That prejudice, then, is only a mere survivor of those Rousseauian ideas that with Jefferson he held at the outset of his career. So, while Lyon views Gallatin's frontier experience as a "participation in the basic experience of American national life," Adams thinks there cannot have been much enjoyment in it for him or entertainment for the reader. Accordingly, he passes quickly over them.

In contrast to *The Life of Gallatin,* the biography of Randolph offers us a cautionary tale. Adams gives Randolph's life unity by his failure to profit from the education experience offers him. Although he is shown early to learn from his humiliation as a freshman congress-man, his need for personal power, which for a time existed fruitfully with his admirable political principles, ultimately destroys his career. In Adams's hand, Gallatin's development reflects the shift in political thinking from admirable, impracticable principles to a theoretic, ef-fective nationalism. Randolph moves, along with the region he repre-sents, from advocacy of the same unworkable principles to revolt against any nationalism not subordinate to the debased needs of the South. His revolt uses fragments of those once great principles per-versely in the service of those needs. While Gallatin reaches his fullest stature when he has surrendered his hope of power, Randolph deteriorates to an irrationality and morbidity beyond even his own defense by sacrificing all other aims to his quest for power. In Adams's view, his political action becomes the vehicle for personal power just as the principle of states' rights becomes the degraded rationale for the will to power of the slave states.

J. C. Levenson early pointed to the importance for Adams of the eighteenth-century view of history as a series of exemplifications of enduring moral and political principles. Adams found ample evidence of this in his family's writings, from John Adams through John Quincy Adams down to his own father.[3] However, in imbuing Gallatin's education from politician to statesman with the underlying metaphor of growth and development, Adams suggests a view of the self rather different from the one he found there. The eighteenth-century view implies a sense that character is unchanging and that an account of a life embodies qualities of character. This view is considerably modified in Adams's thinking by the impact of the evolutionary ideas of adaptation and by the germ theory of history, which was itself influenced by evolutionary ideas. Adams, with other historians who were trying to account for the rise first of English and then American political institutions, likened their development to the transfer of a germ from a foreign, more primitive culture to a new environment in which it develops in new ways, modified through adaptation. Such a view of an organism growing from some nucleus of potentialities that sets direction and certain limits but does not dictate the nature of the mature organism is the one which largely supplants in Adams's biographies the older sense of the relationship of character and the mature self. In Adams's biographies, the eighteenth-century sense of character as inborn, glimpsed in childhood, and revealed fully by early manhood is replaced by a view of the self as something larger than its character, shaped only in part by the response that character permits it to make to the circumstances of life. These circumstances, then, are no longer the events which figure forth the character and its enduring moral principles but take on some of the attributes of a natural environment shaping the organism. It is important to note that, for Adams, this power of circumstance is balanced by the continuing power of character, now seen as an original germ of the self. They are both components in the same process. The two ways of looking at biography are also integrated by the view of experience as education. This allows Adams on the one hand to show the power of character to set direction and limit the nature of education and on the other hand to make conscious and integrate into the self what would otherwise be a mechanical and alien shaping force.

While Gallatin's character permits experience to educate him for practical statesmanship, Randolph's character permits experience to educate him for political terrorism. We have seen that Adams takes the occasion of Gallatin's achievement of political prominence during the Whiskey Rebellion to show a man committed to law yet responsive to circumstance. Adams shows Randolph acting on principle but with no regard for circumstance because he is driven by something not found in Gallatin. Randolph's part in the Yazoo claims controversy is in Adams's view one of the decisive moments of his career. The people of Georgia had responded to a corrupt land sale by the Georgia legislature by electing a new legislature, which rescinded the so-called Yazoo land grants. Some purchasers had their money returned; others had not. The federal government took over the rights to the Yazoo land from Georgia and reached a compromise with the surviving claimants. Jefferson, Madison, and Gallatin supported the compromise. Randolph opposed it on the grounds of state sovereignty, but, more effectively to Adams's mind, he denounced it as a corrupt combination involving northern democrats, Federalists, and executive influence.

Adams describes Randolph as right to defend Gallatin's original repudiation of the corrupt Yazoo sales. He presents his views as sound and his actions as courageous and without selfish or personal motives. But when Adams says "selfish or personal" he means only that Randolph didn't want office. Overall, Adams feels, and wants us to feel, that Randolph is in the wrong. Part of his feeling is accounted for by his sense that Randolph had nothing useful to gain politically for the country by preventing a compromise that would lay to rest a problem bristling with legal and political nettles. He nonetheless opposed and insulted his party's leaders and in Gallatin the one he admired and respected most. In Adams's eyes, Randolph's inability to subordinate his own views to the administration's decision once the argument had been thoroughly aired is a fault not balanced by his courage in acting alone. When Gallatin's point of view is overridden he submits and continues to produce the best results he can for the administration under the conditions.

Yet Adams does not present Randolph as a man who follows principle above all else. Where was principle in the Louisiana Purchase, Adams asks. Where was consistency of principle when in 1804 Randolph criticized a bill for not providing remedy enough against

British naval depredation in American ports? Then he would have had the navy struggle until it was annihilated. Both stands were against every republican principle, but in these instances strict construction submitted to the slavery interest, and antimilitarism surrendered to what Adams calls "fault-finding" and "temper." In the Yazoo affair Adams wants to expose a more central flaw in Randolph's behavior, not mere inconstancy or personal eccentricity. He has already told us that Randolph saw himself entering the political arena as a Gracchus. Now, striking that note again, Adams shows that all Randolph's positive qualities—adherence to principle, courage, and indifference to personal gain—appear in the service of something more dangerous to the Republic: "only a classical, overtowering love of rule thus ventures to defy the opinion of others . . . he willingly flung his chances [for office] away but only to grasp at the higher, moral authority of a popular tribune" (81).

Randolph's extravagant spiritual claim is shown to be unaccompanied by the intellectual and moral qualities that might give it credibility. As the leader of the government case in the impeachment of Justice Chase, Randolph appears as a man who cannot grasp the implications of the proceedings, who cannot apply himself to the necessary hard work, and who cannot carry on an extended, reasoned argument. He cannot command the case either in broad vision or in small detail, and his claim to authority is exposed as mere rhetoric. In short, he lacks the "scientific" qualities that distinguish Gallatin.

Adams calls the impeachment of Chase a turning point in Randolph's career and follows it with an account of his failure in Congress to stop the appropriation of money to buy the Floridas. In this attempt is summed up the elements of his ruined career. His motivation is the hatred of Madison that seems to fill the vacuum created when Jeffersonian theory was, in Adams's phrase, "silently discarded" (130). He removes himself from his party, calling himself a tertium quid, destroying his own power, and begins a long period during which he no longer represents important historical trends.

According to Adams, in these years of political isolation, Randolph develops to the highest degree of effectiveness a political art based on what Adams calls terror, a combination of verbal aggression, insult, brutality, ridicule, and vindictiveness. By 1819 he has laid the foundations for the identification of slavery with states' rights, and Adams sees him as "the legitimate and natural precurser of Calhoun" (178). The terrorism is wedded to the possibility of political power, and

Randolph becomes again for Adams "an important historical character." His inability to carry on an extended reasoned argument is unimportant for a man whose rhetoric successfully exploits the fear of the slaveholder that he will lose his slaves and holds up the specter of bloody revolt. Adams presents him as having "at last got hold of a deep principle, and invented a far-reaching scheme of political action" (185). In 1806, the last time he had been able to act on a principle in a position of power, he disrupted only his party. Now he was the architect of the attack on the Union.

The greatest contrast with Gallatin, then, is not only that Randolph is a man ridden by theory and arrogant moral claims, without self-control or powers of reason, while Gallatin is a practical man with a sense of human limits, and a highly developed capacity for reason. The great historical contrast is between the man who represents the consolidation of the union and the man who represents the threat of its disintegration. Whatever the theory Gallatin began his political life with, his efforts fed the centralizing trend of the early nineteenth century through which, as Adams saw it, the true political form of the United States emerged. Randolph represented a degraded form of the theories of 1798, which he basely manipulated in his fight against the new political structure that had been shaped by the compromise of theory with circumstance.

III

In both biographies, the historical role gives value to the personal qualities. Behavior is characterized according to historical consequences, and therefore, moral qualities are created by those consequences and do not preexist them. In a different perspective, adherence to principle might easily appear in a catalog of virtues. A man broken by that adherence would appear tragic. A man who forsook principle for circumstance would be described in less flattering terms. But these views would hold if character were seen as something that preceded not only historical significance but action itself. We see the extent, then, to which Adams's judgments of these men's actions departs from the eighteenth-century view which was his heritage. Randolph's and Gallatin's actions are morally defined by their historical context and consequences, as revolutionary an approach to the writing of history and biography in America as any brought by the pragmatic and progressive Charles Beard.

In a letter to Henry Cabot Lodge, Adams wrote about Gallatin in terms his grandfather would have understood, terms compatible with an enlightenment morality: "The inevitable isolation and disillusionment of a really strong mind—one that combines force with elevation—is to me the romance and tragedy of statesmanship."[4]

But the narrative itself, as we have seen, does not support such a view. In it, Gallatin's life is neither a romance nor a tragedy. Adams's narration emphasizes too clearly the achievements and satisfactions of Gallatin's life after he ceases to wield power. Furthermore, Adams does not convince us that Gallatin ever refused power, although he argues such an interpretation in the biography as well as the letter. He expresses admiration for Gallatin because he "could and did refuse power when he found out what a vanity it was and yet became neither a cynic nor a transcendental philosopher" (314). Yet, this statement seems just a little inapplicable to the Gallatin Adams has created for us. That Gallatin was driven from power by foreign war and domestic faction. Nothing in his correspondence or his actions as Adams reports them supports the view that if he could have truly exercised power he would have refused it.

Nor has Adams been able to convey to the reader as he does in the *History* that there is no such thing as the true exercise of power. He never makes us feel that the war and domestic faction are simply instances of those conditions which always and everywhere prevent it. In the biography we feel rather that Gallatin refuses John Quincy Adams's offer to take up a cabinet post because he understands thoroughly that the base of power lay in the party and that he no longer possessed such a base. The offer of the cabinet post, then, appears as the offer of difficult labor and responsibility, not power. It is made in recognition of the value of Gallatin's efforts in Jefferson's administration and as a reward for his commanding role in the peace commission of which John Quincy Adams was nominal head. For the reader to feel that Gallatin was isolated and disillusioned, Adams would have had to show a much greater sense of Gallatin's loss as circumstances turned him away at the brink of realizing republican ideals and led him to those actions which would bring about the centralized government he once hated. The Gallatin of the biography is too resourceful, too strong, too absorbed in the management of the aftermath of the defeat of those ideals to play the part Adams assigns him in the letter. Adams has made the work Gallatin could do after his loss of power of greater value than the work he was prevented from doing.

The disparity between the letter and the narrative highlights a repeated feature in Adams's shaping of his materials. He created a hero who surmounted the loss of power, but this was not enough. He had to see him as a hero who refused power because it is an illusion. Here, at the beginning of his career, Adams found the figure who first enacts the often repeated failure to command power we find in his writings. Outside his correspondence, Adams never depicts this failure as romantic or tragic. In the *History*, it gives rise to a pervasive irony. In *Mont-Saint-Michel and Chartres*, it is played off against the achievements of art and philosophy by which men and women momentarily transcend it. In the *Education,* it is at once the source of his ironic view of nineteenth-century ideas of the self, the education which will at last fit his countryman for their lives, and the motive and material for his dynamic theory of history. From the first, the realization of powerlessness is accompanied by a compensating accomplishment, but it is real and always threatens the value and significance of human life.

Although the pervasive sense of powerlessness in Adam's later works may have been aggravated by his wife's suicide, its presence in the *Gallatin* very much weakens the most recent argument that the tragedy of his middle years accounted for much in the late masterpieces.[5] Early in his life, his own disappointment at being merely an observer of politics, of coming at the end of a declining family of publicly powerful men, combines with the sense that his father's talents were not fully used by a country insufficiently appreciative of his diplomacy in England. His earliest letters give a glimpse of the fantasy of power that lay behind his desire to be a political journalist. While serving as his father's private secretary, he ran a great risk writing for an English newspaper in the hope of affecting public opinion and the course of the Civil War. Even this fantasy of political power wielded indirectly through his writing might have had some chance of realization if Adams were living in pre–Civil War America or in New England directly after the War. But in the America of the eighties and nineties, the intellectual was losing status as a shaper of American ideals. The career of William Dean Howells as editor of the *Atlantic Monthly* shows us how the hegemony of the New England sage retreated from the country as a whole to hold sway for a little while within New England itself, giving way steadily to writers from the West and ideas and ideals shaped by the commercial life of the nation. Howells's novels show the businessman usurping the intellectual's place as an arbiter of American values. Even in Henry James, the businessman can act the part of the hero, while the journalist cast as newpaperman or woman is fit only for comedy or worse.

However, whatever the personal sources for Adams's choice of his great and all-absorbing subject, from the first, as we see in the Gallatin biography, his shaping imagination found compensation for power lost. This compensation is of two kinds, both of which will reappear in his later work. First is the emphasis on the work that can be done without power; second, is the identification of the self with the issue of events and a surrender of any goal conflicting with that issue. These goals are themselves seen as mere theory, fragile in the face of actual experience. The self becomes to an extent passive; surrendering its claims to power, it identifies circumstances as the source of power and posits wisdom as lying in response to circumstance, rather than in domination of it. This is the pattern of the Gallatin biography; it is the pattern for the artist in *Mont-Saint-Michel and Chartres* who surrenders his own taste for the taste of the Virgin Mary, and it is the pattern Adams strives to fulfill in the dynamic theory of history. In the *Education*, the impossibility of Adams ever wielding political power becomes one of many examples of the impossibility of commanding any of the traditional forms of power, all of which are associated with vanity. But just as Gallatin's "really strong mind" is the source of both his disillusion and his transcendence of it, so Adams seeks in the *Education* to know the issue of events, so that through his knowledge and through his response, he may participate in their power. Adams's positive response to Comte and Marx is illuminating in this regard. It is a response to thinkers who also wanted to enable men to participate in the power of circumstance. The identification of historical phases hasn't a merely intellectual interest for any of these men. To identify with the historically significant is to make one's own action significant, to fill it with the power of history.

That is what it means to be a type in Adams's *History,* and like Marx who believed that the proletariat could become conscious of the historical significance of its actions, Adams strove for a theory of history in which men could not only be types but would know it, thereby transcending the ironic world of the *History* where they were not only ignorant of their merely exemplary nature but believed they could exercise powers in their own person. Only in this perspective can we understand Adams's failure in the *History* to compare the emerging centralized America to the older republican aims of polity. He never speaks comparatively. He chooses the evolutionary metaphor not because he is in the grip of evolutionary theory—he is critical of it—but because it enables him to emphasize that history is what happens, not speculation or theorizing or moralizing but the events themselves.

Gallatin's ability to respond to the demands of power in his world was the means by which he became identified with the historically significant and made his own actions significant. In contrast, Randolph risked insignificance and therefore failure as well as moral opprobrium to the extent that he advanced the claims of some imaginary personal power against the power of events, of history itself. The evolutionary metaphor in Adams's history emphasizes the end of a process, an end by which all the events that have led to that end are ordered and valued. In the *History*, although the centralized form of American political organization that finally emerges is the touchstone for judging all action, the web of opposing motives and energies, the unforeseen and unforeseeable are fully realized, and the outcome is never made to appear inevitable. However, by the time he wrote *The Education of Henry Adams*, Adams believed that future events could be predicted through a graph that plots the velocity and direction of change. He wanted to make the new man, through his realization of the future, powerful with its significance. Ultimately, then, Gallatin's ability to detach himself from those efforts that failed, those events that did not "happen," and to serve those that did, became Adams's paradigm for creative action of any kind and the type of the only kind of power any individual could hope to wield.

3 *Mont-Saint-Michel* *and Chartres* and the Road to Scientific History

Critics often approach Adams's vision of medieval civilization in *Mont-Saint-Michel and Chartres* (1904) from the perspective of Adams's later expressed desire to show a society shaped by ideals that control all its modes of expression. Consequently, observers look for the kind of opposition between the Virgin and the dynamo that Adams established in *The Education of Henry Adams*. Because of this misapprehension, *Mont-Saint-Michel and Chartres* is often made to contrast with the historical world of Adams's earlier work and thus appears to transcend history in a protomodernist vision.[1] Yet *Mont-Saint-Michel and Chartres* remains profoundly historical and is a meditation on historical change that shows Adams moving away from ironic history toward the dynamic theory that would restore human agency without claiming more power for the individual over circumstance than Adams thought he possessed.

The strain, the conflict, the irony, the ambiguity of motive, and the gap between intention and consequence that characterized the narrative of the *History of the United States of America during the Administrations of Thomas Jefferson and James Madison* are gone. In their place we find an ease, a tolerance, a sense of each possibility of human response and desire receiving due outlet and fulfillment. At the same time, there is a far greater sense of dialectic in *Mont-Saint-Michel and*

Chartres than in the *History.* The earlier work is dominated structurally by the inadequacy to circumstance of one theory of political organization—the Jeffersonian. The centralized political structure that emerges in the *History* is not the successful antagonist of the Jeffersonian state by the consequence of its failure. In *Mont-Saint-Michel and Chartres,* while contradictory historical possibilities are given free play and exhaust themselves rather than defeat each other, there is a highly developed sense of competing, yet coexisting possibilities. The churches, poems, and theology of the past are shown to embody alternative ways of organizing society and understanding reality that are responsible both to reality and to each other as antagonists. Nonetheless, *Mont-Saint-Michel and Chartres,* like the *History,* is marked by the desire to depict and explain change, the fundamental element of all historical narrative. In the disjunction between the Trinity and the Virgin that is at the heart of the book is the disequilibrium that makes for change, a disequilibrium that Adams nowhere offers to transcend permanently.

A good deal of the literature on *Mont-Saint-Michel and Chartres* inadvertently obscures the basic chronological plan by speaking of a division between feeling and intellect or a distinction between masculine and feminine imagination or by emphasizing the section on the Virgin at the expense of the last chapters. These are all important elements in the book, but they are fundamentally ahistorical interpretations and to the extent that the book is history, they distort it.[2]

I

The narrative opens with a powerful image of origination: the Mount emerges *ab ovo.* Opening with the image of Michael, who stands watching over the ocean, "the conqueror of Satan, the mightiest of all created spirits, the nearest to God,"[3] Adams conveys the sense both of a culture emerging from the natural chaos represented by the sea and of a culture so new it is still close to its creator. He repeatedly emphasizes the simplicity of Norman art, both in the Mount and in *The Song of Roland.* At Mont-Saint-Michel, we do not feel the Trinity, the Virgin, or Christ, only the Archangel and the unity of God. "We have little logic here, and simple faith, but we have energy," he writes (8). We learn in later chapters that logic and faith are the primary poles of organization for Adams around which Gothic art revolves. Here, the idea of energy is stressed, the energy that conquers England, the energy of the first crusade. Norman art, we are made to feel, is very close to the source of power, but it is not very differentiated formally. While he sees in the Romanesque "simple, serious, silent dignity and energy," in the Gothic "something more complicated stands in their place"(10). Similarly, the primary quality of *The Song of Roland* is its simplicity.

By characterizing the period of the Mount in this way, Adams makes it a prelapsarian world of mythic unity. God and man are united as they will never be again. The image of their unity is the feudal loyalty of Roland to his liege. Over them both, God is the Lord whose word is always to be trusted. The period assumes the aspect of an ur-text, of which the Gothic will constitute an elaboration and complication once doubt shakes the strong, simple tie of man to God. As Adams presents it, the energy that sends society to the crusade comes back in altered forms, ready to be embodied in different art. Once the connection between man and God ceases to be seen in the unquestioned light of feudal organization, the love of the Virgin and the logic of the schools must help take up the task of organizing the society made possible by the fundamental energy.

While the Mount is seen as the expression of God's power as the Church of the Father, Christ's Church at Chartres is characterized as the Church of the Mother. Christ is "identified with his Mother, the spirit of love and grace" (10). There is no crucifixion at the portal, although each other scene from Christ's life is represented. Here, there is only majesty and mercy; "never once are you regarded as a possible rebel or traitor," in contrast to Norman poetry with its omnipresent Ganelon figure. Adams finds the essence of Chartres is the assertion of divine might in Mary, "apart from the Trinity, yet one with it" (78). Neither she nor Christ is a feudal monarch. She is an imperial power, a kind of authority, in Adams's view, that the people wanted but that was not to be found in Europe and that the fiefs feared. Adams associates her initially with a power "able to enforce justice or to maintain order" (73), but such a role is at odds with the Mary that develops in the course of Adams's narrative.

It is particularly interesting, however, to note that at the outset Adams connects the representation and significance of Mary to the political context. He could hardly have avoided it if he had wished to because, in his view, Mary appears to be represented at the northern entrance as the Queen Mother, an idealized Blanche of Castile. At the southern entrance, in contrast, she is represented as Blanche's political rival, Pierre de Dreux, conceived of her, not as a power that absorbed the Trinity but one subservient to it. There, Christ is enthroned, and the Virgin, at his right without a crown, is equal in rank to John the Baptist on his left, neither with "any power except what Christ gives them" (84). On the gable she appears throned, crowned with the Child on her knee. Adams supposes that Pierre admitted she was Queen Regent.

II

Adams's description of the portal emphasizes the difference in feeling between Chartres and the Mount. He tells us that Chartres embodies sophistication and self-consciousness in contrast to the simplicity of the Mount. This implies a movement from innocence to experience, but because he has also used the metaphors of male and female to contrast the styles, we cannot characterize this progression as maturation.

Throughout, *Mont-Saint-Michel and Chartres* deals with its subjects, the Mount and Chartres, the Trinity and the Virgin, the mystics and Thomas Aquinas, in terms of pairs of contrasting and conflicting elements. Although from the perspective of the nineteenth-century audience, the pairs coexist, they embody different periods within the three hundred years of medieval culture that they encompass. To the extent the pairs do coexist, they are warring elements, as in the rose windows, the portals, and Abelard's debates. In the transition Gothic, these competitions constitute the essence of the period, and they are shown to give way to the trinitarian Church Intellectual of Aquinas. Adams's explanations of why they give way as well as his explanation of the passage from Romanesque to Gothic are, like the explanation of change in the *History,* offered in terms of consequence rather than cause. What emerges as a result of the change is seen as the reason for the change itself.

In the cathedral, the handling of the change from Romanesque to Gothic results in a deft balance of those elements in rebellion against the past and those loyal to it. The old leaps into the new before our eyes, Adams says:

> *The two expressions are not far apart; not further than the Mother from the Son. The new artist drops unwillingly the hand of his father or grandfather; he looks back, from every corner of his own work, to see whether it goes with the old. He will not part with the western portal or the lancelet windows; he holds close to the round columns of the*

choir; he would have kept the round arch if he could, but the round arch was unable to do the work; it could not rise; so he broke it, lifted the vaulting, threw out the flying buttresses, and satisfied the Virgin's wish. (106)

In this moment appears the new Gothic, "a rare and excellent miracle." Adams accounts for this emergence through the narration of an action which resembles the action of the *History* in some respects, although it is significantly different in others. There, too, the first form, the Jeffersonian version of the state, was seen, in some respects, as an ur-state. Because Adams begins by promising to trace the emergence of American political character, the formation of the American state, we must assume that in Jefferson's first administration it did not yet exist.[4] In the *History*, too, there is the view of the first state of things as simple, too simple to account for the complexities of experience and the political needs of man, just as the relation between man and God represented in the Mount and in *Roland* cannot provide for all the needs of man.[5] However, in contrast to the action of the *History*, the change from the first state of organization to the second is effected by an intentional act. While the actors in the *History* had intention, the grand theme and source of irony in the *History* is the way events ran counter to intention. In the *History*, state one and state two are said to be fundamentally different ways of political organization, but here "the two expressions are not far apart; not further than the Mother from the Son."

The familial metaphor appears to describe both the art and the artist. Not only is one art as close to the other as parent to child, but the artist, as Adams notes, only unwillingly drops the hand of his father and grandfather. As he creates he looks back to insure compatibility. When he must surrender the round arch, he surrenders it because he perceives that it was simply "unable to do the work." So he does what is necessary, as the actors that Adams most admires in the *History* do. He responds, like Albert Gallatin, to the demands of circumstance and works that rare and excellent miracle, the creation of the new.[6]

We feel the weight of Adams as an American historian here, with the sense he expressed at the opening of the *History* of the great conservatism of the American people and the American ambivalence toward the past. Adams sympathized with the particularly American need to free itself of the past but felt its great weight as not easily put down. Similarly, in his own psychic economy, the weight of his familial past was a source of both pride and guilt. His imaginative engagement with ways of envisioning change has its roots in both a social and a private need to see change as something other than a parricidal act engendering guilt and punishment. These factors feed his treatment of the element of intention and help to explain his commitment throughout his career to the importance of the element described here as the ability or inability to do the work. In the *History* the degree of the agent's responsibility for change is impaired because, although he has intention, he cannot effect it.

The agent's responsibility in *Mont-Saint-Michel and Chartres*, however, is also impaired because, although he can effect his intention, his intentions are not truly his own. Left to himself he would not have dropped his father's hand; he does it because the Virgin wishes it. All the chapters on Chartres insist that all the architecture and decoration are designed to please the Virgin's taste. Even the use of the Romanesque motif of the rose window is explained by the Virgin wanting it. The Cathedral of Notre Dame, we are told, does not please the Virgin: "it is too architectural; too regular and mathematical; too popular; too impersonal" (120). At Chartres the choir ignores the newer Paris scheme in a way that is inexplicable to Adams's architectural authority, Viollet-le-Duc. Adams says of the Chartres choir that it carries "a sort of violence—a wrench—in its system as though the Virgin had said with her Byzantine air: I will it!"

Adams, as we have seen, also explains the changes in style by invoking "the work," the technical requirements of the building. Adams speaks of the use of the wooden shelter roof and the flying buttresses both made necessary by the decision to lift the vaulting. Because the light columns that were desired were incompatible with heavy vaulting, the architect built light stone vaults that he protected from the weather with the wooden shelter roofs and added flying buttresses to distribute the weight they would have to carry. But the necessities of the work all reach back to the original decision to lift the vaulting, which is simply the Virgin's taste and wish. In the end we are left with a sense of the technologically imperfect solutions used by the Gothic architect as the logic of his craft gave way to the demands of the Virgin.

One of the most striking instances of this is in Adams's description of the west rose at Chartres. It is the rose the Virgin looks at, and though it was planned at the same time in the thirteenth century as two other rose windows, perhaps by the same architect in the same work-shop, it is in the twelfth-century spirit of the twelfth-century facade and portal that it dominates. Adams accounts for this design by examining the relationship of the rose to the facade and portal. When he finishes, he adds a striking figure that gives the intention and responsibility to Mary. In an earlier chapter, he described the sculpture of the figure of Abraham about to sacrifice Isaac that flanks the figure of the Virgin just inside the entrance of the cathedral. His stated intention is to show how the sculptor, knowing how the Virgin shrinks from pain, tried to make even this subject, "with the compound horror of masculine stu-pidity and brutality," pleasing. He returns to this metaphor to explain how the thirteenth-century architect came to build the twelfth-century rose window. "The architect," Adams writes in this instance, "is listen-ing, like the stone Abraham, for orders from the Virgin, while he caresses and sacrifices his child." Then we know that "Mary and not her architects built this facade" (115).

In the breaking of the rounded arch, Mary guided the artist to the miracle of the new. She was the agent of change that he would not have chosen. But in the creation of the west rose, she is the agent of a change that is a return to the old. Once again, she has relieved the artist of responsibility and taken away his freedom. And again, he has surren-dered personal motives for her service. In breaking the arch, he gave up his father; here in the twelve-century manner of the west rose, he sacrifices his child. There the Virgin's wishes were identified with logic of the work; here is emphasized the arbitrariness of the action. The violence of the metaphor of the statue of Abraham echoes an earlier one in which the architect is said "to injure his own work by sparing that of his grandfather." On reflection it is possible to say, yes, but the effect is surely to enhance both the architect's work and that of his grandfather. Yet Adams's text works to inhibit such a reflection. It emphasizes the injury and sacrifice of the artist's own work, as if what he produces under the command of the Virgin were not his own. And of course, this is the effect of the rhetoric, to make the art the Virgin's, not the artist's.

There is a striking difference here from the earlier instance of the Virgin's intrusion. The metaphor for the creation of the new was much gentler, a natural letting go of the father and an implied realization of the self. Here, maintaining integrity of style against the passage of time and the rise of yet a newer style is the equivalent of maintaining that self, a self that acts and achieves but whose intentions are never his own, a self freed from the burden of responsibility. But this maintenance entails great costs.

As we have seen, the vision of action in the political world of the *History* is ironic and frustrating. The vision of action in this world of religious art presents another version of the mortification of the self that hardly seems to be compensatory for the suffering of history. Behind the figure of the sculptor listening to the commands of the Virgin is the "compound horror of masculine stupidity and brutality" that Adams calls the story of Abraham and Isaac. It is made pleasing to the Virgin by Isaac, on whose face is "an expression of perfect faith and confidence" while Abraham caresses him with "a movement that must have gone straight to Mary's heart, for Isaac always prefigured Christ." In the metaphoric action of the sculptor, Mary replaces Jehovah. On one level, the violence threatened in the sculpture of Abraham is unfulfilled because Isaac is saved and a lesser sacrifice is accepted. By analogy, the art of the architect is saved, also in the sense that a lesser sacrifice, that of his own thirteenth-century taste, is made and the twelfth-century art in accord with the Virgin's taste is saved. Yet at the same time, he is said to "sacrifice his child"; the violence is not averted. Furthermore, the work and the credit are Mary's. There are no personal failures in this view of action, but no successes either.

This metaphor of the Virgin's taste is in fact analogous to the tendency toward central government in the *History*. It is another way of seeing the end result of a process as its explanation. The Virgin's taste is merely the Gothic itself emerging against the forces of conservatism, logic, and technological common sense. It is the same transitional Gothic persisting even after new forms of the Gothic have evolved. However, in the *History*, the status of the agents was clear. They were essentially ignorant of the ends of their actions. Centralization exists as an explanation for these actions only in that it provides, in retrospect, a gauge of their significance or futility. Because centralization is what emerged, it turned everything that preceded it into the process which created it, turned it from happening to history. But centralization as an explanation does not change the actors into effective agents. The status of the artist in *Mont-Saint-Michel and Chartres* is more ambiguous. In the rhetoric the artist seems to be aware of the end of the process of which he is a part. He is made to choose, to reject, to sacrifice. What he chooses and what he sacrifices to is the Gothic itself, which comes into existence only through his choice and sacrifice. At the same time, by making the artist sacrifice his own taste to the Virgin's, the rhetoric simultaneously denies his awareness of the full significance of his own act, for in such awareness how could his deference to the Virgin seem to be sacrifice? Furthermore the rhetoric insists on the element of the arbitrary and illogical in the Virgin's taste so that it cannot wholly be grasped by the artist it commands. Finally, the fact that the artist's action takes place always in this realm of rhetoric serves to make insubstantial the element of choice and awareness that are part of that rhetoric. This insistence on metaphorical narrative leaves ambiguous the status of those elements in reality.

Mary's role in the shaping of the Gothic at Chartres is consonant with her power as it is seen elsewhere in the text. The world of the Trinity is the world of order and justice.[7] The Virgin's power is outside that world. It is arbitrary as her demands on her architects are arbitrary, the result not of law but personal preference. Adams sees Mary as the embodiment of the medieval idea of favor, as opposed to law or equity. She represents not what was man's due or his desert but what was unearned: "God was Justice, Order, Unity, Perfection; He could not be human and imperfect, nor could the Son or the Holy Ghost be other than the Father. The Mother alone was human, imperfect, and could love; She alone was Favour, Duality, Diversity" (261). She represents what is "irregular, exceptional, outlawed; and this was the whole human race." She is not "respectable" and saves criminals who are loyal to her. In her glass, the Last Judgment becomes merely a "jewelled decoration which she wore on her breast" (145). The splendor of the glass becomes, in Adams's rhetoric, a "Paradise [that] contains and hides it." She swallows up Christ and the Trinity and supplants their justice with her favor.

III

For while change is seen as the work of an agent who has no freedom, who wants one thing but does another, for whom self is vanity, it is also seen as arising out of the failure of any one kind of organization to meet the needs of diverse and lawless humanity.[8] Adams's organizing impulse that first makes the energy of life visible in the forms of Norman art dominated by God the Father now counters with an insistence on the Virgin as Empress. Her power is independent of the Trinity. However, the effort to make her power swallow up all power is counteracted by vivid passages where the Virgin appears as subordinate to the Son or the Trinity. Most effective are the passages in which the description of the cathedral leads Adams to the political conflicts between the men and women who built it. The chapter on the nave and the choir at Chartres, which he calls the Court of the Queens of Heaven, shows how Adams strives to express both his fidelity to those diverse and lawless human beings who built it and his formal need to see the source, if not the expression, of their energy as one.

He begins with a study of the windows whose most striking aspect is their lack of unity and whose charm is in their "vanity . . . and sometimes even [in their] downright hostility to each other" (179). They reflect the diversity of a people who, Adams says, are united only by their love of the Virgin. But the diversity is narrowed and organized around the great opposition between the rose window representing France and that representing Dreux. As in the smaller windows, the war of the roses of France and Dreux represents actual social conflict, Blanche of Castile versus Pierre of Dreux. It is also a conflict of the woman and the man, for Pierre "with all his masculine strength . . . wants to rule by force . . . [and] carries the assertion of his sex into the very presence of the Queen of Heaven" (183). Here we are also being reminded of the distinction between the world of the Mount and the world of Chartres. In addition, Pierre is "no courtier," so we are reminded of the opposition between the warrior world of *Roland* and the courtly world of the romances.

The rose of France shows Mary as regent for her Son even as Blanche is regent for Louis, and it asserts her rights as Queen Regent of Heaven against Pierre, "the rebel" who asserts "rival right" (184). The use of the term *rebel* is striking here as being in contradiction to Adams's earlier assertion in his description of the entrance of Chartres that Mary's mercy and grace filled that space so utterly that there was no rebel or traitor there. The reappearance of the rebel, like the references to the masculinity and force of the world of Norman art, signals a different realm, one where conflicts are real and fundamental. For every assertion in Adams of a state of being that subsumes conflict, an organization that integrates every claim, a law that explains every case, there is the countervailing recognition of the ineradicable antagonisms of history as well as the anarchy of the natural world. His most impressive vision allows for what Santayana would call different realms of being and gives full justice to the claims and possibilities of each.

At this moment in the text, the world of art, like the world of philosophy in the later chapters, is made to enact the conflicts of history, not transcend them. Not only does France support the claims of the Virgin, but in the windows beneath the rose, it supports the "royal and divine pretensions" of St. Anne, the Virgin's mother. And the figures from the Old Testament that flank her are seen as trampling on the tribe of Pierre de Dreux. On the opposite wall, the rose of Dreux defies Blanche. In it, Christ as King is surrounded by the figures of the Apocalypse and the angels and kings who symbolize the New Jerusalem. In the windows beneath are the Evangelists and the Prophets and directly under the Christ is the Virgin. This Virgin has been brought down one step so that she is on the same level with St. Anne. "She is the Virgin of Theology . . . but she is not the Virgin of Chartres," writes Adams. Even the armorial decorations are seen by Adams as weapons in the conflict between Pierre and Blanche, and Pierre's pledge of fealty to the Virgin is a blow against Blanche. The Virgin in Blanche's rose sees only enemies as she looks around the church, Adams tells us. The warfare is in the color itself as "Blanche flames out on us in splendid reds" and the images of the glass are aggressive as she "flings her Spanish castles in our face." At the same time, the "brutal energy" of Pierre's southern transept "shows itself in Prophets who serve as battle chargers" and in the Evangelists who "serve as knights."

After this splendid evocation of political passions and theological divisions, Adams returns to the unifying elements he has exploited throughout the text. First, he appeals to the taste of the Virgin, which is the touchstone for the artist. Second, he defines the spirit of Chartres as the spirit of the western portal and the twelfth century. The passions of the thirteenth century and the artists of the thirteenth century give way to the continued vision of the Virgin of Chartres as the Virgin of Grace. In Adams's view, the passions of Blanche and Pierre have their place, their "legal" place in the transepts, but from the throne above the altar the Virgin cannot see them, as high above the "agitation of prayer, the passion of politics, the anguish of suffering, the terrors of sin," she looks down, "crowned, throned, glorified" (192). The Virgin who loves the Romanesque rose window and who causes the thirteenth-century artist to sacrifice his work for the twelfth century, holds together the three centuries that elsewhere in the text are so clearly contrasted.

The essence of Adams's achievement here as an historian is not to set medieval unity against an implied modern multiplicity barely men-tioned in the text. His success lies in showing how the multiplicity of the medieval period, the distinctive forms of eleventh-, twelfth-, and thirteenth-century life, was integrated in Chartres while evoking for us the sequence of changing political, esthetic, and intellectual forms that characterize the passage from the eleventh to the thirteenth century. Charles R. Anderson speaks of some of the ways Adams creates an illusion of unity by telescoping time. Otherwise, he suggests, the Middle Ages would appear to be a period of "motion and flux like any other" (135 ff.). Our analysis here shows that, as a historian, Adams uses the elaborately worked figure of the Virgin's taste to help us keep the movement of time and the change of architectural practice that accompanies it in mind at the same time that he shows us that Chartres owes its glory to the thirteenth-century architect's willingness to diverge from thirteenth-century practice. The Virgin's taste accounts for a privileged moment in the world of art, when changes in style are suspended to permit the fulfillment in one period of the conception of an earlier one. For Adams, this is a rare accomplishment in human endeavor and worthy of celebration. Were there not other, equally worthy stylistic possibilities to be rejected, the triumph would not be so great. Never does Adams let us forget that the Virgin who is Empress of Heaven is only one of several possible ideals of human relationship to the divine. Her glory is defined by the order, law, and unity her love stands apart from.

In Adams's discourse, the Virgin as ideal exists on two levels: one is governed by the perspective of the artist whose action is controlled by her taste; the other is governed by the perspective of the worshiper who is granted her favor. At the same time, Adams shows her as a creature of history, with her roots in the Byzantine Empire and her development shaped by the needs of people living in a feudal society. Her status as an ideal, therefore, depends on the people who need her, and Adams makes clear that these are the needs of men and women of a particular period. The Virgin, though an ideal, is not eternal. Adams often treats her as if she preceded her realization in aesthetic and religious forms and shows her, that is the ideal she represents and hence the needs she fulfills, to be the force that creates the forms. At the same time he lets us see that she is the culmination and realization of the significance of the forms, not their source. While Adams, in *Mont-Saint-Michel and Chartres,* is not primarily concerned with showing the way ideals arise out of changing social circumstance, his sense of that connection is powerful enough to make us feel the pathos of the change that is going on all around these formal islands, particularly around the Virgin and her cathedral, just as the ocean of time from which all forms emerge separates us from Normandy at the opening of the text.

It is typical of Adams that the forms are never cut loose from circumstance and that the power they wield is seen as borrowed from and essentially inhering in the conflicting needs and drives of men and women. Just as the Virgin's taste was the outcome of the process by which the Gothic emerged, so the Virgin, Herself, is the outcome of the historical process whose constitutive elements are religious, social, political, and aesthetic events. If we deal with the question of historical change by calling all literary, aesthetic, and religious conventions and ideals in Adams "fictions," as Melvin Lyon (following Elizabeth Stevenson) does, and say that "the individuality of historical periods is due to the change in fictions produced by the forces of history" (110), we make a distinction between history and conventions and ideals that is foreign to Adams's way of thinking. We separate history from the very elements that are history and run the double danger of ascribing either more or less autonomy to these "forms" than they possess. They are neither dependent on history nor independent of it; they are history.

Adams shows that the religious, social, and aesthetic forms combine to realize certain possible social ideas and perforce to exclude others. Fundamental to this process is the relationship of multiplicity to unity. For Adams, the relationship is inherently unstable and changes in that relationship constitute a major explanation for historical change. The Romanesque ideal of power embodied in the figure of the Lord to whom all owe fealty produces an art of extraordinary cohesiveness and solidity, which, seen from within, presents no reason for change. But seen from without, it is clear that the Romanesque does not integrate all the forces of its contemporaneous society, and its failure to do so, the failure of any form to do so, lays the foundation for its decline. Adams is most moved by the Gothic of 1188–1225 because it encompasses in its unity of form the tension of multiplicity. Its unity is not won so much by exclusion of contradictions as by balancing antagonistic elements. Sometimes Adams expresses this by a formulation in which the transition Gothic balances faith and logic or love and intellect; sometimes he expresses it in the depiction of the Virgin, who is power as she is love and who is anarchy as well as salvation; sometimes he expresses it through the figure of the sacrificing artist. The achievement of this period makes it all the more vulnerable to change because it is subject to disintegration from within as well as pressure from without, and, indeed, in the perspective of three centuries of medieval art, it is relatively short-lived as a distinguishable style within the Gothic.

IV

In the concluding three chapters, Adams makes more explicit the implications of the ways unity and multiplicity are related. In them, he makes clear that the solutions found by the Gothic in the years of the transition, the solution reflected in the fable of the artist who sacrifices his will for the Virgin's taste, is not one he can rest in any more than in the solution of the Romanesque.[9] He will follow the path of medieval philosophy to Thomas Aquinas, whose Church Intellectual completes the triad begun by the Mount and Chartres. Thomas's church finds a solution unavailable to Romanesque art or the art of transition Gothic. While the Mount sacrificed the individual will to an ideal of power and Chartres sacrificed the will to the ideal of love, Thomas found a way to maintain both the individual and the unity he yearned for.

Adams's approval of Thomas and his evident identification with him are of great significance for his career as an historian. The worlds of the Mount and Chartres are dead, while the world of Thomas, as we shall see, is identified in the imagination with modern science and thus is still alive. In the chapters on the Mount and Chartres, the view of individual power and responsibility in historical change is similar to that of *The History of the United States of America during the Administrations of Jefferson and Madison;* they are slight. The worlds of the Mount and Chartres are free of the corrosive irony of the *History,* however, because the individual surrenders his own will, which he recognizes as ineffectual, to sources of real energy: God and the Virgin. But Adams has no wish to make such a surrender. Adams occupies his last years in a search for a theory of historical change free of the irony of his early years while allowing a nonromantic view of man as an agent in history. Thomas is part of that search.

Adams's account of medieval "science" begins by setting terms for the problem he wishes to solve. He focuses on the unbridgeable separation between unity and multiplicity that divides Abelard's nominalism and William of Champeux's realism. Realism begins with unity, with "the universal, the ideal, the type," with God, and cannot get to multiplicity, "the concrete, the observed fact of experience, the object of sensual perception," to Socrates (291). Nominalism begins with multiplicity and cannot get to unity.

Furthermore, for Adams realism ends in pantheism. Because only the universal is real, all energy resides in it, that is, in God, and all other energies in the world, such as nature's or man's, are only apparent. All energy is God's, and free will disappears. For the nominalist, on the other hand, only the concrete is real; therefore ideals, types, God are only names. Nominalism ends in materialism and free will again disappears. Adams cannot believe that the army or the church or the state are merely concepts. The army, he says, is "an animal that thinks, creates, devours, and destroys" (299). Concepts, Adams argues, cannot "constitute" either the individual or the whole—either the soldier or the army. Names have no energy. And, of course, in this he is correct. Adams wants both the army and the soldier to be real, to be centers of energy. "The attempt to bridge the chasm between multiplicity and unity," he writes, "is the oldest problem of philosophy, religion, and science, but the flimsiest bridge of all is the human concept, unless somewhere, within or beyond it, an energy not individual is hidden; and in that case the old question instantly reappears: what is the energy?" (299). Santayana would have answered that the energy is in matter, whose forms the human imagination gives phenomenal shapes and names but whose energy remains hidden, unknown, uncontrollable by man. William James would have said that the energy is in the soldier and that whatever energy ideals have they have through man's belief in them and action based on that belief. But Adams wanted man to be a source of energy, to possess free will, and he simultaneously wanted universals to be real, to possess energy.

Melvin Lyon finds Adams philosophically closest to Abelard, and, although Adams's assertion that the army is an animal contradicts such a view, Abelard does represent the classic position that gives the same reality and energy to the concrete that Adams does. However, Adams cannot assent to materialism, and the difficulties of his dynamic theory arise from his trying to envision a science that is neither materialist nor empiricist.

Moreover, Abelard's view of God and the Trinity also lead to positions that Adams cannot find useful in the solution he is seeking to the riddle of unity and multiplicity. On the one hand, Adams ascribes Abelard's condemnation by the Council of 1121 to his application of the theory of concepts to the Trinity. As an explanation of the process by which unity could produce diversity, conceptualism would destroy the Trinity by identifying its components in terms of human concepts. In the first two-thirds of the text, Adams himself referred to God and the Virgin as human concepts. In this view of the Virgin's power, where was the source of energy if not in the people who worshiped her? But what was acceptable to Adams in a study of art was not apparently acceptable to him in a study of philosophy. It was not that Adams required the unities of philosophy and religion to be true while he required the unities of art only to be coherent and significant. He admires Aquinas's Church Intellectual for being coherent and significant, although he doesn't believe it to be true any more than he did the Virgin as represented in Chartres. But Aquinas believed the Church Intellectual to be true, and Adams doesn't see how Abelard, once he applied conceptualism to the Trinity, could have the same belief in the Trinity. Abelard destroyed the coherence of his own philosophy.

The mystics did not believe that scholastic logic would find the way to God, and Adams often appears to agree with them. He is drawn to their rejection of intellect because it mirrors his own distrust. Francis is a radiant figure for Adams, but paradoxical. Adams says of him that he represents anarchy as opposed to organization and the forces of nature as opposed to intellect, but he is also a pantheist who knew God through the absorption and disappearance of the self in the mystic union. The conclusion of the section on Francis speaks of the lines of gratitude for "our sister death" that Francis added to his Cantico del Sole on his deathbed: "the long-sought, never found sister of the schoolmen, who solved all philosophy and merged simplicity in unity" (341). Implicit in this is the recognition that the surrender to anarchy and to nature does not bring the freedom and potency of the self that Adams seeks. Whatever the extent of Adams's skepticism, he never descends to the depth of "contempt and hatred for human intellectual processes" he recognizes in Francis's mystic union. In fact, Adams's most profound identification is with the intellectual science of Thomas Aquinas.

In the first two of these three concluding chapters, Adams refers repeatedly to later philosophers—Descartes, Spinoza, Pascal—who represent to Adams similar ways of dealing with the problems that the medieval schoolmen and mystics wrestled with. More rarely, in these chapters he refers to scientists such as Farraday and Haeckel, to show that he is dealing with perennial intellectual dilemmas. While in the earlier sections on art, he invited us to return to an openness of feeling that children lose as they mature, in these masterly pages on medieval thought present and past are of an age. There is no gulf, either of feeling or intellect, that needs to be bridged. In the last chapter, however, medieval philosophy is brought particularly close to his own day and interest through the multiplication of scientific allusion and analogy. Thomas is put into a conversation with a "modern mechanic." Thomas says, I see motion, I infer a motor, not an infinite series of motors, "an intelligent, fixed motor" (347). The mechanic answers, "we can conduct our works as well on that as on any other theory, or as we could on no theory at all, but if you offer it as proof we can only say that we have not yet reduced all motion to one source, or all energies to one law, much less to one act of creation, although we have tried our best" (347). Adams calls Thomas the extreme of scholastic "science" and sees his achievement as the result of two hundred years of "experiment and discussion . . . among thousands of men . . . who discussed little else." Not only is this an implied analogy to science but also an implied hope that science will some day point to a solution as impressive as Thomas's.

Most striking of all is the following comparison between Thomas's philosophy and the science of Adams's own day:

> *Avowedly science has aimed at nothing but the reduction of multiplicity to unity, and has excommunicated, as though it were itself a Church, anyone who doubted or disputed its object, its method, or its results. The effort is as evident and quite as laborious in modern science, starting as it does from multiplicity as in Thomas Aquinas, who started from unity; and it is necessarily less successful for its true aims, as far as it is science and not disguised religion, were equally attained by reaching infinite complexity; but the assertion or assumption of ultimate unity has characterized the Law of Energy as emphatically as it has characterized the definition of God in theology. If it is a reproach to Saint Thomas it is equally a reproach to Clerk-Maxwell. (371)*

Nowhere has Adams made clearer this awareness that science was not in its essence a path to unity, and nowhere does he admit it with greater equanimity. The pain that this recognition cost him is excluded from these pages, though it dominates the pages of the *Education*. He comes perilously close here to accusing the Law of Energy of being at odds with scientific aims. But Adams is a writer preeminently responsive to his immediate context, and his context here is the sympathetic presentation of Thomas's philosophy. The comparison of religion to science is not here to criticize Clerk-Maxwell but to enhance Thomas. There is little questioning of the scientific assumption of unity even where there is ample reason to question it, Adams is saying. Why then, goes the implied question, should we not allow Thomas the same latitude? Especially, and this is characteristic of Adams, if it will let him get the job done.

This pragmatic side of Adams comes not only from his commitment to science but also from his fascination with the relation of any form to the particulars that make it up. In spite of his unwillingness to surrender the realist view of universals like the army or the state and his insistence on their having an energy of their own, not merely the energy of the particular soldiers or citizens that made them up, he doesn't think of those forms as eternal, as existing prior to their materialization in a particular set of relationships among soldiers or citizens. Sets of relationships emerge through the interactions of particular men, as the shape of the American union emerged in the *History* or as a work of art emerges through numerous choices of the artist. For Adams, the same sense of the relation of form to its constituent elements maintains in biology, politics, and aesthetics. Once the elements attain a particular relationship to each other, they become a new organism with an energy of its own that cannot be explained in terms of any of the constituents. Because the form doesn't preexist but emerges through historical process and exists as a function of its parts, such a view allows for the actions of particular men to count; they may facilitate or impede. Such a view allows for a concept of human agency that will become very important in the development of his dynamic theory of history.

Thus, Adams's meditation on how Gothic style emerged from the Romanesque and how it changed marked his reengagement with the questions of historical process that he dealt with in the *History*. There he defined one of the chief problems facing America in 1800 as the creation of a stable political form. He looked then and he looked in these last three chapters to science, not to art, to help him understand the process that his study of the Gothic embodied.

Thomas has a privileged status for Adams because the job that Thomas is trying to get done is what Adams sees as science's job, as well, what Adams calls "getting Man and God under the same roof" or "bringing two independent energies under the same control" (371, 373). It is accomplished by making God the object of man's free choice.

In Saint Thomas' Church, man's free will was the aspiration to God and he treated it as the architects of Chartres and Laon had treated their famous flèches. The square foundation-tower the expression of God's power in act—His creation—rose to the level of the church fa-cade as a part of the normal unity of God's energy; and then, sud-denly, without show of effort, without break, without logical violence, became a many-sided, voluntary, vanishing soul, and neither Villard de Honnecourt nor Duns Scotus could distinguish where God's power ends and man's free will begins. All they saw was the soul vanishing into the skies. (373).

Remembering the analogy between Thomas's science and modern science, the reader sees in such a passage that Adams thinks less of science as an objective way of knowing the truth, different from and opposed to art, and more of science as an activity governed as art is by aspiration, consistency, and coherence. In this perspective, Thomas can serve as an exemplar to modern science and to Adams as one who places great hopes in it.

Neither Abelard nor Francis, though their appeal to Adams was great for each spoke to a part of his own thought, could get man and God under one roof, find the connection between unity and multi-plicity that kept both real, both centers of energy. Similarly, as we have seen, in the relation of man to God in the Mount and man to the Virgin in Chartres, man yields all power and sacrifices his will. The symbolism and materialism that are the possible outgrowths of Abelard's concep-tualism and the pantheism that comes from Francis's mysticism both deny human agency. Limited as that is in the *History of the United States of America during the Administrations of Thomas Jefferson and James Madison* and in the biographies of Gallatin and John Randolph, it is real, and the rest of Adams's intellectual life is a struggle to achieve a scientific view of history that will still have room for some form of human agency. The faith that this is possible, not faith in the religion of art, is what *Mont-Saint-Michel and Chartres* embodies. Adams's last comment on Thomas's church is contained in a meditation on the symbolism of the Gothic style:

Of all the elaborate symbolism which has been suggested for the Gothic cathedral, the most vital and most perfect may be that the slender ner-vure, the springing motion of the broken arch, the leap downwards of the flying buttress—the visible effort to throw off a visible strain— never let us forget that Faith alone supports it, and that, if Faith fails,

Heaven is lost. The equilibrium is visibly delicate beyond the line of safety; danger lurks in every stone. The peril of the heavy tower, of the restless vault, of the vagrant buttress; the uncertainty of logic, the in-equalities of the syllogism, the irregularities of the mental mirror—all these haunting nightmares of the Church are expressed as strongly by the Gothic cathedral as though it had been the cry of human suffering, and as no emotion had ever been expressed before or is likely to find expression again. The delight of its aspirations is flung up to the sky. The pathos of its self-distrust and anguish of doubt is buried in the earth as its last secret. (377)

This entire passage is a reflection of Adams's own rededication after a period of intense distrust of the world and of himself to the intellectual task that occupied him when his wife killed herself. It reflects the strain of his own continued belief in unity and in the universe as significant throughout, not simply in patches and instants. It speaks of his questioning of the powers of the mind, his fear of the inadequacy of reason. Yet out of just such elements, for the Gothic style and for Thomas, there came a great triumph. So for him, too, this book marked a new outpouring of his own aspirations. It was the beginning of a period of great exertion and risk taking marked by his willingness to attempt the mastery of a whole new intellectual world, the world of modern science, and to incorporate that knowledge into a structure worthy of Thomas, not as an artist but as an historian rededicated to bringing American historiography into the scientific age.

Nor do I see any will to believe in God balancing Adams's sense of history in *Mont-Saint-Michel and Chartres,* as such different readers as Levenson and Blackmur perceive. The book is energized by the vision that all cultures embody a fundamental organizing principle that con-stitutes, for each one, the truth of experience. Adams was one of the first to read a culture as if it were a work of art and tell us the figure in the carpet. The radiance of medieval art was enhanced for him, not by the desire to believe in that organizing principle, but by his hope and faith that his own fragmented culture might also emerge into whole-ness through the discovery of the yet unarticulated principle of its being. So too, Santayana was urging America to follow the example of pre-Renaissance cultures, not by borrowing their principles, but by imitating their method whereby America would be loyal to the charac-teristics most truly its own and make them the foundation of a vision of wholeness. Like Adams, while he wrote about the medieval imagination, he believed science could be the foundation of a culture as great as any that came before.

As Adams moved from *Mont-Saint-Michel and Chartres* to the writing of *The Education of Henry Adams*, he moved from the re-creation of a field of force that had decayed because it had grown too large and complex for the magnets at its center to the effort of persuading his own world to come into the new field of force created by the magnets of science. Or rather he saw the new field of force as potential to be actualized by our understanding of the patterns of its power and by our realization of the way our own lives as creatures of history would be made "once more intelligible" (177) as the light through stained glass at Chartres made its world intelligible.

Levenson quotes a passage Adams marked in his copy of Pascal as evidence that Adams shared Pascal's profound religious fear: "The empire founded on opinion and imagination reigns for a while and is sweet and unconstrained, but the empire of force reigns forever" (296). I see here rather a sharing of the unblinking view of a universe not ruled by Providence. This view pushed Pascal into religion but propelled Adams to an even more determined effort to discover what the universe was ruled by. Adams feared that empire of force, certainly, but he was afraid of its effects on his self-direction, on his rationality, on his separate existence and energy. He wrote to his brother Brooks, who was searching history for its laws and was not afraid of mechanist explanations, "To me, the new economical law brings us or ought to bring us back to the same state of mind as resulted from the old religious law—that of profound helplessness and dependence on an infinite force that is to us incomprehensible and omnipotent."[10] In the fear of that profound helplessness lies the source of Adams's ambivalence to Brooks's line of thought.

Yet he was not always so frightened of mechanist explanations. In 1884, when he was just beginning his *History*, he wrote a letter to Francis Parkman that contemplates blithely enough what it means to be a citizen of that empire of force if he could but understand its principles: "The more I write, the more confident I feel that before long a new school of history will rise which will leave us antiquated. . . . I am satisfied that the purely mechanical development of the human mind in society must appear in a great democracy so clearly, for want of disturbing elements, that in another generation psychology, physiology, and history will join in proving man to have as fixed and necessary development as that of a tree; and almost as unconscious."[11] Indeed, not only does he look forward to it, but, as we have seen, he saw his own work as part of the future school, while his joining of himself to Parkman as a fellow antique is purest courtesy.

4 The Dynamic Theory of History

The letter to Parkman quoted at the end of the last chapter makes us aware that when Adams invoked scientific history he meant something quite beyond the objectivity and presentation of documents that was the rallying point of the followers of Ranke. Further, scientific history appears to mark a surrender of human freedom in its search for what John Carlos Rowe calls "totalizing order."[1] Yet as Adams develops the dynamic theory of *The Education of Henry Adams*, we can see how it is an attempt to bring the energy of man and the energy of nature and of history under the same roof. It would be the salvation, not the surrender, of human freedom. This freedom would, however, be redefined, shorn of the illusions and pretensions of the nineteenth century, in fact, very much in danger of not looking like freedom at all. But the effort to find the underlying principles of history was in the service of this freedom. Otherwise history remained merely experience, and experience, as the *Education* is at pains to show, teaches man nothing he can use as a guide to action. Without underlying principles, history, like our private pasts, is an ironic comedy in which rational life is impossible.

In the *Education*, Adams comes to grips at last with the meaning of the phrase *the forces of history* in order to establish the relationship between man's energy and the energies of nature and history and to decide whether history can be said to have its own energy after all. Adams makes it clear that the forces of history can only refer to the forces that make history, not those that belong to it. History is the account of those things that do work or help to do work: man, nature, symbol, thought, ideal. Any of these may be force, and Adams uses the word *energy* interchangeably with *force*. Most importantly, the forces in the universe are not distinguished by their constitution, but by their function. Material, spiritual, intellectual—all these may constitute the "body" of a force.

In "The Rule of Phase Applied to History" (1909), Adams argues that man's conception of the dominating form of energy distinguishes different phases of culture. Acknowledging Anne-Robert-Jacques Turgot and Auguste Comte as his masters, he posits four phases, the religious, mechanical, electric, and ethereal.[2] The ethereal denotes the phase of society in which force is seen as mathematical in form. In that phase, physicists are no longer experimenters. The empirical world is left behind. The mathematician lives "in the Hyper-Space of Thought; he could exist only by assuming that all phases of material motion merged in the last conceivable phase of immaterial motion—pure mathematical thought."[3] The culture heralded by Bacon is no more; like science it has entered a new phase, in which ultimate reality is mathematical relationship. Nevertheless, Adams goes on to say, "Always and everywhere the mind creates its own universe, and pursues its own phantoms; but the force behind the image is always a reality,—the attractions of occult power" (310).

I

In the *Education,* man's conception of the energy that makes the universe work, whether he sees it as divine, as material, as electric, or as ethereal, is the primary shaping force of his society. Progress is the development and economy of forces, "man is the sum of forces that attract him; his body and his thought are alike their product; the movement of the forces controls the progress of his mind, since he can know nothing but the motions which impinge on his senses, whose sum makes education" (474). But while this statement, as Adams says, "takes for granted [that] the forces of nature capture man" and that man "suffers" and "is attracted," such a passive view of man's education by experience is contradicted by a following image of a man as a spider. In it, man watches for "chance prey," which are the forces of nature, and the spider "pounces on them when he can," for man does not merely suffer the world. He acts on it, seeking to "assimilate other forces as he assimilated food" (474). "The spider mind," Adam goes on, "acquires a faculty of memory, and, with it, a singular skill of analysis and synthesis, taking apart and putting together in different relations the meshes of its trap."

Man's web, then, is woven by his skill of analysis and synthesis, which along with memory makes a changing mesh, i.e., changing concepts for the trapping of different forces. These qualities of intellect, although presented under the image of a natural function that makes man one of the forces he seeks to trap, are not in fact inborn as in a real spider. They are taught to him by other forces of nature—fire, running water, other animals, even grasses and grains. And these forces continue to act on him, with his mind "needing only to respond, as the forest did, to these attractions."

Man is a part of nature but without the instincts of other animals; he requires education but gets it passively through an inborn capacity to respond as other natural forces and existences do to each other. This education includes the view of the universe as a unity. With no explanation Adams calls this an education "on the same lines of illusion which according to Arthur Balfour, had not essentially varied down to the year 1900" (476). Education then is seen here as a natural evolution that produces a man who believes in unity. The grounds on which Adams knows this belief to be an illusion can only be a new evolution, a new education which, of course, has been the subject of the book. The new evolution is the experience of the nineteenth century, which led Arthur Balfour to question the assumptions of nineteenth-century science. Adams, like Balfour, has put himself through the new science by which he has been attracted and is a new man. No wonder the conversion of St. Augustine seemed to Adams an appropriate model for his autobiography, just as the Church Intellectual of Thomas was a model for his dynamic theory. To students of American literature, Adams's call for the new man who appears in response to new surroundings and new laws has an ancestry reaching back to Crèvecoeur's *Letters from an American Farmer* (1782). To readers of the *History,* the twentieth century answers in the affirmative the question Adams posed at its opening: whether it could "produce or was compatible with the differentiation of a higher variety of the human race."

However, man as he emerged five thousand years ago, the "old" man, made an attempt to cultivate through religion the force he imagined to be a unity. Since he could not define force as one, he symbolized it as such. In other words, symbolic thinking took the place of explanation and understanding. Nonetheless, Adams regarded the infinity thus symbolized as real as food and hunger for they are all aspects of man's desire to assimilate power. In order to arrive at this conclusion, Adams had to maintain two perspectives. In the one, the infinite is real and the value man sets on the universe when he worships it is real. In the other, man's conception of the unity of the universe is illusion. The first set of statements comes out of Adams's sense of the infinite power and therefore infinite value of the forces of nature. His contemporary, Santayana, who wished to separate value and power and thought that religion made a great mistake when it tried to posit moral energy in the power that energized the world, urged his readers to recognize the true source of values as the hearts and minds of men and women. Adams is willing to posit value in the forces of nature. Or I might better say that sometimes he is. He is at this point in the *Education*, and he is when he is attracted to Francis and mysticism in *Chartres*. But when he speaks of the chaos of nature earlier in the *Education* and recounts the story of his sister's death, then the absence of value is one of the lessons learned, and he adopts the second perspective. This contradiction comes from Adams's groping for a way to do justice to what men, in his view, have justifiably believed, but ought no longer to believe. He is trying to provide a relationship between the world dominated by those beliefs and the new world he sees rapidly taking shape around him. His theory is not fully formed; he wants it to provide a way of seeing everything in Western history as part of a single, integrated, process. Rather than separate past and present by asserting that the past was wrong and the future right, he insists that history is a single process in which the past explains the present. Yet he feels disjunctions in history he cannot entirely overcome and to meet them turns to his theory of phases, which will allow for both underlying continuity and novelty. In the *Education,* he does not develop the implications of the rule of phase. Part of him is in a debunking humor and seeks to degrade religion as motivated by an appetite for power. Part of him wishes to mock established culture from his own position of privileged knowledge.

When he speaks of specific events in history, however, his own analysis stands out in relief. New forces appeared without society willing it, and the widening of men's minds and their ability to assimilate the larger field of experience came ultimately from the attraction of the new force. "The fiction that society educated itself, or aimed at a conscious purpose, was upset by the compass and gunpowder which dragged and drove Europe at will through frightful bogs of learning" (483). The climax of this process was Bacon's urging that "the mind should observe and register forces . . . without assuming unity at all" (484). This change like the others, Adams sees as mechanical, not voluntary. The new forces accelerated in their appearance, and mind responded, although painfully and reluctantly. In 1900 the new forces were no longer to be known empirically, and a new phase of science's response to nature is heralded, to be accompanied, it seems implicit, by new social relations just as every previous accession of new force has been. Adams makes no distinctions between technology and science. For him, they both encompass spontaneous appearances and mechanical responses to spontaneous appearance. When he speaks of the success of Bacon's science, he says a new variety of mind had appeared. But whereas both the slave system and religion failed Rome, the new forces of nature to which Bacon's followers submitted did not fail them. The key to their success is in their submission. To them, science meant "self-restraint, obedience, sensitiveness to impulse from without" (486).

At this point, a subtle shift in Adams's view of human action becomes evident. In his references to earlier periods of man's development, Adams presents events as reactions, but he also insists on man as a force. Early man, not yet characterized in particular social terms, is defined by his natural ability to assimilate other forces. As man becomes a social creature, the reactive nature of his behavior is emphasized. Whatever the action or actor, Columbus, Luther, the Puritan settlers of Boston, all responded to the attractive forces of nature; not one realized what he was doing. But with Bacon and his followers comes action that is self-reflective and voluntary. Adams may call it mechanical; nevertheless he characterizes it in terms of choice. And we are reminded of the image in Chartres in which the architect and sculptor sacrifice their own intentions for the Virgin's taste. In Adams's account the process of forces reacting on each other is seen as giving rise to a kind of purposeful effective behavior in man. This behavior, however, is purposeful passivity. It is a kind of endless play—that is what characterizes the new kind of mind. Newton watched an apple, Franklin flew a kite, and Watt played with a teakettle. Adams quotes Bacon's dictum, "Nature, to be commanded, must be obeyed," and when Newton, Franklin, and Watt held out their hands, "nature stuck to them" (486). Just when Adams seems to use this imagery as a prelude to formulating a new level of consciousness, he explicitly denies this possibility and repeats the figure of men obeying as trees obey heat and light.

The dynamic theory of history makes no place in history for conscious choice and intention. The scientist must observe and register forces, but he appears to do this in a state of unreflective passivity and because his constitution requires it. Unlike the artist, who has work to get done, the scientist and the historian stand outside a system of forces that expands and changes direction and speed as a result of the disequilibrium created by mutually attractive forces. The historian stands in fact at two removes from history. He explains change, not in terms of observable forces, but in terms of what scientists tell him about those forces. And that is true whether the scientist is religious, Darwinian, or atomic.

The failure that is the governing image of the *Education* is from one point of view inevitable. It is the failure of any age to educate the next generation for new conditions of life. It is the failure that moved Gallatin and Jefferson to claim that each generation is free from the influence of the past. This idea of failure is already very strong in the *History*. It is the sense that established concepts about experience constitute an inertia that resists the reaction to new forces. As a consequence, the inevitable reaction is retarded and made more tortuous.

Although particular minds are limited in their capacity to respond to new forces, Adams sees the mind, in general, as flexible and expansive. As new forces have multiplied and accelerated through the interreaction of man and nature, consciousness "has been induced, expanded, trained" (487), and men's faculties have risen and widened. When acceleration has actually brought society from one phase to another, as in the Renaissance, a new variety of mind appears large enough to encompass the new force, to assimilate it, and to maintain itself as a separate reactive entity. In 1900 the world stood on the threshhold of such a new phase.

Adams sees in the history of science repeated threats to consciousness by the "unknowable and unthinkable." In these circumstances, the mind tries to return to its sense, literally to think and know in terms of its empirical predilections. In this activity the mind enjoys a high degree of success, able as Adam says to "bar chaos out, but always assimilating bits of it" (461). The mind is not lost in the attractive forces; it is even mildly aggrandizing. It owes its expansion to its assimilation. Adams describes this process as a process of control, for in 1900, he writes, "the avalanche of unknown forces . . . required new mental powers to control." The new chaos is "supersensual" and mind must "merge" or "succumb." When Adams says "merge," he doesn't mean lose identity; he means to become supersensual, too, so that mind can continue to assimilate. The way mind does this is to enter the hyperspace of mathematics, as he calls it in "The Rule of Phase Applied to History," where, as we have noted, the scientist turns from physics to mathematics.

In spite of the searching criticism directed at Adams's use of science,[4] Adams unquestionably identified the crucial change in science that he had lived to see. It surely would be a change of phase when a society's scientists ceased to apprehend the ultimate constituents of the universe in empirical terms. The power of the *Education* to make us feel how fundamental science's changing concept of nature is to our sense of ourselves in the world and to our possible actions is unique in its time. Adams's long quarrel with Charles Lyell and Charles Darwin came from his belief that their science was contaminated by an unscientific assumption of unity. He found that their observation and recording of forces did not generate this unity and that the society that ordered its life on such assumptions was due for just that much more of a shock when the forces of nature became clearly uncontainable in such concepts. We must grant the force of William Dusinberre's argument that Adams's sense of the catastrophic as a force in history was fed by his wife's suicide; he wrote that every anniversary of her death brought his sense of the world's impending end to him.[5] Nevertheless, his notion of catastrophic change as opposed to small variations under uniform conditions comes out of the argument over Lyell's geology that predated his personal tragedy. It is an idea that not only describes the revolution of atomic physics in his own time but has survived to have its day in modern evolutionary theory.

The argument of the *Education* does not move, however, from science to society but from society to science. The major portion of the text is an account of Adams's failure to find continuity and unity in any area of his experience. If science urged these qualities as inherent in nature, it must be mistaken, and indeed Adams's exploration of the newest science finds, to his bitter satisfaction, that the older science is as mistaken as the science of Thomas.

Adams sees mind expanding and rising to maintain itself as a force in the new supersensual chaos and thus ascribes to it awareness and understanding, though neither autonomy nor dominance. Once the operation of the mind is conceived of as assimilation, Adams's conception allows the mind to partake of the energy that attracts it. It is no longer powerless, only less powerful.

II

But what of force when it is manifested in society on the level of historical event? Rowe, pointing to Madeleine Lee in *Democracy* and the young Henry Adams of the *Education,* says acutely that they are both seeking "that engineer of power who is the agent of historical change" (120). Both of them are defeated in their search because, as early as *Democracy,* as early as the years of the first conception of the *History,* Adams sees men not as engineers of power but as its "stokers and pitmen." In 1882 in a letter to William James, he argued against hero-worship like Carlyle's because, although he admitted that the progress of human thought depended on a few hundred men, he sees them as prisoners of the convolutions of their brains, like trains who have the free will of "half an inch on 3,000 miles."[6] He insists that they cannot tell us anything worth knowing. This image comes up again in the *Education,* where "a score or two of individuals" have shown the capacity to manage steam, electric furnaces or other mechanical power:

> *The work of internal government has become the task of controlling these men, who are socially as remote as heathen gods, alone worth knowing, but never known, and who could tell nothing of political value if one skinned them alive. Most of them have nothing to tell, but are forces as dumb as their dynamos absorbed in the development or economy of power. They are trustees for the public, and whenever society assumes the property it must confer on them that title, but the power will remain as before whoever manages it, and will then control society without appeal, as it controls its stokers and pit-men. Modern politics is, at bottom, a struggle not of men but of forces. The men become every year more and more creatures of force, massed about central power-houses. (421)*

This passage contains an idea of management that is different from that of control. Those who manage mechanical power are separate from politics and as ignorant of the significance and social effects of the forces they manage as the forces themselves. They understand how to develop or economize force; as industrialists they are entrepreneurs of force, and if their businesses are nationalized the nation will no more control the force than the original managers did, with the additional drawback that when the forces are no longer separate from government, there will be no appeal from their power. When Adams talks of John Hay's success in foreign affairs he describes it as coming, much as Gallatin's did, from knowing the dynamic realities of economic forces relative to the merely inertial effect of political power. The kaiser, the czar, and the mikado, Adams asserts, had nothing to teach Hay. Politics as politics knows nothing.

Adams writes of what he sees of the new forces on his return to New York City in 1904 in these terms: "Power seemed to have outgrown its servitude and to have asserted its freedom. The cylinder had exploded, and thrown great masses of stone and steam against the sky. The city had the air and movement of hysteria, and the citizens were crying, in every accent of anger and alarm, that the new forces must at any cost be brought under control" (499). He sees Roosevelt's battle with the trusts as a battle against revolutionary forces that upset the values and conventions of the old society. The trusts were "obnoxious because of their vigorous and unscrupulous energy," but he envisions the problem not as how to "control" them but how to create the society to "manage" them. The distinction between the words *control* and *manage*, blurred in Adams's earlier use, is clearer now, as is his conception of the sort of men who can manage as well as the society that can manage. Insofar as control means domination, Adams rejects the proposition that men can dominate the energies to which they react. As we saw above, he believes, rather, that men can develop and economize these energies. Men can come to understand their nature and function and facilitate their operation so that they produce the most work with the fewest obnoxious effects. Adams sees the forces themselves as spontaneous, amoral, and potentially destructive. They are tamed by men who are sympathetic to the way they work and can think in terms compatible with them. Underlying the ideal of their management is the image of their domestication, but a domestication that requires the man to change more than the beast and that leaves the man the servant of the beast. Adams's alternative to the image of the beast is the image of the bomb. Just as science is shaped by the objects of its study, so society is shaped by the energies it seeks to manage or is destroyed by them.

Adams knows he has not restored the idea of human agency—man as the engineer. He says of his view of history that it was "profoundly unmoral and tended to discourage effort" (501). But he found an immense satisfaction in his view of man's relation to the forces by which he was attracted. That satisfaction is reflected in his characterization of the new mind that the forces of 1900 would bring into existence. "The new American," he says, "must be either a child of the new forces or a chance sport of nature." Typically, Adams casts this prediction in the form of a choice. It is not, of course, a choice, although it is part of his satisfaction to cast recognition of truth as a choice rather than a submission. What he means is that either we understand the new man to be the "child of the new forces" or he will remain the other. The image he uses is not the servant, the stoker, the broker, the engineer, but the child—an image encompassing organicity and legitimacy. Otherwise we are left only with accident. To choose consciously to respond to the forces that in any case attract us integrates us in a natural process. Without process, we have only contingency.

III

In the account of this view of history as we have traced it, there appears a separation between science and history. The scientist reacts to the forces in a way that allows him eventually to recognize and demonstrate their nature. In other areas of life, politics preeminently, people do not perceive their actions as responses to forces, nor can they identify the forces that cause them. But process rather than contingency can only be established in our understanding of history if the participants are conscious in the way that scientists can be. Or so Adams asserts. The logic of the situation he describes seems otherwise. We are all children of the forces willy-nilly. Consciousness of this fact seems redundant. How can consciousness affect the truth of history?

Furthermore, consciousness becomes equal to force only through its interreactions with it. Consciousness is the end of the process and cannot, in the terms of Adams's theory, exist within it. In the *Education,* Adams seems to have the idea that education can facilitate its development or at least "encourage foresight and . . . economize waste of mind" (501). It is not clear that mind as Adams describes it ever makes a connection between the force it is able to assimilate and the historical events caused by the mind's "managing" of the force. In Adams's view, the separation of these two realms of experience cannot be bridged by the active participant in events, by the Roosevelt who battles trusts, but neither can it be bridged by the scientist, or by the financier or industrialist who understands his force as the scientist understands his. Yet

Adams scholarship has recognized how future oriented the dynamic theory appears to be. It has an exhortatory dimension, even a prophetic tone. "Sleeper awake!" is its text. But as Adams describes it, to awake is to be outside the process. Experience no longer can be an education, but history, which comes into existence retrospectively, can. Implicit in Adams's theory is a view of history as the bringing into consciousness what has been unconscious. The hero of history, then, becomes the historian, for he alone can bridge the gap between cause and effect. In Adams's description, science cannot stand for intellect or consciousness. Its "knowledge" of force is also reactive, an instinctive adaptation. Science is as much a part of experience as politics and cannot educate us. That privilege is reserved for history.

While we can see that in Adams's conception of the function of history, the multiplicity of experience has its place, in his descriptions of the historian at work and his vision of the study of history in the university that multiplicity is very weakly felt. Indeed, he had warned us that in the 1890s, before he ever undertook his investigation of modern science, he already felt that history "had no use for multiplicity; it needed unity; it could study only motion, direction, attraction, relation. Everything must be made to move together" (377–78). In the conclusion of the *Education* he speaks of history as the movement of a meteor stream whose study by the historian consists of the measurement of its acceleration through the development and economy of forces and the plotting of its past and future orbit. In his final vision of history in a letter attached to "The Rule of Phase," he sees it as the center of university education where all subjects, including the sciences are "grouped about" it. History would be

> *a main current of thought branching out, like a tree into endless forms of activity, in regular development, according to the laws of physics; and to be studied as a single stream, not as now by a multiversal, but by a universal law; not as a scientific but as a historical unity; not as a practise of technical handling, but as a process of mental evolution in history, controlled like the evolution of any series of chemical or electric equilibria, by one general formula. University education organized on this scheme would begin by ceasing to compete with technical education, and would found all its instruction on historical method. (784).*

What we live through as actors with an illusion of choice and intention is not history, and Adams no longer wishes to arrange it. In order to reach the level of significance in history Adams feels, he must rise to levels of abstraction in which history is no longer narrative. "The Letter to American Teachers of History" (1910) and "The Rule of Phase" are the frantic scrambling of a man working in self-imposed intellectual isolation to arrive at some way of implementing his vision, feeling death at hand, his ideas confused by his own concentrated effort to assimilate a great deal of new intellectual matter that he only imperfectly understands.

Although the arithmetic is embarrassing, the naive and arbitrary choices of numbers for his logarithms and square roots must not, however, obscure for us Adams's wide-ranging and often powerful attempt to bring the writing of history into relation with what science told the late nineteenth century about the human psyche and the energies that constituted the world. He was an acute judge of the historical profession's assumptions. If, as followers of the genteel tradition, history teachers wanted to teach that "not instinct but Intellect is the highest power of a supernatural Will;—an ultimate, independent, self-producing, self-sustaining, incorruptible solvent of all earlier or lower energies, and incapable of degradation or dissolution,"[7] Adams wanted them to choose this position consciously with the knowledge that it was at variance with science. He saw that for a long time American intellectuals were at peace with science because evolution seemed to make the same assumptions about the unity and progress of the human experience that religion made.

The arguments of the last works, "A Letter to American Teachers of History" and "The Rule of Phase Applied to History," are attempts to establish the limits on historical thought that science demands. In "A Letter," he admits that social energy, which the historian existed to describe, "could not be reduced directly to a mechanical or physico-chemical process" (10). Therefore, he believes the historian to be, of necessity, a vitalist, who exists as a force independent of mechanical process. But if he were a thoroughgoing vitalist, what was to keep him from seeing this force as self-producing and self-sustaining, as the university believed intellect to be? He also argues that the movement of history is dictated by the law of thermodynamics. What necessary connection is there between the law of thermodynamics and this vital energy that would make Adams view history as the progressive loss of a fixed initial amount of energy and the modern period as running rapidly toward entropy? To a vitalist, social change is not bound to occur as reaction to natural forces, so he clearly does not envision a vital energy independent of material process, distinct perhaps but independent never. But as his definition of force in the *Education* shows, he assumes that ideas can do work and are forces.

Twice in June 1910, after reading "A Letter," William James tried to make Adams see the distinction between value and energy. First he wrote that the value of human institutions "has nothing to do with their energy budget—being wholly a question of the form the energy flows through."[8] In his second letter he gave him an elaborate illustration: a hydraulic ram in a brook will "symbolize the machine of human life. It works, clap, clap, clap, day and night as long as the brook runs *at all*, and no matter how full the brook (which symbolizes the descending cosmic energy) may be, it works always to the same effect of raising so many kilogrammeters of water. What the *value* of his work as history may be, depends on the uses to which the water is put in the house which the ram serves" (347). But for Adams crosses and compasses are equivalents. Adams sees ideas as powerful in themselves, as if they had not been thought by particular men and women. He is not, we remember, an admirer of Abelard's conceptualism.

So the theory confuses because Adams can be neither a vitalist nor a materialist. Furthermore, it confuses because after the Middle Ages, all the ideas that Adams calls forces seem to be scientific and are no longer distinguishable from material forces. Similarly, after 1900 Adams seems to be saying that although ideas will be scientific, they will be mathematical and will again in his view be nonmaterial. At times, then, as we read Adams, history seems to be the account of physical energies that dominate the world, and, at others, it seems to be the account of man's changing conception of the structure of the world. An incurable dualist, who will not sacrifice one reality to another, Adams insists both that social energy exists independently of mechanical process and that the law of entropy governs that social energy and explains changes in society.

William Dusinberre, writing from the perspective of the achievement of the *History*, sees chiefly the destructive aspects of Adams's turn away from narrative as the right form for the historian and views both Adams's turn to the arts and his ventures in "arithmetic" as "two forms of a single reaction against the demanding detailed analysis of the *History*" (213). Yet we cannot do justice to the heroic effort of Adams's last years unless we realize in them the effort to go beyond the ironic mode of his historical narrative, to come to some understanding of why the old ways of looking at human action inevitably left men as fools, and finally to reestablish a sense of human agency, even if the arena for its operation is largely shifted to the future. Through the actions of economizing, facilitating, and predicting, the human mind would have its maximum effect on what was about to happen. Human agency, as in Marx, would exist, perforce, always on the forefront of history. There, practice and intellect would be brought together, and people would cease to be alienated from their own lives.

5 History as a Model for the Novel: Henry James

While Henry Adams confirmed himself in the belief that historical narrative would never show how things really happened if it continued to be written as a variant of biography, Henry James's fictional narratives also moved away from the model of biography toward the model of history. Written in a span of five years, *The Bostonians* (1886), *The Princess Casamassima* (1886), and *The Tragic Muse* (1890) all constitute, as Adams's *Education* would, a critique of the idea that the world exists for the education of man. They embody a rejection of the Emersonian view that individual consciousness is adequate to the meaning of experience. Rather, they attempt to find coherence and continuity by invoking a realm of action that, as historical, can tolerate the elements of antagonism, contradiction, and real change without diminishing in significance. Dominated by the sense of irony that comes from the confrontation of individual claims to power and actual events and from the variance of intent and outcome, these novels show that what is at stake in the move away from biography toward history is the fate of the individual will. They end in the containment of the explosive forces of history and in the establishment or reestablishment of an equilibrium that was threatened by the action of the narrative.

The Bostonians, The Princess Casamassima, and *The Tragic Muse* have for some time now been thought of by James scholars as the novels most influenced by the ideas and practice of the French naturalists. Most recently Sergio Perosa described them as "experimental" in Zola's meaning of the word: "marked that is by an awareness of social and environmental problems and by a reliance on the principle of full documentary exposition."[1] Although I am not persuaded that we can best get at these novels through such a term as *documentary,* James clearly had an idea of the novel quite different from the one he embodied in *The Portrait of a Lady* (1881). As he said in the preface to *The Tragic Muse,* the novel is much like a Tintoretto painting in which more than one thing is going on while the subject remains one. Although he did not comment on it, the space in the Tintoretto is public. The difference between *The Portrait of a Lady* and these novels is, indeed, the difference between a portrait and a fresco, between a biography and a history: in the one, the aim is to understand a person, the important actions conceived of as those which are characteristic of the person and explain her essence; in the other, the aim is to understand the relations among a series of events in which character is not wholly private but serves to connect and explain the events. In a history, whether painted or printed, character cannot be understood without reference to a sequence established among the events on the canvas.

I

We may come to understand better, through James's use of a biographical model in *The Portrait of a Lady,* the attractiveness to him of the more inclusive historical model. *Portrait* is a novel entirely consonant with the view that experience is the education of consciousness. It starts with ignorance and ends in knowledge. Its heroine is all potential at the outset, all finished form at the conclusion. It begins with unmarried innocence and ends in married experience. The birth, growth, maturity, and self-discovery of the heroine through the paradigmatic subject of a choice of husband controls the depiction of a world whose events are never explained in any terms but personal. Individual psychology is sufficient. What Isabel comes to know about herself is her attachment to a certain moral view of life that transcends particular historical moments. She returns not to Osmond but to the idea of marriage. Little attempt is made to give the manners so acutely observed any historical explanation. Even when a novel is so attentive to social detail that it can serve a later age as an historical document, it may not present experience historically because the author does not desire to explain central events or relationships in terms of the relation of past to present or to focus on moments of threatening or actual change.

Yet if we compare the conclusion of *Portrait* with that of any of Jane Austen's novels, in which the heroine enters a social world that complements and continues the self-discoveries that their experience has provided, we see indeed that Isabel Archer's situation is radically different from Emma's or Elizabeth Bennett's. Isabel's education brings her to a knowledge of the discontinuity between herself and the world and a preference for the world of beautiful but completed forms over the contingent world of ongoing choice and contradictory emotions. Like Henry Adams, who chooses the great abstraction of force that can be measured instead of the confusion of events, Isabel chooses unity and coherence over multiplicity, which she feels as chaos. Like Adams's education and unlike Emma's, Isabel's education is compromised, though not entirely failed. It comes too late; she has already made the marriage that marks her maturity.

In this disjunction between experience and the consciousness it educates and in James's denial of the chance for that knowledge to make a difference in Isabel's happiness, we see an ambivalence toward the relation of consciousness and experience. Her decision to remain with Osmond is in a fundamental way a confirmation of the self that chose him initially. Although in one sense Isabel seems now, by her loyalty to her empty marriage, to have surrendered her girlish ideal that there must be no disparity between what she is and what she seems, her loyalty is also an affirmation of that ideal. She is not tempted by Warburton or Goodwood, because they challenge an idea of herself to which she is already firmly committed. Although she appears finally to be acting as Henrietta told her one day she must—to please no one, not even herself—she is in the most important sense choosing and pleasing herself.

When James moves toward a model of history, the power of the central consciousness is markedly reduced. The explanation of his characters' fates is conceived more broadly than they are able to comprehend. Unlike Isabel, who is raised to her greatest prominence by her final choice, Verena and Hyacinth are in different degrees obliterated. When Basil throws his cloak over Verena and takes her from the Music Hall, part of her self is submerged; her identity is hidden, not proclaimed. Hyacinth not only kills himself, but, in our last view of him, his body is covered by the Princess. Both Hyacinth and Verena, it is true, come to understand many of the determinants of their positions. Neither, however, comes to the full understanding that Isabel achieves, an understanding that allows the reader to feel her triumphant in spite of her losses and denials. The design of the narratives of the two later novels provides, through the more extensive historical significance of the events, a sense of explanation and therefore a sense of external constraint and necessity that is not one of the effects of *The Portrait of a Lady.*

II

In exploring "the sentiment of sex," as he called it, in late nineteenth-century America, James sought for genuine historical explanations. We can understand *The Bostonians,* and the lives of its characters only through the events of their shared American past. For instance, Miss Birdseye's efforts in the great reform movements before the Civil War are central in forming an estimation of all their lives: "The great work of her life," James calls it without irony, was "her mission repeated year after year, among the Southern blacks. She had gone among them with every precaution to teach them to read and write; she had carried them Bibles and told them of the friends they had in the North who prayed for their deliverance."[2] She brings from the past a belief in justice and social progress that the events of the present do not justify. The awakening of moral sentiment for the eradication of social abuse that she thinks she sees in the ferment of Boston's Gilded Age is in fact a multiple degradation of the ideal of reform. Reform has become a subject for advertisement, newspaper report, and entertainment for the masses, as it will be if Verena speaks at the Music Hall, and for the mindless rich, as it has been when she spoke at Mrs. Burrage's soiree. In its passing from Miss Birdseye to Olive and Mrs. Farrandar, reform has been cut loose from genuine moral consciousness and transferred to the narrow sphere of personal injury and ambition. In Olive, a sharp but limited understanding of social reality combines with a powerful will and intense but poorly understood emotional needs. The energies this combination releases lead her to a martyrdom not entirely un-sought and a removal from the arena of social action in which the ideas she carries can have an historical future.

So committed is James to historical explanations that even Basil's love for Verena is presented as best understood from a historical per-spective. The defeated Southerner, the embodiment of the chivalric masculinity whose social basis has been destroyed by the war, Basil comes north. Like many young Southern men of his generation, he adopts the commercial ways of the society that has proved itself stronger. Basil's sexual response to Verena is intermingled with his feelings of resentment about the North, which seems on the verge of defeating him again. The result is that his will is made unexpectedly powerful. His need to see himself as the heroic protector of woman- hood comes from his fight against psychic disintegration and his drive to reassert his Southern identity as much as from his love for Verena. Out of his need, he sees a truth about Verena. He sees that she is not committed to feminism, that she is a conduit for other people's ideas, and that even in private she falls into stock phrases and mere forms of argument. To the extent that Basil assumes that a fundamental part of human nature can be distinguished from the social forms that express it—that personality is not subsumed wholly by social role—to this extent his views are James's. We ought not to assume that he speaks for James, however, when he asserts that he knows best which social form expresses Verena's essence. In fact, as a social theorist, he is frequently a figure of fun, with his ideas from Tocqueville and Carlyle and his groundless intellectual self-satisfaction. Yet as David C. Stineback points out, his ideas are not wholly deprecated by James.[3] He is also an outsider through whom the commercial, democratic North can be measured. The ambiguities that some readers find in James's attitude toward the woman's movement and toward Basil spring from James's willingness to permit in the characters a multiplicity of conflicting, yet coherent views of experience.[4]

Verena, as she is presented in the novel, is also a product of historical events. She is the daughter of a charlatan in whom the spiritual needs and questions of pre–Civil War New England are trans- formed into spirit rapping and faith healing. Her father has no essen- tial self apart from his meretricious roles. That is why his wife is never able to catch the slightest private admission from him that there is anything dishonest in his séances, for example, and why his greatest bliss is to find his name in the newspapers. Verena's mother comes from an old abolitionist family now allied, through her impetuousness, with a man who will sell his own daughter. Verena has been taught, then, to believe in social ideals, but her teachers have been hypocrisy and shoddy commercialism. On the basis of the historical model, the novel should move through these conflicts toward victory for the person whose historical dimension provides a connection and fulfillment for a girl with such a history.

To give that victory to Basil's Southern conservatism and sense of sacred private values rather than the Northern reform that Olive stands for makes a handsome formal reversal of the Civil War. The Southern defeat is reversed, yet Miss Birdseye's hope that a real Southerner will be brought around to the cause is, in a witty maneuver, given new hope. Verena's desire for a life's work like Miss Birdseye's mission in the South is given ironic fulfillment in her marriage. She too will have a mission in the South, and it too will be tumultuous. Of those tears she sheds when she leaves the Music Hall with Basil, James tells us, "in the union, so far from brilliant, into which she was about to enter, these were not the last she was destined to shed" (466). With that word *union,* James reminds us that society and individual lives are shaped by the conflicts of the past. Here the ending specifically invites us to see continued conflict, not resolution.

However, there is a narrative force operating against the sense of continuing conflict at the conclusion of *The Bostonians.* When we look at the action from Verena's point of view, we observe the biographical model in operation. Verena is yet unformed when we meet her. Stineback suggests that Olive and Basil are attracted by her "childlike weakness" (85). She is a consciousness waiting to be awakened to herself and to the world. She even agrees to forswear marriage for the movement because she is ignorant of her own sexuality. The drama lies in the emergence and education of her consciousness. For this reason, when Burrage and his friend mock her and Mathias Pardon offers to make a good thing of her financially, Olive's appropriation of her seems defensible because it contributes to a broadening and deepening of Verena's experience. Similarly, in New York, when Olive at her worst is tempted to marry Verena to Henry Burrage, she provides the increasingly amorous Basil an opportunity to seem to be offering Verena a larger, truer life. By the third part of the novel, Verena has been educated to the point where she must make the kind of choice that biographies from their earliest versions as saints' lives and exempla present their subjects; she must choose between good and evil and reveal her own moral essence. The most profound lesson of her education is the lesson of her sexual nature. Her choice of Basil is the choice of a privacy deeper than any he conceives of, for she is not choosing marriage as the social form that most justly embodies sexuality. She is choosing sexuality itself, for the sake of which she must surrender her loyalty to other social forms she admires and endure forms that are sure to bring her pain.

This biographical model of narrative interacts with the historical model to produce a great complexity and richness as well as a degree of uncertainty of interpretation, but it also competes with the historical model in the sense that Verena's choice is made without reference to the historical model. If we understand Verena's decisions as personal and biographical, then the historical conflicts involving past and present, public and private, North and South, and the possibility of changes in relations between men and women seem almost irrelevant. Verena's great summary choice does not seem to illuminate the historical themes.[5]

Still, in spite of the competition between the biographical and historical models, *The Bostonians* seems to be a novel that shows James's confidence that history as an explanation of events in the public realm and biography as the account of the education of consciousness are compatible and that it is possible to make sense out of experience, not merely to be reduced, as was Henry Adams, to measuring it. The fact that we experience the models as competing rather than wholly complementary reflects the strain James sees in the relation of private and social experience, the biographical and the historical determinants of our actions, and the high cost by which consciousness maintains its integrity and masters experience.

III

In *The Princess Casamassima,* there is almost no difference between the biographical and historical determinants. Like *The Bostonians, The Princess* works toward a public explosion that never takes place. In both novels, a moment of violent social change, the culmination of historical actions represented in the narrative, is averted by a personal violence that contains it.[6] Within Hyacinth's personal experience are repeated enough of the class tensions within society to make us feel that the full range of society is represented, even if on reflection we miss industrial workers. Indeed, James was probably historically correct in omitting a representative of that class from his depiction of the anarchist groups. In *The Bostonians,* Verena's experience can be interpreted in different ways, depending on whether the model of biography or the model of history dominates; in Hyacinth's experience, however, there is very little disparity between the two models. In fact, Charles Anderson, who argues that the social conflicts are to be understood only as an externalization of Hyacinth's internal dilemma and that James's theme was, again, not the coming revolution but the familiar one of awareness, creates a dichotomy that James's narrative avoids.[7]

Hyacinth's awareness, indeed, is embedded in the course of history, to use Auerbach's phrase, and his tragedy is the tragedy of history. The growth of his awareness as the hero of a novel on the biographical model takes him to the point where he cannot carry out his pledge as an anarchist. Once he becomes aware that the glories of civilization and its abominations are inextricable, he cannot act to bring it down. The story of his own family, in which his ill-treated working-class mother murders his aristocratic father, becomes a prophecy he cannot fulfill once he recognizes himself as his father's son. The relationship with the Princess thus represents one possible reparation for the historical injustice that is inseparable from Hyacinth's private life. With her, the injustice, his illegitimacy, is turned to possible advantage in two senses. First, it is the source of his "gentleness," that is, the nobility that makes possible his visit to Medley and his openness to the beauties of social form and art. Second, a relationship with the Princess marks the transcendence of class hostility and initiates the possibility of new kinds of social organization that will make reparation for past wrongs. The danger that Mme. Grandoni warns of is the lack of any basis for such relationship beyond the Princess's whim. The Princess neither seeks to compensate Hyacinth for the suffering her class has inflicted on him, which is Lady Aurora's motivation, nor can she transcend class and establish new relations on the foundation of common humanity. She is drawn to Hyacinth precisely because he is an anomaly within his class, not for any qualities seen independent of class. Her only worry is that having known Lady Aurora, he may not be as fresh a specimen, as innocent of the beauties of civilization, as she had supposed.

Moreover, the relationship with the Princess is marked by fantasy from its beginning, when she is indeed a princess from a romance, the same romance in which Hyacinth imagines he will be recognized by his father's family. After his return from Europe, the fantasy persists in the scenes where he feels a companionable intimacy with her at her fireside in a relationship that mimics the domestic side of marriage. In Pinnie's death scene, James reminds us of this romance, which is such an important part of Hyacinth's relationship with Pinnie, by having her voice the fantasy that during his absence Hyacinth has been with his aristocratic family, who will now recognize him to compensate for the depravations of his life with her.

The meeting of the anarchists, which precipitates Hyacinth's declaration that he will pledge himself to "immediate action," begins with Poupin's sense of the way social injustice is embodied in Hyacinth—in

his origin, in his "mother's disaster. . . . He was *ab ovo* a revolutionist."[8]
But James provides more than this rather mechanical explanation of
Hyacinth's revolutionary impulses. He vividly depicts the miseries of
London that Hyacinth absorbs on his long walks, "and as in that lower
world one walked with one's ear nearer the ground the deep perpetual
groan of London misery seemed to swell and swell and form the whole
undertone of life" (233). When Hyacinth learns that Hoffendahl is in
England for some purpose yet unknown, he becomes exalted by the
vision, "immensely magnified, [of] the monstrosity of the great ulcers
and sores of London—the sick, eternal misery crying out of the darkness in vain, confronted with granaries and treasure-houses and places
of delight where shameless satiety kept guard" (241). Aware that Paul
Muniment is keeping Hoffendahl's secret plans from him, a secret
Hyacinth sees as an opportunity for his own devotion, Hyacinth's
tension mounts; out-of-doors he attempts to relieve his nerves, but he
is caught between the sense of suffering humanity and the abject
helplessness and blundering counsels of the people in the room he has
left. Alone in the street, he has the vision of action that becomes
inseparable for him from Paul Muniment: "If he had a definite wish
while he stood there it was that that exalted deluded company should
pour itself forth with Muniment at its head and surge through the
sleeping world and gather the myriad miserable out of their slums and
burrows, should roll into the selfish squares and lift a tremendous
hungry voice and awaken the gorged indifferent to a terror that would
bring them down" (243). His relationship with Paul contains the alternative resolution to his disinheritance. In the brotherhood of the anarchists, Hyacinth might find both the emotional fulfillment he craves
and the new social relations to replace the class structure that he hopes
to destroy.

Hyacinth, James reveals, is as mistaken about what Paul can give
him as about what the Princess can. J. M. Luecke argues that Hyacinth's
tragedy originates in this fallible consciousness that makes him so
misjudge the two people he has most counted on.[9] Such a view is
certainly true to the education of consciousness that the novel contains,
but it takes an unnecessarily narrow view of the significance of Paul's
and the Princess's failing Hyacinth. Hyacinth is not merely experiencing a sense of abandonment by the people he loves in those hours
before his suicide. His anguish at the novel's conclusion, although fed
by his relationships with Paul and the Princess, stems primarily from
his indecision over the rightness of the anarchist views that have

brought them together. The fundamental change in his life comes
from his visit to Europe, where "the sense of the wonderful, precious
things" society has produced came to dominate in his mind "the idea of
how society should be destroyed" (321). After his pledge to Hoffendahl, James tells us, "a change had come over the spirit of his dream.
He had not grown more concentrated, he had grown more relaxed"
(321). Why should it be, as Lionel Trilling maintains, that Hyacinth's
decision to give his life to the revolutionary cause frees him "to understand human glory"?[10] What is the connection, never articulated by
Hyacinth nor understood by him but contained and explained by the
narrative, between the pledge to kill and die and the discovery of the
riches of civilization?

Initially, Hyacinth's entry into the world of beauty involves a
guilty separation from his foster mother, Pinnie, and a disloyalty to his
class as defined by his suffering mother. Pinnie's fantasy of his aristocratic family feeds both his own fantasy and the guilt that accompanies
it, which seems to make her death and the denial of his mother the
price for his new life. But the pledge of his life to the cause of the
suffering poor atones for his guilt and makes possible his acceptance of
money from Pinnie and Mr. Vetch. James writes of his "sense that since
he was destined to perish in his flower he was right to make a dash at
the beautiful, horrible world" (322). Furthermore, the antagonism
inscribed in his parentage is between the suffering poor and the exploiting rich. Before he goes to Europe he does not make the identification of beauty and power that will exacerbate his guilt and make it
impossible to surrender his pledge. In the Keatsian world of Medley,
sensual delight has nothing to do with power.

In Paris Hyacinth identifies with his revolutionary French grandfather and experiences his most exalted vision of history as mixed
destruction and creation, as blood and glory:

> *he had recognized so quickly its tremendous historic character. He had
> seen in a rapid vision the guillotine in the middle, on the site of the
> inscrutable obelisk, and the tumbrils, with waiting victims, were sta-
> tioned around the circle now made majestic by the monuments of the
> cities of France. The great legend of the French Revolution, a sunrise
> out of a sea of blood, was more real to him here than anywhere else;
> and, strangely, what was most present was not its turpitude and hor-
> ror, but its magnificent energy, the spirit of destruction. That shadow
> was effaced by the modern fairness of fountain and statue, the stately*

perspective and composition; and as he lingered before crossing the
Seine a sudden sense overtook him, making his heart falter to an-
guish—a sense of everything that might hold one to the world, of the
sweetness of not dying, the fascination of great cities, the charm of
travel and discovery, the generosity of admiration. (331–32)

Hyacinth appears to be preparing to take on the mixed guilt and power of a revolutionary, but in the last lines, he withdraws to a life of passive appreciation.

Yet the emotional intensity of the life that Hyacinth imagines as possible for himself becomes clear in the letter he writes to the Princess explaining his new feelings about the cause. Far from forgetting mankind's suffering, he has a more intense sense of the achievements they have been capable of in spite of it:

They seem to me inestimably precious and beautiful and I've become
conscious more than ever before of how little I understand what in the
great rectification you and Poupin propose to do with them. . . . The
monuments and treasure of art, the great palaces and properties, the
conquests of learning and taste, the general fabric of civilisation as we
know it, based if you will upon all the despotisms, the cruelties, the ex-
clusions, the monopolies and the rapacities of the past, but thanks to
which, all the same, the world is less of a 'bloody sell' and life more of
a lark—our friend Hoffendahl seems to me to hold them too cheap
and to wish to substitute for them something in which I can't sonehow
believe as I do in things with which the yearnings and the tears of
generations have been mixed. (334)

The cause now appears, not in the image of the French Revolution, which has been a great destroyer and creator, but as a "redistribution" based on "invidious jealousy." He fears this desire to take and to have in himself and ascribes to Hoffendahl the desire to "cut up the ceilings of the Veronese into strips, so that everyone might have a little strip" (335). Experiencing a "deep mistrust of . . . the intolerance of positions and fortunes that are higher and brighter than one's own," he fears, indeed, that such an intolerance has been his motive in the past. To take any part in the action of history, then, is to be guilty. Hyacinth imagines that to be only an admiring spectator of the results of its energy and horror is to be free of both the suffering and the guilt of action. He conceives of his revolutionary act as performed without the desire for possession that would leave the stain of envy on his soul. He cannot abrogate his pledge for he is caught even more surely by a second form of guilt, the guilt that comes from his recognition of the inextricability of beauty from the horror of power. Even scourging envy from his own heart will not free him of that guilt.

To this point in the novel, the claims of the revolutionary attitude have been strongly advanced, principally through Hyacinth's experience of the cruel London streets, based on James's observations of London, and through the pathos of Pinnie's life, with its suffering despite its unquestioning acceptance of social inequity. In a letter of 1886 to Charles Eliot Norton, James remarked that "the condition of [the English upper class] . . . seems to me to be in many ways very much the same rotten and *collapsible* one as that of the French aristocracy before the revolution—minus cleverness and conversation; or perhaps it's more like the heavy, congested and depraved Roman world upon which the barbarians came down. In England the Huns and Vandals will have to come up—from the black depths of the (in the people) enormous misery. . . . At all events, much of English life is grossly materialistic and wants blood-letting."[11]

The Princess, herself, makes much the same comment to Hyacinth at Medley, but her historical judgment is compromised by her manipulations of her husband, the comedy of her sacrifices, her love affair with Paul, and her failure to see that she is being used. Of course, James make clear that every position is compromised by the limits of the people who espouse it. As in *The Bostonians*, here, too, the model of history does not permit a privileged perspective. Because characters are in the midst of history as experience, no one of them can encompass fully the significance of the action as it progresses. And, indeed, James, himself, was ambivalent about social injustice and revolution. Two years before he wrote that England was ready for a blood-letting, he published *A Little Tour in France* (1884) in which he recorded his response to a bombing in Lyons:

> *Of course, there had been arrests and incarcerations, and the "Intransigeant" and the "Rappel" were filled with the echoes of the explosion. The tone of these organs is rarely edifying, and it had never been less so than on this occasion. I wondered, as I looked through them, whether I was losing all my radicalism; and then I wondered whether, after all, I had any more to lose. . . . I failed to settle the question, any more than I made up my mind as to the possible future of the militant*

democracy, or the ultimate form of a civilisation which should have blown up everything else.[12]

Like the irresolute James, Hyacinth, on his return from France, makes a half-hearted attempt to repudiate his pledge. In the scene with Paul Muniment at the park, Hyacinth shows that his desire to strike a revolutionary blow is inseparable from his desire to be loved by Paul. He cannot imagine how, if Paul cares for him, he can contemplate Hyacinth's death, and Paul's reasonableness chills him. He says he will not repudiate his pledge, but he seems to want Paul to tell him not to carry it out. Clearly, Hyacinth regards Paul as having arranged his pledge, and the reader is left with the sense that Paul will not let Hyacinth off the hook, exploiting Hyacinth's affection and admiration for himself but giving no emotional response in return. The "healthy singleness of vision" (379) that James credits him with permits him to remember the "immeasurable misery of the people" and to respond to this cause alone. Although there are no contradictions in Paul as there are in the Princess and he never claims to be something more than he is or to disguise his aims, we feel his inhumanity compared to the pathos and generosity of the Princess. Furthermore, Hyacinth's sense of Paul as a man of action and power makes Hyacinth's yearning to identify with Paul, to be his brother in social action and in love, another source of guilt as well as a reason to stand by his pledge.

Like Hyacinth, who both takes possession of the aristocratic point of view and seeks to repudiate any point of view based on class resentment, the Princess also seeks to free herself from class. She is trapped, however, by her money. In the comedy of her life, we see her trying to make middle-class bad taste take the place of poverty. But in its tragedy, we see her become aware that only the money and the husband she detests give her a chance to be a part of the movement, that her life is at its core a contradiction. Like the contradictions of history, her personal contradictions are the source of her glory and her destructiveness. She is capable of conceiving and projecting a beautiful idea of social revolution, and by this she constitutes yet another tie that binds Hyacinth to the pledge he gave Hoffendahl, even as she becomes ever more anxious to free him from it.

Hyacinth seeks before his suicide to escape the irreconcilable contradictions that are a part of his relations with Paul and the Princess. His desired return to Millicent would be a return to his origins, to unquestioning membership in the class that marked his childhood. Yet James has represented Hyacinth as alienated from this class by the contradictions of parentage and the peculiar upbringing resulting from it. His air of superiority and refinement make him attractive to Millicent, just as it is what involves him with the Princess, and indeed, it is what makes him Hoffendahl's choice for assassin. Furthermore, Millicent lives in the world of appetite and sensuality where history does not exist. He cannot return there.

He has not lived there since the visit to his dying mother in prison with which the book opens. Pinnie feels rightly the decisiveness of that visit, that in taking him there she has done something needing forgiveness, for she gave him then the burden of his own history. Hyacinth tells her quite mistakenly that that "dismal far-off time . . . had ceased long ago to have any consequences for either of them" (313). His last view of his situation before he chooses suicide is that he cannot bear to commit an act that would not only be a personal repetition of his mother's crime but would also be a blow struck at her by bringing her "forgotten, redeemed pollution" again before the world. In Hyacinth's despair lies the final view of history as a crime reenacted in succeeding generations. To such an idea dwindles the magnificent notion of a world-historical action.

At the moment of crisis the two warring visions of the fulfillment of his pledge are embodied by the Princess and his mother. In the last meeting with the Princess, she argues so eloquently and looks so beautiful that "the image of a heroism not less great flashed up again before him in all the splendour it had lost—the idea of a tremendous risk and an unregarded sacrifice" (495). But at the moment before action, he sees again the revolutionary act as a murder committed out of envy. His mother's act blots out the sublime vision of the French Revolution, "a sunrise out of a sea of blood." When Hyacinth expresses to the Princess his horror at the thought that anything should happen to her, he is speaking not only of his love but of his need for the splendor with which she invests history and human action, against which he feels always the tawdry drag of his own experience. She, in contrast, asks why she should be outside common human destiny. She cannot find her way into history from the world of romance and comedy in which Hyacinth along with the other men in her life and her own ambivalence imprison her.

The disagreement in the critical literature over whether Hyacinth's suicide is an act of heroism or weakness comes from confusing the immediate emotions that compel the act and the significance of the act for the view of history the novel embodies.[13] What Hyacinth as a character feels is loneliness, rejection, alienation, guilt, and the desire to expiate what he experiences as his own envy and selfishness. All of this is mixed with shame at not being able to redeem the pledge he made on behalf of the suffering millions whose claim to justice he still recognizes. But the significance of his action is far beyond what he himself understands it to be.

Ironically his suicide is the reenactment of his mother's action, a striking out at the oppressor class made futile by its private character, a denial of the revolutionary act. In a context where history is seen as the bloody transfer of power and the forms of civilization are inseparable from the class that exercises power, Hyacinth's act also denies a vital part of history. Preoccupied with the forms of the past it forgets or has no faith in the capacity of power to create new forms as it is wielded by new hands. Yet the pledge of the revolutionary act had released in Hyacinth both the response to beauty and the belief in his own capacity to create it. Hyacinth's self-destruction aspires not only to expiate the guilt of hunger and the guilt of power but to bring an end to the cycle of blood and sunrise he imagined history to be. His suicide strikes at once at the lust for power and at creativity, for if we identify power and splendor how can we deny our desire for the one without surrendering the other? The identification also dismisses claims to justice, yet the suicide constitutes a refusal to take part in civilization's injustice or in the destruction of its beauty. His alienation from Paul, the Princess, and Millicent speaks to the alienation that is both his birthright and his destiny. It is not merely the revolutionary act he cannot perform; he can undertake no action because he has no foothold from which to act. Yet every life must be lived from a particular point of view. History is made by the collision of warring and self-justifying perspectives, and we all live in history or not at all.

IV

As a novel written on the model of history, *The Tragic Muse* is less occupied with explanations of the present in terms of the past or with consequences of the past than with the attempt to embody the social history of the late nineteenth-century artist in fiction. The idea of social change as a road to more just relationships and the satisfaction of desire among those excluded from the ruling class is given a different turn than in *The Bostonians* and *The Princess Casamassima.* Through Nick and Miriam, James continues to explore the relationship of personal experience and the shared experience of history, but this time the tragic and sardonic elements of the earlier novels give way to a comedy that forbids suffering. James turns his back on the power of historical action to create and destroy. On his way to the entirely private worlds of the later career that open in the end to myth but never again to the power of the historical dimension, he shuts down the possibilities of significant political action and transfers all the energies of men and women competing for power to the world of art.

In the preface, James compares his novel to a play in which there is no "usurping consciousness."[14] In *The Tragic Muse,* there is no central intelligence against which all the events ultimately are measured, nor is there a figure like Verena or Hyacinth who advances on the biographical model to maturity. Miriam's training in her craft is a way of showing what it means to be an actress, not an initiation into selfhood. From the first, the characters exhibit a self-knowledge or a lack of it that is not altered by events. Their ability to muster the courage and perseverance to choose what is right for them and the clash between fully realized ways of being in the world are the main lines of interest in the narrative.

At the heart of the novel is a fundamentally historical action. Nick's choice of art over politics is an act of rebellion, a revolution against a way of life established by his father and maintained by his mother and Julia Darrow. In Lady Agnes's fate are embodied the social consequences—loss of power, privilege, ease, and status—that the choice signifies. James says of the Dormers at the outset, in the scene at the Salon, that they are "finished creatures . . . ranged there motionless on their green bench" (4). The exhibition carries a threat to them in bringing to Nick the feeling of "youth in the air, and a multitudinous newness, for ever reviving, and the diffusion of a hundred talents, ingenuities, experiments" (22).

Nick's revulsion from politics is not based on the realization that he hasn't the talent for it. On the contrary, he seems to have the abilities to make a great career: he has "the trick" of speaking well; he knows how to appeal "to stupidity, to ignorance, to prejudice, to the love of hollow idiotic words, of shutting the eyes tight and making a noise" (103). Nor is the choice of art merely a choice of one great life over another, for Nick sees politics as emptied of the meaning it had in his father's lifetime. He has come to believe that the parties have no programs, only the wish to be in power; Mrs. Dallow cares little for social improvement, wishing merely to preside over a political salon.

In the episode at Mr. Carteret's house, Mr. Carteret's prodigious memory of old cabinets and elections makes the past weigh heavy in politics and cuts politics off from life, as if parliamentary affairs were not ultimately the affairs of the nation. When Nick expects to see 1830 on his wristwatch, the reader feels further that politics was always so, a matter of form and precedence never filled with the excitement and splendor of human aspiration and rivalry. This is the English political sleep that the revolutionaries of *The Princess Casamassima* wish to disturb. Yet amidst the ruins of the Abbey on the grounds of Mr. Carteret's estate, Nick has a vision of England through the centuries, a combination of history and landscape that seems to make serving his country a relation of love reciprocated.

Whatever ambivalence the reader feels is dissipated in the unpleasant air of financial and emotional blackmail by which Mr. Carteret and Lady Agnes seek to maintain Nick in the life of politics. Nick can more easily free himself to perform his revolutionary act than Hyacinth can because what he rejects has little value in his own eyes. What he chooses is not only an affirmation of what he knows to be his authentic self but is a rejection of the hypocrisy and sordid manipulation that politics means to him.

James is not especially successful, as he admits in the preface to the New York edition, in making us feel what the life of art means to Nick. Oscar Cargill claims that James had no "fund of positive ideas" to give Nick the "quality of creative genius."[15] He wishes James had attended the exhibition of the Fauves and laments his conservative taste in painting. However, James knows a great deal about the stage, and through Miriam he is able to make clear the significance of the life of art to Nick and to herself. Through her relationship with the diplomat, Peter Sherringham, we realize the sense of power and freedom that Miriam's life in the theater gives her and the satisfactions art offers to rapacious drives. When Peter first asks her to give up her career to be "a great diplomatist's wife," she asks what he will do about "the demon, the devil, the devourer and destroyer" in her nature (254). She rejects the notion of keeping it under but approves when he says he "will gorge it with earthly grandeurs." Nevertheless, only when she feels the full extent of her power as an actress does she believe he has felt it sufficiently to make a mere actress his wife. Her anger that he should believe her to be "the perfection of perfection" and yet imagine she should give it up to be "a muff in public" for him is held in check by what she feels she owes him and by the sense of her own splendor, independent of him, transcending anything society can offer in position, money, or privilege.

The egotism and the desire to dominate and manipulate show most crudely at the outset of Miriam's career, and as she discovers her voice and flowers as an actress, they are the source of the prodigious energy of the process that culminates in the splendor of her presence on stage. James celebrates the power that makes her irresistible to Peter and to the audiences that she enthralls. The power, however, has as its dominion the realm of art. James repeatedly shows that Miriam uses gestures and postures from her roles in social encounters, so that we feel how insignificant the "real" Miriam is. The face, voice, step, spirit, turn of head, and wonderful look that Peter imagines will make her supreme in his world as they do on the stage will turn to mere manner in a diplomat's wife, while on the stage they constitute truth. The real Miriam is the woman who marries Dashwood because she needs such a man to manage horses, rehearsals, tickets, and publicity. Only on the stage is she the exalted being Peter loves. The freedom and power of art is not transferable to the realm of action.

The reader cannot suppose that Nick will attain that freedom and power. It is one thing for the classless Miriam, outside convention by racial heritage, to take up a life subversive to society. Nick declares his independence of his father's world, disinherits himself, and by forcing his mother to surrender Broadwood, destroys for his family the way of life it represents. But Nick's fate is a comedy. The world, in the person of Mrs. Dallow, will not let him go, and his love of her speaks of his imperfect freedom from it. She makes good the damage he has caused, restores his family to Broadwood, and marries his sister to Peter. The reader feels the danger of Gabriel Nash's prophecy. Julia and her way of life may prove too tolerant of Nick's art, and he will be integrated into the life of weekends in the country.

Miriam and Nick both rise above the unpleasant life that social and personal history seem to dictate for them. Verena, however, appears doomed to a continuation of the Civil War and fails to achieve freedom along with her sexual identity. In *The Bostonians*, James represented heterosexuality as a powerful conservative force, but it does not remove Verena from political life. Such a removal is Basil's fantasy, but the reader sees that such a fantasy itself is part of the political world. Every act in the earlier novel is political and part of history. Hyacinth, however, is destroyed by the contradictions of history and politics, for which James could imagine no resolution and no transcendence and whose explosive force he feared. The "demon, devourer, and destroyer" in Miriam that are inseparable from her artistic drive are a part of every action insofar as action is conceived of as the expression of the desire to possess, to dominate, to transform, even to enjoy.

Although Gabriel Nash is a version of the English aesthete, Quentin Anderson, in seeing him as a version of James's father, points to an important link between the way James was brought up to see action in the world and his devotion to art.[16] James, senior, advocated being as superior to doing, just as Nash does, because it is in doing that the demon is unleashed. In the world of *The Princess Casamassima*, there is no way to have something without taking it away from someone else. In the world of haves and have-nots, the have-nots can become haves only by destruction and expropriation. In *The Bostonians*, Olive Chancellor's character is developed with a sharp eye to its self-delusion, its narrowness, its intellectual and emotional ungenerosity in the first half of the narrative, and Olive reaches her moral nadir in the pages where she seems ready to conspire with Mrs. Burrage to marry off Verena in a way that will secure Olive's emotional dominance. At this moment in the narrative, Basil appears as a liberator, and to love him appears to be the choice both of self and of a larger life. Yet as Basil becomes more powerful and persistent, he becomes more problematic a figure, while Olive is given the moving scene on Cape Cod where she is overwhelmed by shame and loss, and Verena feels the cost of her alliance with Basil. Ultimately Basil is represented as capturing and carrying Verena off in a demonstration of domination more ungenerous than anything we have seen in Olive. In Paul Muniment, as in Basil, we see the singleness of vision that James associates with successful action, while both Verena and Hyacinth are torn by their awareness of contending perspectives. Both Paul and Basil share the rapaciousness that Miriam is aware of in herself but that is harmlessly expressed in the symbolic domination and possession of her art, while Nick does not.

All three of these narratives are carried forward by the interaction of different centers of consciousness with antagonistic ways of seeing events and organizing experience. They are pervaded by the ironies arising from these multiple perspectives, and therefore they withhold from the reader a firm moral center. In both *The Bostonians* and *The Princess Casamassima*, the past is morally equivocal, creative and destructive. The present is the continuation, not the resolution of that conflict. In *The Tragic Muse,* James envisions the artist as being able to free himself from history and live without the burden of ambiguous morality: freedom and power without guilt. But in the life of action, those who exercise power tend to be morally obtuse. In James's view of history, both as past and as contemporary social experience, power and justice cannot be united. All the revolutionary forces that James evokes in these novels are held in check by the very moral equivocality that brings them into existence. That is why, like the formal works of history by Henry Adams, these novels on the model of history reveal history to be comedy. But, while Adams strove to make his dynamic theory a gateway to men's participation in the amoral energies of historical process and to a recapture of power, James eventually moved away from history to define a realm in which all personal and social experience could be depicted entirely in biographical terms and a moral life rediscovered.

6 History as a Model for the Novel: William Dean Howells

In *A Hazard of New Fortunes* (1890), William Dean Howells's far-reaching and original historical imagination comes to some grief and must ultimately resort to myth to prevent consciousness from being submerged by experience, but not before it has brought into existence an impressive novel on a historical model. The novel is so compelling in its historical explanations that it enables the reader to see beyond the limitations of the central character, whose biography is both a part of the historical action and a biographical pattern competing with it. That there is no wholly independent biographical pattern is part of the meaning of the action; there is no wholly private explanation of Basil March's experience in New York, and there is no way to lead a private life in the New York of this novel. That is the education March's consciousness undergoes. Coming to the city as the editor of a new magazine, he sees the economic injustice of the city first as an exotic landscape, then as picturesque subject for his writing. But his sense that as a writer he is above the world of economic strife, beyond the power of employer over worker that he comes to understand is the reality behind the suffering he sees, gives way finally to the realization that he too is a hired hand and leads as precarious an economic life as any worker in the country.

I

Power in March's world is in the hands of Dryfoos, the newly rich natural gas magnate from the Midwest, thrust from his proper sphere of small-town life where he had the proper scope for the productive exercise of his limited personal abilities. The luck of the gas fields and a talent for the stock market have driven him to a social sphere where he feels lost and inept. He is led about by the impulses of his daughters whom he is no longer competent to educate, looks to the past for a memory of love, and seeks irrationally to bring to heel the son who has no wish to share his father's economic power. The values that acted as a brake to his will and vanity were lost to him when he left his land, and the social gospel of late nineteenth-century Christianity, which his son represents, seems contemptible to him. As a new capitalist Dryfoos finds his proper antagonist in Lindau. Lindau, a refugee from the Europe of 1848, a man who gave his arm in the Civil War and refuses to take a pension from an unjust government, finds Dryfoos's views abhorrent.

Through these men, the economic forces that explain what March sees in the streets of New York and what he feels in the end he must make the subject of his writing are dramatized. Because March refuses to fire Lindau simply to gratify Dryfoos, he comes face to face with his own economic insecurity. Howells gives parallel heroic actions to March and Lindau as they both choose the freedom of poverty and moral action. However, Lindau and Conrad, in his Christian view of the justice of the workers' demands, both act out coherent alternative social responses to poverty, responses from which March is inhibited by his sense of responsibility to his family, his liberal views that encourage a fear of excess, and a sense of his own limitations. One of the most interesting things about the book is how Howells compromises March's moral heroism, first by showing how it is made possible by his wife's small private income and ultimately by having Lindau refuse to work for Dryfoos, thus depriving March of the gesture he has mustered his courage to make.

By means of Lindau and Conrad, Howells is able to enact the violence that he fears is inseparable from economic injustice at the same time that the moral but peace-loving March rejects it. For March himself can go just so far in understanding Conrad's death in the strike in terms of economic forces. Before Conrad's death, March is drawn to the Christian theorists who tried to respond to economic injustice. He goes from church to church on Sundays, reporting to his wife who finds it fantastic and menacing: "She laments the literary peace, the intellectual refinement of the life they had left behind them; and he owned it was very pretty, but he said it was not life—it was death in life.

She liked to hear him talk in that strain of virtuous self-denunciation, but she asked him, 'Which of your prophets are you going to follow?' And he answered, 'All—All! And a fresh one every Sunday.' And so they got their laugh out of it at last, but with some sadness at heart and with a dim consciousness that they had got their laugh out of too many things in life."[1]

Nevertheless, early in the strike March applauds his son's common sense viewpoint, which allows him to separate the crank from the social critic in Lindau. Not content to explain how the poor suffer from the financial failures of the rich, Lindau insists also that there is "no need of failures or frauds or hard times," when the boy and his father know "there always have been and there always will be" (261). But after Conrad's death, March has a clear vision of the economic world as "one which men seem to have created," a world where the terrible economic competition cannot be blamed entirely on character because "conditions *make* character." He sees the uselessness of anyone choosing as a solution to live another kind of life because he knows how he himself is in thrall to those conditions. The simple truths of his son cannot encompass the complex reality he has come to know: "people are greedy and foolish, and wish to have and to shine, because having and shining are held up to them by civilization as the chief good of life. . . . we dare not teach our children otherwise for fear they may falter in the fight . . . and the children of others will crowd them out of the palace into the poorhouse" (381). Kenneth Lynn aptly characterizes March's situation as one in which "the traditional intelligence of Howellsian observers is rendered helpless."[2]

Howells has created in Lindau a man not in thrall to these conditions, and March admires him; but he tells his son that Lindau has died in the cause of disorder by trying to obstruct the law. Not to be in thrall to the economic conditions of the world men have created means implicitly to break its laws, to break down an existing order. But Howells cannot imagine any other road to change. March's son makes brief reference to the notion that "we could vote anything we wanted," and March agrees but in agreeing throws doubt on it: "We can," he says, "we can if we're honest and don't buy and sell one another's votes." Howells cannot allow March to suggest that politics, any more than literature, is outside this economic world. But finally the economic world is given limits, and, with the imposition of those limits, historical explanation breaks down.

Conrad's death in the strike is explained in wholly religious terms.

March says of him: "Conrad—yes, he had some business there; it was his business to suffer there for the sins of others . . . we can't throw aside that old doctrine of the Atonement yet. The life of Christ, it wasn't only in healing the sick and going about to do good; it was suffering for the sins of others!" Conrad, the son of the guilty capitalist, gives his life both for the sins of his father and of Lindau.

Here the model of biography interferes with the model of history. From the perspective of March, the historical consequences of economic conflict are intolerable because he is identified with the existing order; his coherence as a person depends on the coherence of that order. Therefore, his understanding of what he sees is limited, and he gives a mythic explanation, an explanation in terms of his feelings and deep needs rather than a historical explanation in terms of causes and consequences. At the same time, Howells himself is aware of the dissonance of this explanation, which is a nonexplanation in a narrative that moves March closer and closer to real explanations. The conclusion, then, caught and shaped by this competition between Basil as the center of a biography and as a character in a history, cannot bring Basil to full mastery of his experience nor can it embrace social change. Conrad's sacrifice interrupts Basil's progress toward an outward break with Dryfoos and the loss of his material prosperity. Instead Basil becomes an owner of his magazine and in that way is delivered from the threat of economic servitude. His new and more realistic view of New York's economic life, we are led to believe, will be incarnated in the magazine, and the cause of realism, if not reform, will be served. The divergent pull of the ending may be seen as what Kermit Vanderbilt characterizes as the absorption of "basic social, economic, and moral problems of capitalism into the issues of esthetic controversy," but it is also a function of Howells's irresolution over the question of the "possibility of individual effectiveness" in reform.[3]

Both the restricted solution to March's social problem, which is limited to aesthetic terms, and the inability to affirm individual potency are the consequence of the competing narrative models. In Howells's model of biography as the education of consciousness, consciousness is seriously limited in its grasp of the meaning of experience and can retain a sense of coherence and mastery only by recognizing the limits of its knowledge and willingly surrendering what it sees as beyond its grasp in any case. In *The Bostonians*, whatever the subject of the biography cannot learn, and in Verena's case that may be a great deal, she learns the essentials of experience. But in *A Hazard of New Fortunes*, while the subject grasps many aspects of experience, the essence must remain a mystery. An awareness of the competing models also illuminates a central contradiction in the novel: that the admonition that people must care more for each other, which is the significance that is most often generalized from the action of *A Hazard of New Fortunes*, is at odds with March's own realization that social conditions do not allow people to.

In his criticism, too, Howells moves from the biographical model to the historical. He says of Ibsen's *Ghosts,* for example, "who is to blame? You feel that nothing but the reconstitution of society will avail with the wrong and the evil involved."[4] The realm of individual responsibility is inadequate to an experience that can only be understood in terms of social change. Similarly, in a letter to Henry James in 1888 he shows more than his personal ambivalence over the possibility of social justice: "After fifty years of optimistic content with 'civilization' and its ability to come out all right in the end, I now abhor it, and feel that it is coming out all wrong in the end unless it bases itself anew on a real equality. Meantime I wear a fur-lined overcoat and live in all the luxury my money can buy."[5] Two ways of looking at his life make for the rueful comedy. His experience viewed as history reveals its true character to him; it is both rational and moral. When he looks at experience as biography he recognizes that his consciousness has not, perhaps cannot, absorb and make use of the truth that his historical vision affords him. As biography, his life remains an amoral contradiction.

Like *The Princess Casamassima, A Hazard of New Fortunes* can be seen as the second in a series of three novels that group themselves together by method and subject and as a group further our understanding of the relation between experience seen as history and experience seen as biography. These are all novels that follow Henry Adams's principle as it unfolded in both the *History* and the biographies of Gallatin and Randolph: personality and character are interesting and significant, not in themselves, but only insofar as they are representative of the particular historical process the narrative embodies.

II

In *Annie Kilburn,* which preceded *Hazard* by a year, the biographical curve of the narrative is entirely compatible with the historical curve. After the death of her father, Annie returns from eleven years in Rome to the village where she spent her summers during her girlhood. She is educated, has an independent income, and comes from one of the old families that the village recognizes as its aristocracy. Impelled by the desire to do some good with her life she believes she will find out how in Hatboro. She views herself as a battleground of good and evil forces and believes that she is the source of her own evil impulses because God, who made her, could not have made the evil in her. She therefore questions whatever she strongly desires. By the novel's end, she will discover how to do good, and she will cease to see life in such morally distinct terms.

The Hatboro in which she seeks to find her place is a farming village turning into a small manufacturing town. Annie's drive down Main Street on her return shows a village complex enough to develop a commercial life including a money economy and class structure. In South Hatboro, it has acquired a vacation community of the leisured class, whose women have fled the fatigues of upper-class city life: "the cares of giving and going to lunches and dinners, the labor of afternoon teas, the drain of charity-doing and play-giving, the slavery of amateur art study."[6] The sense of change is reflected in the commercial, domestic, and church architecture Annie observes on that drive home, and her own inadequacy to the ideals of the American past are summarized in the monument to the Civil War dead she had caused to be erected in the center of town. Appealed to at her residence in Rome, she had overruled the villagers' "simple notion" of an American soldier as "intolerably hackneyed and commonplace." In its stead, she commissioned a winged Victory poised on the summit of a white marble shaft, and as she sees it in its place she feels shame at its failure, its "involuntary frivolity." She feels it to be "such a modern, such an American shape, so youthfully inadequate, so simple, so sophisticated, so like a young lady in society indecorously exposed for a *tableau vivant*" (14–15). Annie's attempt to locate herself in Hatboro is inseparable from her discovery of actions truly responsive to America's best traditions.

The scheme of the "better" people of South Hatboro to finance a social union for the working people by a series of theatricals from which they propose to exclude the workers is the focus for an examination of the relation between rich and poor. This, in Howells's view, is the central issue of American society since the Civil War. Annie's decision whether or not to take part in this scheme will determine whether her life and the life of the class she represents will decline to a state of "involuntary frivolity" or produce an adequate response to a dangerous, divisive problem. She tries to argue on abstract lines with the minister, Peck, about what grounds the rich and poor can meet on, but he brings it down to whether she could feel friendly to the patronizing supporters of the social union and insists that the issue be seen as a personal question. Appealing to her father's ideas that American democracy was distinguished from and superior to the French ideal in that it made no assumption of social equality, only equality in law and in politics, she argues that to mix the classes would be un-American. But Peck reminds us again of the changing dynamic condition of American life. "We don't know what is or will be American yet." In this novel history is not a process completed in the past but an ongoing process not distinguished from experience.

The merchant Gerrish reminds us of the eruption of the new with his brash values and drive to base his public importance on commercial success. Putney, his antagonist, is a man of what he calls the old New England element, the people who were "on the ground first" and "have to manage pretty badly not to leave their descendants in social ascendancy over all newer comers for ever" (119). Howells sees these people, of whom Annie is one, and the poor who have risen out of their class without forgetting it, like Lyra Wilmington, as the possible sources of support for the working class, not the new commercial class. Putney realizes that his alcoholism has been tolerated without making him an outcast because he has tradition behind him, and he vows to help the men without tradition. In *The Minister's Charge* (1886), Howells had expressed his conviction of the complicity of all in the moral life of the community, but he had sought to embody it solely in the personal relations of his characters. The idea of complicity as enunciated in Reverend Sewall's sermon was left ultimately to work in the hearts of his congregation, and the novel sank under the sentimentality of such a view of social change. In *Annie Kilburn*, Howells puts his hopes to the hard discipline of actual possiblities in American society, to those few plastic areas in American life where impulses of the heart can combine with flexibility of circumstance to make some small change in the way individual men and women of different classes treat each other.

Annie's sentimental impulses toward doing good are defeated, and she comes to be ashamed of her illusion of power in sending the sick children of the poor to the seashore when one of them dies there. Yet her self-castigation is exposed equally as coming from an exaggerated notion of what good can be done and what good judgment can encompass. Similarly Peck, who has good sense about class relations, is also shown to err when he is censorious of Mrs. Munger's failure to remember Putney's alcoholism in putting rum in the punch after the theatrical. For all his personal courage and generosity, he forgets to take home his own child, who is asleep upstairs. Indeed his treatment of Idella is a serious shortcoming in Peck's character and yet a likely one in a man so intent on social action. Howells's people are always limited in important ways. He is most successful as a novelist in making us feel the reality of characters who do not entirely understand either themselves or the world. His view of experience as the education of consciousness is always to bring his people to the point where they realize how much they do not and cannot know.

It is typical of Howells's best novels that his characters powerfully urge their own points of view, often successfully undercutting each other, preventing any consolidation of ideas that will put an end to the multiple, shifting perspectives the novel brings to bear on any one aspect of life. This comes in part from Howells's sense of the limitations of reason and of any individual outlook. He says of Annie at the end of the novel that she no longer is sure what she thinks about the morality of Lyra's relation with her husband's nephew: "One of the dangers of having a very definite point of view is the temptation of abusing it to read the whole riddle of the painful earth" (328).

However, a vital aspect of Howells's sense of history and his belief in the possibility of change is also involved here. The conclusion of the novel focuses on the anomalous qualities of the resolutions arrived at as well as the failure of exemplary figures to teach. Peck is killed before he can show practically or even fully explain the usefulness of teaching mill children and living in a commune with workers. This book comes out of the period of Howells's discovery of Tolstoy, but Howells was at the least ambivalent and at the most negative about the element of Tolstoyan thought that took people out of ordinary ways of life into specially organized communities or into any way of life that was not organically their own, thus Howells's criticism of Tolstoy in *The World of Chance* (1893). Peck's idea of the millworkers' commune is not so removed from the world as the commune David Hughes leaves in *The World of Chance*, but it is not presented as an unequivocally productive choice. Furthermore Peck's death is purposely accidental and irrational, in contrast with Conrad's explicitly sacrificial and exemplary death in *A Hazard of New Fortunes*. About Peck Howells writes, "his death was in no wise exegetic. It said no more to his people than it had said to Annie; it was a mere casualty; and his past life, broken and unfulfilled, with only its intimations and intentions of performance, alone remained" (317).[7]

In one important regard, however, Conrad's death, as a mystery, an incalculable experience of suffering that is nevertheless recognizable as typical of human experience, is like Peck's. They both deny a rational basis for resolving the antagonisms and injustices at the heart of social experience. Indeed, Howells suggests that those situations that do not yield entirely to our sense of logic or our desire for clear moral distinctions are the most creative. Putney's alcoholism and his unceasing struggle with it is the root of the workers' confidence in him. Lyra, whose position Howells also characterizes as morally anomalous, not only because of her relation with Jack but because she was a young hand in the mill who married a rich old man to escape, is also a vehicle for new relations between rich and poor. Howells is close to the sense of history of the Adams of the *History*, where contradictions and ironies allow new possibilities for reorganization, where people act without a grasp of the entire significance and consequence of their actions and no analysis of the field of action will bring reason to illuminate all its dark corners. In *The Princess Casamassima,* the terrible and complete understanding that comes to Hyacinth makes new, more just social forms impossible. For James, when consciousness believes itself to understand experience throughout, then it denies change. Hayden White, in his study of nineteenth-century historians, said of Ranke, one of Henry Adams's early heroes, what is true of Adams himself up to the very last years of the dynamic theory of history and true of Howells, that *"obscurity at some point in the analysis is an unquestioned value,* is required by the apprehension of the historical field as a place where essential novelty intrudes itself under conditions and impulses which are *intrinsically unknowable.*"[8]

The biographical form of the narrative brings Annie to a sense of how she can be useful in life and where she fits into Hatboro society that is on the one hand radical and on the other conciliatory. Midway through the novel, she tells Dr. Morell that life is much more complicated now that she realizes that charity is no solution for the poor. At the same time, although she is convinced that justice can only be done by giving those who do most of the work in the world a great share in its comforts as a right, she also sees that until that can be accomplished, charity must continue provisionally. Shortly thereafter, impelled powerfully by her love for Peck's daughter, Idella, but also by her conviction that Peck's ideas of social justice make it reasonable for her to share in the life of the commune he seeks to establish, she offers herself and her money to his experiment.

Like the social union financed by the "better" people of South Hatboro, Idella is an occasion for the further playing out of the question of class. Her father does not wish her to rise out of the life she was born to but to prosper only as her class prospers. This is the motif Howells first worked with in *A Minister's Charge,* where Lem Barker's rise in the world is halted by his sense of responsibility to his working-class sweetheart. But the justice of his point of view is never established clearly either there or in *Annie Kilburn.* Because Lem's relationship with a young woman of higher class is fulfilling to both, his turn away from her is made to appear in part quixotic, and Reverend Sewall's initial conviction that Lem belongs back in the country with his family is revealed to be founded on an incomplete understanding of the family's financial plight. Ultimately, the novel hints as it ends, Lem will not sacrifice himself to his first love but will marry his superior lady. Social mobility seems denied in *The Minister's Charge* largely by misplaced, youthful idealism. Bromfield Corey speaks of Lem as the next generation's upper class, and his rise from poor country boy to sophisticated city man as typically American.

In *Annie Kilburn,* however, the distance between the classes is looked at from a different perspective. Peck tells Annie, and she ultimately recognzies the truth of his judgment, that she could not endure the life of the mill hands in Fall River and cannot come to the commune. At the same time, Idella plays a part in Annie's discovery that she need not sacrifice her own desires on the assumption that self is bad. Events support Annie's emotional conviction that she is the best mother for Idella against Peck's conviction that Idella must live the life she was born to and Annie's quixotic notion that Idella will compensate Mrs. Savor for the loss of her baby—a loss for which Annie unreasonably feels guilt and responsibility. With Idella comes the surrender of the notion of self-sacrifice as an ideal and the acceptance of the mixed morality of her own desires. But Idella also signifies Annie's adoption and fostering of Peck's Christian socialism. She becomes the heir of his radical ideas.

Nevertheless, although Howells speaks of Peck's death as merely accidental, it is striking that direct action is thwarted here as it is by Conrad's death in *A Hazard of New Fortunes.* In both novels, Howells denigrates boycotts and strikes and supports the vote as the road to social justice. But attempts at change through political action are not to be found in his novels. In *Annie Kilburn,* where there is nothing to approach the extremes of class and the depth of suffering in New York City, the resolution of the novel incorporates a modest degree of social change presented in a tone of gentle irony that defuses the antagonism, downplays the power either of reason or moral judgment, and yet leaves us with a sense of the openness of experience and the reality of positive change. Because much of the money from the original theatrical is rightfully the workers', Annie gives it to them to form their own social union. Annie has a rightful place in this organization based, on the one hand, on genuine common interest and, on the other, on a business arrangement whereby she is paid for keeping the books. She is aware of how makeshift an arrangement it is: "She owns this ridiculous, like all the make-believe work of rich people; a travesty which has no reality except the little sum it added to the greater sum of her superabundance. She is aware that she is a pensioner upon the real members of the Social Union for a chance to be useful, and that the work they let her do is the right of some one who needs it. She has thought of doing the work and giving the pay to another; but she sees that this would be pauperizing and degrading another. So she dwells in a vicious circle, and waits, and mostly forgets, and is mostly happy" (326–27).

This is how Howells sees the contradictions inherent in his capitalist society when it seeks to do good, but the contradictions are consonant with his sense of the contradictions of the moral life. Like Peck and Annie, Howells makes everything personal.[9] There is a little distance here between the biographical model and the historical. The individual moves toward a moral life in the same compromised way that society moves toward social justice. In *Annie Kilburn,* written before *Hazard,* Annie serves as the link between moral experience and historical change. She is the vehicle by which history can become morally progressive. In *Hazard,* individual moral experience has less connection with history. March's discovery that the relations of owners and workers make the world that so troubles him leads ultimately to a practical solution of his own problems: he becomes an owner. While this action provides the highest degree of personal freedom Basil can hope for in his historical situation, it does not integrate his moral insight in a creative way into his life as a creature of history. March's moral insight does, however, suggest a new idea of what literature can be and enables him to transform his writing from the remarks of a tourist to a form of social action.

III

Howells's memoir of his boyhood, *A Boy's Town* (1890), sheds light on his preoccupations during this period. In it, Howells writes of his older brother who was quite different from himself as a boy. The brother, he writes, had "an ideal of usefulness while my boy only had an ideal of glory . . . and his brother was a calm light of common sense, of justice, of truth, while he was a fantastic flicker of gaudy purposes which he wished to make shine before men in their fulfillment." His boy is gray before he begins to "have any conception of the fact that he was sent into the world to serve and to suffer, as well as to rule and enjoy."[10] Just so Conrad serves and suffers, while, for all his offer to suffer, March comes to rule and enjoy. Looking back at his childhood, Howells tells us, on the one hand, that to be a boy is to believe in one's uniqueness and to be ignorant of what harm is, that to grow up is to realize how much people have in common and that harm to others is greater harm to oneself. On the other hand, he recounts an emotionally central experience of his boyhood in which he found himself unable to act out these moral teachings of his family.

Howells's father was a Swedenborgian, and Howells was taught to believe in a "hell which each casts himself into if he loved the evil rather than the good, and that no mercy could keep him out of for a man's love was his very self" (12). At the same time, he discovered that even in his simple world where no one was very rich or very poor there were higher and lower, and "he was taught by precept and example to take the side of the lower" (22–23). He comes to have a friend who is poor, passive, and not very intelligent, thought of by his family and other friends as low. He tries to reform him, influencing him to attend school and helping him with his lessons. The crisis comes when Howells must acknowledge the friendship at school, and though he manfully makes the public gesture, he cannot avoid feeling embarrassed. The experiment fails, and the relationship is destroyed. Howells speculates that his friend felt as a wound "the shame that the boy [Howells] had tried to brave out" (193).

A Boy's Town is permeated with the limitation and fearfulness of the boy's life, and the profound sense of failure at the core of the story of the friendship is generalized in repeated comments on how boys' schemes always come to nothing. Also related to that sense of failure is the fear of death expressed through the boy's phobias and through his writing, where, when he imagines a character dying, he becomes afraid that he is that character. Howells appears to cast himself into emotional hell as punishment for failing to love the good sufficiently. *A Boy's Town* opens with the story of a tragedy at a military post. A soldier, condemned to hang for an act technically considered desertion, is hurriedly executed by the officer in charge moments before a reprieve arrives from the absent general. This anecdote, with its sense of blurred moral distinction, muddled judgment and responsibility, and ultimate failure of justice, is Howells's reentrance into boyhood and the eponymous historical action that governs his personal origins. Whatever the sources of these feelings of guilt, failed reparation, and punishment in Howells's relations with his family, he clearly associates them here with his lifelong concern for social justice, and they are the emotional core of his creative work during the period of *Annie Kilburn* and *A Hazard of New Fortunes*. *A Boy's Town* shows how deeply rooted was the effort to surmount in action the separations of social existence and how deeply rooted as well was a sense of the impossibility of this charge and the attendant, ineradicable guilt this sense of limitations produced.

The book also shows one of the vital sources of Howells's ability to tolerate the tensions of his complex response. Because Swedenborgians were never numerous enough to have their own church in the boy's town, he learned the lesson that there was nothing to fear in being different from others if he believed he was right, and he came rather to like being different. But the warmth and strength that comes from the combination of people for shared public purposes was outside his experience. He might have pushed toward group action in any case. Certainly, John Dos Passos was even more throughly deprived of an identification with a group and sought assiduously for it in his early adult life. But Dos Passos had not the strength of Howells's early lessons that a man was actualized in what he loved as well as in what he did, nor did Dos Passos's isolation have the spiritual warrant Howells's had.

Nevertheless, in the memoir, the conviction of community is the mark of maturity. Many boys go through life thinking they are unique, but they are boys who never grow up, he tells us. So for Howells, as for Adams, experience as a failed education is an often realized possibility. Furthermore individuality is downgraded, a mark of the boy, associated with all the failures of the boy in moral perception as well as with his impotence and fear.

The boy who reached maturity convinced of the importance of what he shared with others developed as an adult the idea of complicity expressed in *The Minister's Charge*. There is nothing in that idea not explained by the Swedenborgian upbringing detailed in *A Boy's Town*. But for all the development of social context in *The Minister's Charge*, the world of that novel is not historically dynamic. Lem's difficulties are part of the conditions of life, not part of a process. In *Annie Kilburn* and *A Hazard of New Fortunes*, society is historically dynamic, and the stories of Annie and Basil March are complete only when they come into relationship with that dynamic process, Annie through Peck's credit union, Basil through a new view of literature.

There is a difference between *Annie Kilburn* and *A Hazard of New Fortunes* similar to the difference between the *Bostonians* and *The Princess Casamassima*. *Annie Kilburn*, like *The Bostonians*, depicts a simpler more innocent world. In both, the Civil War is a symbol of the past as it affects the present; the conflicts are familial. In *Hazard*, as in *The Princess*, the world is larger and older. Through Lindau the historical past includes both Europe and America's own revolutionary past and ideals as well as the Civil War. The divisions are more profound, the suffering more acute. The social and economic changes embodied in Dryfoos are put in the perspective of America's historical ideals and not only explode in the strike and Conrad's death but find neither resolution nor integration. James, as we've seen, turned away from his vision to a rejection of the political world and a view of the artist as safely acting out the impulse to power in another realm. Howells too turned away from narrative on a historical model for several years.

IV

He returned to it in 1893 with *The World of Chance*, and in that novel we see many of the attitudes of Henry Adams toward the concepts of intention and action, a like diminution of human agency and an emphasis on looking at action as the outcome of events not initiated by us. Even more than in *Hazard*, the narrative gives us multiple points of view without a humane synthesizing figure like Basil to serve as a moral touchstone. The idea has been advanced that the book shows Howells unable to resolve his own conflicts.[11] The view that the antagonistic ideas of Hughes, Kane, Denton, and Ray show a novelist who cannot integrate his own fragmented intellectual life depends, it seems to me, on the frustration necessarily attendant on a search for a biographical model, with its view of experience as the education of consciousness. The reader without such an expectation finds a novel that exploits its historical model to an impressively integrated effect.

The limiting biographical element of the novel is the experience of the young writer Shelley Ray, who comes to New York with a first novel that serves as a gentle mockery of variations on Howells's ideal of realism in fiction as well as an affirmation of Howells's confidence that the novel's rightful subject is the common man, its rightful audience, the masses, and its rightful aim, social reform. Howells's historically modeled narrative is concerned with social reform and economic justice. The center of this narrative is David Hughes, who carries the tradition of reform from Brook Farm to Tolstoy. He comes to the city fresh from the dissolution of a commune in New Jersey, which he saw as suffering from the same shortcomings as Tolstoy's efforts to live his socialism. According to Hughes, Tolstoy retired into peasantry as into a monastery, away from the scene of struggle. To Hughes, political action is the proper course of reform. Howells, however, uses the skeptical and ironic Kane to undercut Hughes's idealism: "He sees now that the right way to universal prosperity and peace is the political way and if he could live long enough, we should see him in Congress—if we lived long enough."[12]

Kane shows us what is distorted in Hughes's altruistic philosophy. A post-Darwinian man, as Hughes does not seem to be, Kane finds Hughes's philosophy unrealistic because unlike Hughes he does not believe the altruistic can be separated from the egotistic any more that the spiritual can be from the animal. Nature, he thinks, "through a million blunders" and the destruction of "myriads of types" arrives at imperfect man. "If our human intelligence could be put in possession of the human body, we should have altruism at once. We should not get hungry three times a day." Instead of the stomach we have, we should have one "responsive to all emotions of philanthropy" (99). Kane sees "these reformers" as very like the old-time abolitionists and thereby puts political efforts at reform in the same impotent frame as Hughes puts Tolstoyan efforts.

Hughes's son-in-law, Ansel Denton, embodies a pathological strain of reform, a dangerous mixture of religion and reform that has been typically American. When Denton searches for the meaning of the suffering caused by economic injustice, he does it in terms of individual responsibility: "Someone must be responsible. Someone must atone. Who shall it be?" (196). He feels that his invention, which gave a man's job to a machine, was a sin and asks, "How shall the sin be remitted?" This is the language, not of moral responsibility, but of religious mystery. Howells has pushed past the position he allowed Basil March to take in *A Hazard of New Fortunes,* in which the death of Conrad in the strike was a type of Christian suffering that constituted for those who watched it an imitation of Christ. But that significance was wholly a matter for the observer. Conrad had no such motive or intention. Howells's creation of Denton seems to suggest that Howells saw that Basil's claim for Conrad was, on the one hand, mere metaphor and, on the other hand, constituted a great danger for men and women dedicated to alleviating economic suffering and made desperate by their impotence.

Hughes tries to make one important distinction for Denton between religious mystery and moral responsibility by saying, "Men have nothing to do with the remission of sins; it is their business to cease to do evil" (247). Hughes's daughter, Peace, also urges on him "justice not sacrifice." Denton responds, "What is justice but sacrifice?" Peace says, "Yes, it is self-sacrifice. All our selfish wishes" (248). The guilt, frustration, and fear of punishment that we saw as part of Howells's psychic economy in *A Boy's Town* appear here in an unstable mixture that finally explodes in Denton's attempt to sacrifice Peace and in his own suicide. Denton is a madman, but Howells does not represent him as alien to normal humananity. Rather he presents him as an exacerbated part of it kept harmless in the sheltered life of the commune and held in check briefly by Peace's understanding and loving-kindness. His crisis comes when he must live in the ordinary economic world, where his sense of guilt and responsibility and his repressed anger cannot be soothed by human relationships and there can no longer be peace for him.

Hughes has no sons, and Denton's death raises the question of the future of reform. Ray appears in a filial role as he visits Hughes daily in his last illness. Hughes passes on to Ray the same conviction Basil came to and Howells himself held. He advises Ray to make the literary department of the periodical that he has been hired to conduct ethical: "literature should be the handmaid of reform" (290). He regretted that he had not cast his own views in the form of fiction. At this point it appears that Ray will be Hughes's intellectual son, not Denton, the religious maniac, or Kane, the Darwinian skeptic. Yet Ray's novel hardly seems a successor to a philosophic tract. With its modern version of Romeo and its romantic elements intermixed with realistic characters, it seems rather what comes to replace philosophy and social aspiration in American literature, just as it is chosen by the publisher explicitly in preference to Hughes's book. Howells puts space between his own esthetic ideals and Ray's book by having one reviewer praise it for moving from gross realism to spiritual realism and having a Southern lady interviewer suggest that its success rests on the readiness for psychological realism in an audience weary of the "photographic, commonplace school." How often was Howells criticized in his time for his gross realism and his photographic, commonplace art! Nor are we given any reason to believe that the novel was merely the work of Ray's youth, to give way to the kind of art Hughes urges on him.

Furthermore Peace brings to a halt her budding romance with Ray, offering no explanation beyond a change in her feelings. Ray also proves to be half-hearted in his love and to accept her rejection with relief. Not merely an example of the realist's programmatically resolute rejection of easy romantic conclusions, the failure of their relationship is also a denial to Ray of the healing and binding experience of love that Peace incarnates. It leaves Ray, as Howells did not leave either Annie Kilburn or Basil March, without an emotional center and significance in his life.[13] For Annie, Dr. Morrell meant humane tolerance for limitation, skepticism over the efficiency of large gestures, and a belief in the satisfactions to be found in spite of a morally ambiguous world. To choose to love him when she might have worshiped the idealist Peck is an affirmation of a real though limited order in life. Basil March's marriage is shown to be capable 'of withstanding the strain of his economic education, and his commitment to his family is integral at once to his danger, to his moral courage, and to his moral limitiations. The romantic relationship between Margaret Vance and Conrad, though it is tragically unfulfilled, embodies the idealism and self-sacrifice of the Christian socialism that brought Conrad to the strike. It was a terrible accident that he was killed, but, as Basil tells us, he had proper business there, and his death, to which Margaret sent him, had significance for the life of society for onlookers enabled to see that men, as Howells put it in *A Boy's Town*, were put on earth "to serve and suffer, as well as to rule and enjoy" (185).

The ending of Ray's relationship with Peace is the significant culmination of the narrative on the model of biography. Experience has proved to be a failed education for him. Ray's interaction with Hughes never supposes an involvement on his part in the issues that

Hughes stands for. Ray is capable of human sympathies and a sense of obligation toward the Hughes family in their suffering but nothing beyond that. Howells's narrative insistently cuts off what happens to Ray in his search to succeed as a writer from the ongoing process of historical change in which Hughes's life has been immersed. While Basil's education opens his eyes to the true causes of suffering and his part in the economic relations that rule the world, Ray's education reveals to him the absence of any ruling principles. The book opens with a conversation overheard by Ray in which a business man describes his failure: "I've heard about the law of demand and supply before. There's about as much of a law to it as there is to three-card monte" (22). He discovers that the publication of his book, its success, and the end of its popularity are all equally inexplicable. It is striking that in an area where Howells might have emphasized the place of ability, not only in the novel, which we are shown is a very weak affair, but in Ray's work as a journalist, Howells specifically downplays the efficacy of Ray's talent and effort, and the accident of his success in becoming an editor even exceeds that of his novel.

Kane responds to Ray's questioning of causes, not with a denial of cause, but with a separation of it from its effects:

> *"Why do we always seek a law for things? Is there a law for ourselves? We think so, but it's out of sight for the most part, and generally we act from mere caprice, from impulse. . . . I couldn't honestly say that I've seen the cause overtaken by the consequence more than two or three times. . . . Consequences I've seen a plenty, but not causes. Perhaps this is merely a sphere of ultimations. We used to flatter ourselves in the simple old days, when we thought we were preparing tremendous effects, to follow elsewhere, by what we said and did here. But what if the things that happen here are effects initiated elsewhere? . . . Everything in the universe is related to that book, if you could only see it properly. If it has stopped selling it is probably because the influence of some favorable star, extinguished thousands of years ago, has just ceased to reach this planet." (360)*

Lest the reader of *The World of Chance* not take Kane, the skeptic, seriously enough, Howells concludes with Ray's less ironic recapitulation of Kane's conclusions: not only did chance govern the economic world, but "he had found the same caprice, the same rule of mere casuality in the world which we supposed to be ordered by law—the world of thinking, the world of feelings. . . . yet somehow we felt, we knew, that justice ruled the universe. Nothing, then, that seemed chance was really chance. It was the operation of a law so large that we caught a glimpse of its vast orbit one or twice in a lifetime. It was Providence" (374–75).

Certainly we see Howells in the teeth of his own admission that experience did not bear him out, clinging to the notion of a moral and orderly significant universe. His response to the failure of experience to educate us in the causes of things is to broaden his perspective. Like Henry Adams he holds on to order by surrendering the belief that we can come to it through experience.

The narrative on the model of biography, which was so power-fully united with the narrative on the model of history in *Annie Kilburn* and *A Hazard of New Fortunes,* is severed from it. It is not so much a question of a growing pessimism in Howells's historical perspective. Certainly the two earlier novels cannot be said to be optimistically expectant of social improvement. Nevertheless, people achieved an understanding of their own lives only through the transcendence of the merely personal; they entered the realms of significance and au-thenticity through a social experience conceived of as historically dy-namic. Howells, like the young Adams, at one point believed that history could be made rational by individual moral behavior. Until it was, history would remain just what happened before and after a moment of time, but once the world of thinking and feeling was brought into conjunction with it, history would lose its contingency. Indeed, David Hughes dies secure in that belief. The pathos of the ending of *The World of Chance* is not the discovery that history as it is manifested in economic circumstance and its attendant suffering is a world of accident, but that if the world of thinking and feeling is what Ray thinks it is, then history will always be accident, and the only view we can take of David Hughes is Kane's mockery. The idea that justice or Providence was a law so large that "we caught a glimpse of its vast orbit once or twice in a lifetime" is the serious side of Kane's joke that he would see Hughes in Congress if he lived long enough. *The World of Chance* marks Howells's surrender of an intense preoccupation and a rewarding mode of narrative. As decisively as James, Howells turned away from narrative on the model of history in favor of the model of biography, biography distinguished by the psychological realism he humorously ascribed to Ray's novel.

7 Biography as a Model for the Novel: Theodore Dreiser

Theodore Dreiser's most powerful novels are written on the model of biography, but the idea of experience as the education of consciousness, the foundation of the novel on a biographical model throughout the nineteenth century, no longer informs them. The idea of character that was already changing in Adams's biographies of Gallatin and Randolph is further revised in Dreiser's studies of the relation of the self and power. In Adams's biographies, character, seen as the innate germ of the self, set direction and limits to the shaping force of circumstance. Because experience was still seen as education, the force of circumstance, historical circumstance in Adams's narrative, became conscious and was integrated into the self. Historical energy, then, instead of remaining mechanical and alien, became the energy of the biographical subjects' own lives. Whatever significance or power they had was inseparable from the historical process. They were not then subject to it nor were they its victims; they were inseparable from it.

Dreiser's fictional biographies question more ruthlessly the educational possibilities of experience and conclude that there is no distinction between self and character. Nor is there a distinction between the self and its circumstances, nor any means to make conscious the significance of the natural process that both the circumstances of the self and the self comprise. How then can there be an education? Who would be its subject and what its object?

Dreiser's novels are all accounts of experience as failed education.

His characters do not learn, change or grow in the way James's and Howells's do. They discover the scope the world offers for their appetites. They come to feel their strengths and weaknesses, but the significance of their own lives lies beyond them. Indeed, readers of *Sister Carrie* (1900) and *The Financier* (1912) are often made to feel that the meaning of the characters' lives is simply the play of appetite in the world. In his greatest novel, *An American Tragedy* (1925), written after long reflection on the significance of humanity in a universe made of atoms in unstable combination, he so epitomizes the frustration of desire as to make its inevitable and therefore legitimate demands and equally inevitable and legitimate defeats appear as truth, not only about appetite but every aspiration.

Dreiser, too, is impelled by realism's demand to show things as they really happen. Much of his work is a reaction against what he saw as the moral hypocrisy that pretends, as he says in *The Financier,* that there are other laws that govern human behavior than the "subtle will and power of the individual to achieve."[1] At the same time, his novels establish a present time as inevitable and natural, and in it the historical dimension that characterized realism in James and Howells disappears into a representation of events as a natural process in which actions are variations on a few unchanging basic patterns of appetite and will. He looked neither to the past to explain present events nor to collective social experience to explain his characters' lives. The elaborately realized social circumstances of a Frank Cowperwood or a Clyde Griffith are given to show us the objects of their desire and the possibilities for its fulfillment or frustration. We are not invited by Dreiser to imagine changes in these circumstances by which the events in the novels might be changed, lives more fulfilled, tragedies averted. Not that he shows us a static world. On the contrary, it is always in motion, but its dynamic is the dynamic of philosophical naturalism, not history. There is movement, but no real change, just the repetition of certain patterns of growth and decline. Historical events are mere epiphenomena of the underlying reality, a physical process in which people and their circumstances are an integral part. Yet his analysis of crime and punishment in *The Financier* and *An American Tragedy* constitutes a remarkable counterpart to the analysis of constitutional law that characterized so many of Charles Beard's books. Like Beard, Dreiser strove to destroy abstractions by showing in practice both crime and society's response to it. But while Beard sought thereby to show that what was made by individuals with certain interest might be changed by others with different concerns, Dreiser sought not so much to effect changes in social arrangements as to remove cant from our thinking and to make us responsive to the moral equivocality of experience. When other writers, responding to the cry of realism to show things as they are, turned to economic, political, and social events to supplant ideal explanations of conduct and institutions, Dreiser could not follow them. To him they were merely part of the changing phenomenon of existence; they did not explain.

Howells, James, and Adams had all turned away from the search that Emerson had told another generation was the "dream of youth and the most serious occupation of manhood," the search "after the great man."[2] But it was something very much like this search that Dreiser undertook. "I should like to see," he wrote in 1911, "a race of people for once on this earth who like Niccolo Machiavelli could look life in the face."[3] What he shows us in *The Financier* is not the superman that some critics have called Cowperwood,[4] but the eponymous hero of such a race.

Eager to defend Dreiser from the charges of immorality on the one hand and intellectual muddle on the other, some critics have put the book into a moral context[5] and have seen the sympathy Cowperwood's rise aroused in the reader as something to be explained by his virtues and his opponent's vices.[6] But Cowperwood is best understood in the context that Dreiser's naturalism established for him, not in the quite foreign context of the moral education or the conflict between the individual and society that define so many other novels with ambitious protagonists. As Donald Pizer has eloquently argued,[7] the question of how Dreiser is a naturalist is not simple, but it is inextricable from his use of biography as a model for fiction and from the power of his novels.

I

Frank Cowperwood is a man like the managers of force Henry Adams called for in *The Education of Henry Adams.* He understands the lines of true force in his society and in manipulating them prospers. He is not distracted by sentiment, morality, ideals, or conventions. He feels the energies of his own sexuality and, understanding the connection between that appetite and his drive for power, he draws strength from his belief that through this appetite he shares in the energies that drive the world. As in Adams and in Emerson before him, the question of the relation of the individual to power refuses a clear-cut resolution. But even to put it this way is to suggest a dualism, a separation of the individual from the social and material order that Dreiser denies. As Eliseo Vivas has said, relationships with society in Dreiser's novels are "integral and internal," not external. Society is "an organic pattern and it makes the individual possible as much as the individual makes it possible"(35). But that pattern is above all else dynamic: its relations are in continual readjustment. Cowperwood understands his appetites and the part of the social organism his energies contribute to. He trusts to the legitimacy of his own impulses and like Emerson sees the conventions of society as in conspiracy against his manhood.

Nature speaks its lesson to the young Frank in the much-remarked-upon parable of the lobster and the squid. It is a measure of how far Dreiser is from Emerson that the lobster and the squid are not in a natural environment but confined in unnaturally close quarters by human hands. In a natural context, the contest might have been more equal. When Frank observes "that the squid wasn't quick enough" (8), we must add, nor could he be in that small tank. Yet for Dreiser this distortion of society and the injustice society contributes to natural competition is unimportant. Social inequity is subsumed in Dreiser's world to the natural competition of its creatures. Alfred Kazin saw Dreiser in the transcendentalist tradition at least in part because he did not see "this world as something to be ameliorated."[8] But Dreiser's transcendentalism is not only shorn of supernatural sanctions, as Kazin remarks, it also jettisons the idea of transcendence. Emerson thought that great men raised us above the world of affairs where every good has its price and is subject to time. They raise us, he wrote, to a realm of "uncorruptible goods . . . where there is no competition, where to be up another need not be down" (11). In Dreiser's entirely naturalist universe, where all energy lies in the atoms that constitute it, there is no way to be up without driving others down. He would say with Lucretius that every new organism comes into being at the expense of another that is destroyed. Although Dreiser came by his naturalism through nineteenth-century writers, his position is classic. He seems most to resemble Emerson when Emerson is most himself in the tradition of philosophic naturalism, but when Emerson invokes a world of values, when he speaks of the laws of physics being variants of moral law, then his naturalism is transformed by his platonism into the genteel tradition against which Dreiser is in revolt.

Some of the commonplaces about naturalism in fiction do not

apply to Dreiser. Cowperwood is not formed by his environment. Young Frank manifests his abilities early. His heredity, through his Uncle Seneca, not through his father, arms him as the lobster is armed. His father represents, instead, the conservatism and timidity of convention. When Frank buys the soap he happens to see at auction, his father advises him to wait for the notes he had taken in payment to mature rather than to take the cash at a discount. But Frank says he might want his money, establishing at the outset his characteristic strategy of making his money work as hard as it can, making a greater profit through its rapid use rather than through safe investment. This is the strategy by which he both prospers and fails. His father makes "what he considered judicious and conservative investments and because of his conservative, clock-like conduct it was thought he might reasonably expect some day to be vice-president, and possibly president, of his bank" (23–24). But Frank will take a job recommended by his uncle that has no salary but may bring a generous gift at the end of the year.

Maturation is repeatedly deemphasized as a factor in Frank's character. In a single paragraph that begins by telling us that Frank decided to leave school when he was seventeen, we are taken back to his thirteenth year when he becomes preoccupied with finance and then to this fifteenth year when his father becomes cashier of his bank. "Just at this time," his uncle sends him to his first important job at Waterman and Company. Is he fifteen? Is he seventeen? It does not matter. "Already his eyes had the look that subtle years of thought bring" (24). When he looks at the men he works for, they "were already nothing more than characters in his eyes—their business significated itself. He could see their weaknesses and their shortcomings as a much older man might have viewed a boy's" (29).

Frank is an antiromantic hero. He knows that he won't be a clerk for long, that others will work for him. "There was nothing savage in his attitude, no rage against fate, no dark fear of failure" (29). At the same time, Dreiser tells us that "life had given him no severe shocks nor rude awakenings." He hasn't suffered pain or illness, nor has he envied those richer than himself: "He hoped to be rich" (29).

Yet he sees men on the stock exchange as mere gamblers. In back of them he knew were the men with resources: mines, railroads, mills. "A man . . . must never be an agent, a tool, or a gambler—acting for himself or for others—he must employ such. A real man—a financier—was never a tool. He used tools. He created. He led." He saw all this, Dreiser tells us, "very clearly, at nineteen, twenty and twenty-one years of age" (42). Here we are at one of the first moments of risk in Cowperwood's career. The intelligence, personal force, and financial acumen he possesses do not free him entirely from the position of agent. His stock market manipulations for which he illegally used city money were intended to give him control of the streetcar companies. Real force could come only from material resource.

In trying to assess the significance of this conviction for Dreiser, we are in fact coming to grips with a central issue in the book, in Dreiser, and in the philosophical naturalism Dreiser espoused. To what extent is Cowperwood autonomous? What limits him? When Cowperwood fails in the panic caused by the fire, the narrative constitutes an examination of the question, has Cowperwood done wrong? Or better still, it is actually a recasting of the question into a form much more congenial to the critical attack on abstractions in law and social institutions that quickens the work of Henry Adams, William Dean Howells, and Henry James: what do we mean when we say that Cowperwood has done wrong?

Dreiser never questions that Cowperwood broke a law. What his narrative moves to dissolve is the authority and rationality of that law, while at the same time bringing into the light the wide range of social powers that operates without opprobrium outside that law in the financial world it was supposed to control. Real wrongdoing can come only from opposing the true power of a community. Power runs through other paths than those defined by that law, Dreiser tells us. That power defines real transgression and punishes it. The double narrative that follows, first Cowperwood's financial dealings, then his affair with Aileen, is at bottom a single narrative. The drive to have and possess. and enjoy is financially and sexually the human link to the power that drives the world. What Dreiser cannot allow is that either the social law against using city money that Cowperwood broke or the social power of those who already possess and enjoy, which he challenged and which punished him, have any moral authority.

When Stener, whose failures of courage and intelligence are almost as great a liability to Cowperwood in the panic as the downward pressures on the values of his securities, pleads with the politically powerful Mollenhauer to save him from jail, Mollenhauer thinks:

> *This man Stener fancied that he was dishonest, and that he, Mollen-*
> *hauer, was honest. He was here, self-convicted of sin, pleading to him,*

Mollenhauer, as he would to a righteous, unstained saint. As a matter of fact, Mollenhauer knew that he was simply shrewder, more far-seeing, more calculating, not less dishonest. Stener was lacking in force and brains—not morals. This lack was his principal crime. There were people who believed in some esoteric standard of right— some ideal of conduct absolutely and very far removed from practical life; but he had never seen them practice it save to their own financial (not moral—he would not say that) destruction. (200)

In this world morality is esoteric, ideal, absolutely removed, and no other world exists in the narrative. The reform movement cannot figure well here. Dreiser characterizes its representative, Skelton C. Wheat, as "undisturbed by notable animal passions" (224). As his name suggests, he is not truly alive without those passions but lives a life of abstraction, upholding the "theory of the Ten Commandments."

The trial focuses the lines of true power in this world in which Cowperwood is caught. First, he is to be the scapegoat for the politicians who long countenanced and profited from the practice of allowing the treasury to lend city money, keep the interest, and return only the principal. Second, he is to suffer from Mollenhauer's desire to gain control of the streetcar stocks Cowperwood had accumulated. Finally, Butler's rage over what he regards as Cowperwood's seduction of Aileen animates the entire process, insuring a far heavier sentence than Cowperwood might otherwise suffer. The emphasis is on whether Cowperwood deserves the punishment he receives and not on whether he broke the law.

The account of the way the jury works is an opportunity to show how far its decision may be from the truths of experience. "Facts," Dreiser says, "are capable of such curious inversion and interpretation, honest and otherwise" (324). Yet he presents the process by which it makes up its mind in an equivocal light. Having ascribed to the jury a "so-called" mind and a "so-called" truth, he reduces further its relation to experience by giving it an instinct to be "an orderly artistic whole, to present a compact, intellectual front" (325). This would appear to place its deliberations necessarily at variance with the chaos of experience. Yet he also compares this instinct in a jury to other entities in nature: "It would seem as though the physical substance of life—this apparition of form which the eye detects and calls real—were shot through with some vast subtlety that loves order, that is order. The atoms of our so-called *being*, in spite of our so-called *reason*—the dreams of a mood—know where to go and what to do. They represent an order, a wisdom, a willing that is not of us. They build orderly in spite of us. So the subconscious spirit of a jury" (325).

This meditation on juries is quite without a sense of condemnation, then, of their decisions. The realization of the decisions' irrationality, their relation to an order distant from human standards and wishes, does not put them in the same realm as the "mere theory" of the reformers. The order of the reformer, of the Ten Commandments, is false because it has no relation to the physical substance of life. The instinct to be a whole, to achieve intellectual coherence in itself, apart from a commitment to "mere theory," is the bridge between human forms, social, intellectual, or aesthetic, and the arrangements of atoms that make up our physical substance and the world's. Therefore it is a bridge between us and the informing, order-loving power of the universe.

The actual process by which the jury makes its decision and achieves its order involves "the strange hypnotic effect of one personality on another, the varying effects of varying types on each other, until a solution—to use the word in its purely chemical sense—is reached" (326). Thus, the way a jury reaches a verdict allows for a view of action not controlled either by reason or by our conscious goals whether reasonable or not or by any ability to know what really happened in the case it is called upon to decide. But the reason that he rejects as decisive in the process is not the orderly exercise of intellect and judgment that it is often thought of as being. What we unreflectingly pride ourselves on as reason Dreiser dismisses as the dreams of a mood, insubstantial, fleeting, dominated by our wishes. Coherence and truly creative form cannot be expected from such a source. The instinct for order lies deep in our physical being, and the process by which it is achieved in the jury is like that by which it is achieved in all areas of existence, through individuals interacting.

It is easy to see why some observers, like Kazin (11) and Roger Asselineau,[9] should feel Dreiser's affinity with transcendentalism. The surface play of opposing forces and the underlying irresistible movement toward order is an Emersonian bifurcation of the universal. Cowperwood, like Emerson's self-reliant man, acts on his deepest instincts and in doing so manifests the force and influence on his fellows and on circumstance that Emerson predicts will follow the tapping of universal energies. But it is not only the withdrawal of moral values that differentiates Dreiser's world from Emerson's. More importantly, in Dreiser's world self-reliance will not make us Caesar and Adam both. Dreiser never imagines a hero so filled with those energies that he becomes the only self, even momentarily, in the world. The unappeased hunger that every reader feels in Dreiser would indeed be fed were his vision to allow for the great crescive self that Emerson points to, a self that absorbs our fragmentary and frustrated desires into one all-sufficing whole. Dreiser's world tends always to tragedy and loss whatever the magnificent surge of energy because other selves are never wholly subsumed. They, too, are centers of energy, tied to the inexorable waxing and waning of biological forms.

Like the jury that convicts Cowperwood, the judges who hear his appeal have no real foundation for making a just decision. They have legal experience, but no financial understanding. Three of them are responsive to political feelings and the wishes of the bosses. "They fancied that in a way they were considering the whole matter fairly and impartially, but the manner in which Cowperwood had treated Butler was never out of their minds." Two judges thought Cowperwood had been badly treated but didn't see what they could do about it because he had put himself "in a most unsatisfactory position, politically and socially" (352). One of them had a woman in his own life that inclined him to argue against conviction, but he had political connections and obligations that made it unwise. Nevertheless, because the first three judges were going to convict without argument the other two decided to write a dissenting opinion. The case was important and might go to the Supreme Court; other judges would examine the case. A dissent wouldn't do them any harm. The politicians would even think it looked fairer, and anyway they didn't want to be associated with the other three in condemning Cowperwood. Drieser provides this persuasively complicated explanation for their decision, which shows the interplay of the biases that make up an action men feel as impartial.

Dreiser's uses of the judges' opinions goes farther than this, however. Through one of the dissenting opinions, he is able to state explicitly what has been advanced as a justification for Cowperwood's use of city money from the outset. "Any business man," writes one judge, "who engages in extensive and perfectly legitimate stock transactions may, before he knows it, by a sudden panic in the market or a fire, as in this instance, become a felon. When a principle is asserted which establishes such a precedent, and may lead to such results, it is, to say the least, startling" (354). This has been Cowperwood's sense of what happened all along. This perspective works to undermine our commonly held notion of guilt by making guilt the function of circumstance and reducing the individual's responsibility for his action in a much more effective way than in the scene in *Sister Carrie* where Hurstwood accidentally locks the safe while the money is out of it and is thereby committed to crime. In that scene, as in the famous scene when Carrie, drawn on her by her need and by her sensuous temperament, allows Drouet to buy her clothes and apparently without choosing it becomes his mistress, the characters can be seen as having a choice but being too weak or too amoral to make it. In *The Financier,* Dreiser is able to show that there is no freestanding moral good that the individual chooses or rejects. He makes the judge argue against a principle that makes possible transformation in the value and significance of an action. The judge believes with most people that the value and significance of an action can be determined at the inception of the action, where it is seen as expressing stable qualities of character. He is uncomfortable, therefore, with a view that makes the context that contains the action, not the character of the person who acts, the source of its significance and value. Dreiser's narrative argues that we must be confused by our commonly held notions that run counter to the way things really happen. As long as we cling to the older, more arbitrary way of defining value we will have to be prepared for what must appear to us disjunctions and irrationalities in our judgments.

II

Dreiser came early to his perception of the interconnectedness of the individual and his environment. In *Sister Carrie,* Hurstwood's long decline is initiated by his removal from the material world of Chicago that expressed him and allowed him to be fully himself. Unable to replicate that nurturing environment, he is doomed. Carrie escapes the same fate by her imaginative projection of a context that will give material substance to her inner play of desire and changing values. She leaves contexts that do not define her and responds in succession to contexts that express more of the self she is so acutely aware of but so dimly understands. It is through her relationship with her audience that Dreiser most interestingly depicts the reasons for her prosperity. She is able to embody for them the inchoate and transient emotions they cannot otherwise express but understand to be important elements of their being. Her acting is the vehicle both for her and their emotion, and she and her audience become components of a matrix nurturing to both. Her relationship with her audience grows as her relations to men do, but it is more lasting than her individual affairs. This is because her emotions, like those of the audience Dreiser creates for her, are without true objects and can enter and leave the parts she plays in the way vitality in the natural world enters and leaves forms but is neither contained nor finally expressed by any single one. The extent to which Dreiser feels Carrie to be representative of our emotional lives explains his readiness for philosophical naturalism.

In *The Financier*, Dreiser extends his understanding of the way the material world reflects us and we reflect it. Early in Cowperwood's career, when he is building and furnishing a house for himself and Lillian, Dreiser says of him: "We think we are individual, separate, above houses and material objects generally; but there is a subtle connection which makes them reflect us quite as much as we reflect them. They lend dignity, subtlety, force, each to the other, and what beauty, or lack of it, there is, is shot back and forth from one to the other as a shuttle in a loom, weaving, weaving. Cut the thread, separate a man from that which is rightfully his own, characteristic of him, and you have a peculiar figure, half success, half failure, much as a spider without its web, which will never be its whole self again until all its dignities and emoluments are restored" (97–98).

That Cowperwood is building a house at all defines him as the kind of man that makes as well as finds the context that fits him, supports him, and allows him to grow. The opening of the house for entertaining is the occasion for the declaration of his feelings for Aileen. Building the house and taking possession of it marks the discovery of himself. The young man who married a widow older than himself had also created a domestic environment that expressed him. It spoke his precociousness and his early acceptance of the social forms he found. The new house and relation with Aileen marks his affirmation of the primary value of his life, the desire to possess and enjoy, the single vital root of his financial, aesthetic, and sexual acts.

Dreiser does not rely finally on the idea of success as a measure of the value of action. His appeal is to the idea of health, the idea of the integration and full function of the organism. Self-realization and maturity have no place in his world because they are concepts tied to experience and self-knowledge, understanding and insight. Just as Cowperwood's age is irrelevant to his power as a financier, so is his apparent failure during the panic. Stener, once again, is the figure against whom Cowperwood can best be understood. On the verge of indictment, Stener's face is "grayish-white, his lips blue" (240). He is assailed and frightened by his conscience, while Cowperwood had no "consciousness of what is currently known as sin." He knew nothing but strength and weakness: "He must rely on swiftness of thought, accuracy, his judgment, and on nothing else. He was really a brilliant picture of courage and energy—moving about briskly in a jaunty, dappy way, his mustache curled, his clothes pressed, his nails manicured, his face clean-shaven and tinted with health" (241). Moral qualities, hard work, were irrelevant; Cowperwood doesn't feel he deserves or has earned his success. What he has is the serenity, wholeness, and power that Emerson promised the man who followed his deepest instincts.

Although politics and competition over streetcar franchises are important factors in Cowperwood's crisis, the logic of the narrative makes Butler's reaction to Cowperwood's love for Aileen the most profound threat to his way of life. The "instinct" that Emerson urged men to heed was not, of course, the biological impulse that Freud wrote about. It was a profoundly spiritual intuition whose objects, insofar as it was a way of knowing, were the moral energies that ordered the universe. In Dreiser's universe, sexuality was the experience through which we can know the energies of life. He found in Freud's theory of the libido as the source of all energy the scientific expression of his own conviction. Like Freud and Emerson, Dreiser saw the experience of the primal energy as both constructive and destructive. Social forms were fashioned by men driven by that energy. Cowperwood's desire to possess women and art, to build himself a house that embodied his energy, expressed it to the world and gave it an enduring form, is the desire that makes society. But like Emerson, Dreiser saw that men were "infinitely repellent orbs," that this energy possessing a man made his appetite infinite and, therefore, always antagonistic to other men. Society, then, must set bounds to the appetites that brought it into existence and from which it is always in peril.

Dreiser was most drawn in Freud to the ideas about the costs to the self of inhibiting libido. The conservatism and tragic consciousness of an essay like "Civilization and Its Discontents" was foreign to Dreiser. That society could justifiably prosper at the expense of individual satisfaction was not congenial to his way of thinking.[10] Society in his view was not different from nature. It experienced the same turbulent change; it threw up the same myriad members of a group in order that one member should survive and prosper; its combinations were inherently unstable and inevitably gave way to younger and more energetic forms. It was natural that individuals should oppose others, both singly and in groups, to achieve their own satisfaction. Society naturally sought to contain any individual who sought to establish himself and thereby upset an existing balance, but Dreiser could not agree that we should recognize and assent to this process of containment. People who sanctioned any social practice that sacrificed individual striving for some preconceived social good were hypocrites. And for Dreiser, hypocrisy was not a venial sin. Their action was not merely a case of one social practice privately tolerated while another was publicly avowed. It was a clash between a false assertion about the nature of reality and a true one.

Because social forms always received their energy from individuals driven by their appetites, any containment of the individual achieved by those forms was in truth a triumph of other particular individuals. In Dreiser's world, neither society nor civilization benefits. Any change simply signifies that an individual or a group of people benefit at the expense of others. Like Emerson, Dreiser attached all value to the energy, not to the forms the energy made, inhabited, and ultimately left. And like Emerson, he often has a revolutionary air in his attitude toward society: the man in the grip of primal energies may throw down everything in his path. Let him if he can. And let others, singly or in combination, oppose him. In this he turns away from Emerson.

Primal energy in Emerson is entirely constructive; what appears to be destruction is only the energy leaving a form. Emerson never conceives of a conflict between men who are both acting on their deepest impulses. When a man speaks what is true for him at that profound level, he speaks the truth for all, and, as in Whitman, he acts for all. Asselineau sees Dreiser squarely in the tradition of Emerson and Whitman but largely because Asselineau thinks naturalism means only "dull . . . descriptions of . . . society" (102). To him naturalism is a limiting frame marked by documentary realism, stereotypical characters, and crude social determinism. He does not think of it as a tradition that has Lucretius as its fountainhead, includes Spinoza and Santayana, and appears in American letters in Whitman as well as Dreiser. Consequently, Asselineau does not address the crucial distinctions between the way Dreiser and Emerson describe both the individual and the energy he partakes of. Ultimately there is one man acting in the world for Emerson. There are no opposing selves. Furthermore, this energy, which makes everything that exists, is in its essence good. Evil is its absence. Ultimately to be full of this energy is to be raised above the realm of action to the realm of being. Dreiser's energy, on the other hand, remains always natural. There is no platonic strain to transform natural existence into being. Primal energy has no moral qualities. It is necessity. When we act in its grip, we do what we must. For him, too, certain individuals are representative men. But he does not imagine that the energy filling its vessels makes them ultimately one or ultimately all the same. He imagines, rather, the conflict that results when separate selves act to fill their needs and extend their lives.

In Cowperwood's passion for Aileen, he enjoys direct contact with primal energy, and in following the imperatives of his relationship with her he threatens the existing arrangements of family and marriage by which society seeks to contain sexuality. He also confronts an older, more powerful man. When he seeks to win Aileen, he challenges her father's superiority. Butler's power in the city, Dreiser implies, is ultimately dependent on his power as a man. It is linked to his ability to control the women who belong to him, to benefit from Aileen's youth and beauty, to make her sexuality feed his position and power and satisfy his needs by keeping her chaste and marrying her well. His house, which is repeatedly contrasted in Aileen's mind with Cowperwood's and the family it contains, is the embodiment of his energies. To empty it, to devastate it, is to wound him mortally. The contest between the men cannot be properly rendered in Dreiser's imagination without the explicit sexual confrontation in which Butler goes to the house of ill-repute to take Aileen from Cowperwood. Butler goes there intending to surprise them together and to knock Cowperwood down, but once there he does not. He remains downstairs and never sees Cowperwood. The house itself is an expression of Butler's defeat, and we see that he takes Aileen home only because Cowperwood allows it.

Yet Cowperwood alone does not defeat Butler. Aileen, too, is driven by her passion. For her, too, the forms of marriage and social respectability have no reality, and her power surpasses Butler's. We are made to feel Butler's age and his growing bewilderment as the stable forms of his world crumble. The energy that sustained them is dwindling, and his money and political power and parental authority cannot, without that energy, protect them. He still has power to wound Cowperwood, however, and he uses it to send him to jail for a far longer term that he would otherwise have received. Victory in that battle is his, and it represents society's arousal against the anarchist energy that fills Cowperwood.

The interlude in prison, however, is a moment of arrest in a progress that Butler cannot stop. Prison strips Cowperwood down to his unprotected self. We see him without the support of the family that raised him, his father's money or his own, the favor of politicians, or of Butler himself, whose protégé he was. He is reduced to his own resources, his natural talents and character. As in other such interludes in the lives of heroes, Cowperwood is lost to the world, his identity obscured, and he undergoes a trial and a purging of the self only to emerge in a renewed, more powerful form. At the sentencing, Steger, Cowperwood's lawyer, emphasizes, as he has throughout the trial, that Cowperwood was never more than an agent of the city treasurer. As an agent, he was not guilty of misuse of money. In the matter of the bonds he was said to have misappropriated, rather than replacing them in the city account, he was merely following his customary privileges. We are reminded that from the first Cowperwood did not wish to be an agent but wishes to own the tools of industry himself, not trade in stocks that represented other people's assets.

So Cowperwood goes to jail, punished essentially for being another's agent, for not being independent. The conditions of life in prison first confuse him as to his identity, then hide it, then allow his essential self the merest hint of expression. On his arrival at the prison, he remembers walking when he was a child near a prison from which a drunkard or ne'er-do-well called out for Cowperwood to get him tobacco. The boy is shocked by the man's appearance and refuses. In return the man warns him not to get locked up himself sometime. Like that man, he must now enter prison without a friend to accompany him. That is the prison rule. He subjects himself consciously to those who direct him. He is aware of how the prison clothing deprives him of himself but most effective is the hood that makes each prisoner truly solitary. John J. McAleer suggests that the hood not only intercepts his "eye magnetism, the outward manifestation of his force," but also signifies a psychological equivalent of castration.[11] He comes close to losing control of himself. In his cell, with its offal pot and threat of rats, after a meal of tea and bread thrust to him through an opening in the door, he is not sure whether he can endure his sentence.

Yet when the warden sees Cowperwood, he is impressed by some ineradicable essence of the man, and in spite of the fact that he knows

Cowperwood is out of favor with his political peers, he grants him special privileges. In symbolic representation of the warden's recognition of Cowperwood's true self, Cowperwood is permitted his own underwear and shoes. Nevertheless, even for those who were friendliest with him and who tried to help him before he went to prison, he ceases to exist. Both his and his father's houses are sold off. And Dreiser tells us who of Cowperwood's friends and enemies picked up choice pieces of his household goods.

When Aileen comes to see him, although her visit marks the beginning of an increase in his personal comfort through his discovery of the bribable overseer, Cowperwood feels most keenly his degradation. Dreiser has Cowperwood assert his identity: "Only a stoic sense of his own soul-dignity aided him here. After all, as he now thought, he was Frank A. Cowperwood, and that was something, whatever he wore" (411). The pain in his meeting with Aileen comes from his sense of her belief in him, her knowledge of his true identity even where and how he is. Dreiser says he is afraid of her "ardent sympathy." When he is with her, her love is so "soothing . . . that it was unmanning. . . . he lost his self control" (413). He cries as she comforts him: "My baby— my honey pet."

His submission here is similar to the moment in *The Titan* when he accepts a subordinate position to Berenice. In the later book, Cowperwood is shown as the dominating lover in a series of ultimately unsatisfactory relations with women. The women are all only partial embodiments of the energy he believes is contained in the most beautiful and aesthetically sensitive women. When he relinquishes the active role to Berenice, he allows her to define their relation and is willing to be in any relation that will keep him near her. Is there a contradiction in Dreiser's view of Cowperwood's power that at crucial moments in both narratives he brings his hero to a passive dependent posture? I think not. What we see here is the ambivalence inherent in the idea of the individual acting out of his deepest instinct, the question of whether he controls the energy or it merely acts through him. These two moments of submission to the women who are the fullest embodiments of that energy for him at different stages in his life are both moments of solace, reenergizing him at a time of great stress. Just as Aileen refuses to desert him when he is momentarily bested because she responds to his essential power, so Berenice's indecision is ended by seeing Cowperwood at his most embattled, and she too chooses him at a moment when his victory is in doubt. His brief experience as their child rather than their dominating lover is not meant to be nor is it experienced in the narratives as weakness but as a way of indicating the source of his power.

In *The Financier,* this experience precedes the account of Cowperwood's recovery of the sense of his own strength and is a way of explaining what makes it possible. After it, through the homely acts of caning chairs, trapping rats, liming his toilet, and growing violets, pansies, and geraniums in his prison yard, Dreiser shows us Cowperwood taking possession of his world. Once again he creates a "house" for himself, without which he would have no being. From that "house," he operates through an agent in the world outside. Although Cowperwood's business relation with Wingate exists before the visit from Aileen, it is after it that we hear specifically how Wingate manages. As Cowperwood recovers himself in these small ways, Butler, from whose house Aileen has withdrawn its essential energy, dies, and Cowperwood is pardoned.

Once again we see the importance of the sexual relationship in Dreiser. In a narrative that insists its hero is superior to circumstance yet is also constrained by it, who wields a great power that in some sense is not his own, the relation with women can enact the interplay of dominance and submission that characterizes Dreiserian action.[12]

The narrative of *The Financier* follows importantly the traditional pattern by which the hero gains power during a period of obscurity in an underworld. In the conclusion Dreiser, makes clear that we are not to think of Cowperwood as someone who rises and falls because of circumstance. He falls because of the fire, and the meaning of his actions during that time, as we have seen, was actually changed by that circumstance. It may appear to one familiar with the financial history of Yerkes that he recovers his fortune in exactly the same way that he loses it—through a circumstance over which he has no control. And from one perspective, this is certainly true. Jay Cooke's failure and the panic it precipitates are Cowperwood's opportunity. His "great hour" comes, and he has done nothing to bring it. But it is crucial that he has been preparing for and expecting the opportunity. If it had not been Jay Cooke, it would have been another. The instability of his world makes it certain, and he knows that. Dreiser is at pains to show Cowperwood the master, not the creature, of changing financial reality. Dreiser describes Cooke's operation and has Cowperwood criticize it. He as much as predicts the failure of the Northern Pacific as well as its success later. As the panic gets underway, "his instinct told him how widespread and enduring" it would be. "Where many men were thinking of ruin, he was thinking of success" (440). He understands the way the market works, and he sells short to make a fortune. In the midst of apparent chaos, he can follow the hidden channel of power and through it achieve personal triumph. In addition, Dreiser emphasizes the brevity of Cowperwood's period of failure. He comes out of the panic of 1873 as rich as he was in 1871, the year of the fire, and only a little older. And finally, he leaves the market because of its instability. He won't chance being caught again and moves on to Chicago where he will try to live out the insight he had already possessed at the beginning of the book: a man in the market was only an agent. Power lay in the control of material goods.

Larzer Ziff has suggested that those who are destroyed in Dreiser's world "may be objects of compassion but they themselves rarely feel bitterness. . . . They are citizens of nineteenth-century America and they have its creed in their blood."[13] And he cites John William Ward: "If you are not a success look to yourself, not to the system, for the reason for your failure." Ziff is right in identifying what may seem to us a curious lack of bitterness, but I think the reason for it is different from Ward's. Dreiser's people don't blame themselves because they perceive the limits to their power and therefore can accept their failure without the terrible self-laceration that besets the citizens of our own century, which emphasizes the mobility and equal opportunity of society, the strength and mastery of its citizens. Dreiser emphasizes the rarity of strength and mastery: that is why Cowperwood is a hero. Very rarely can people in Dreiser's world exist without the support of their material environment. In Hurstwood, he shows how success is owed to a fortuitous "fit" between a man's capabilities and the circumstances of his life. When something happens to destroy that fit—Stener is another example—the man is destroyed. Here too Dreiser resembles Emerson, who speaks in "Experience" of the mastery of successful men as consisting of keeping themselves where and when their special talent "shall be oftenest to be practised" (349). Even in Cowperwood, who dominates and for a long time creates his material circumstance, we see the dependence on his circumstances. He goes to Chicago because he knows that the circumstances there are "made" for him. Ultimately he will go to New York and to Europe in search of the society in which he will fit. His final stoicism will come not from any belief that for the reason for his failure he must look to himself, but his belief that it is in the nature of things. It is as Henry Adams lamented in *The Education of Henry Adams:* experience never educates; it never fits man for his world.

The meditation on the disparity between the moral principles espoused by society and the reality of experience that has been so important throughout the book dominates its concluding pages. First, Cowperwood's sister, Anna, speculates on the restoration of financial prosperity to her and to Cowperwood's parents following his success. Dreiser follows this with the well-known remarks on *Mycteroperca bonaci*—the black grouper, in which nature shows itself to exercise "subtlety, chicanery, trickery" (447). He asks mockingly of his readers, whom he expects to be shocked by his exposure of a world that is not constructed on the principles of the Ten Commandments, "Would you say, in the face of this, that a beatific, beneficent reactive overruling power never wills that which is either tricky or deceptive? . . . Why were the Beatitudes dreamed of and how do they avail?" (447).

The last three paragraphs of the book, which he called "The Magic Crystal" and which look ahead to the action of *The Titan* and *The Stoic* (1947), make plain that the world that judges Cowperwood on the basis of the Beatitudes rather than nature will withhold a place in society from him and Aileen, but that its real reason will be that it is "outraged by the power of one man; . . . seething with indignation over a force it could not control" (p. 448). Finally, Dreiser puts Cowperwood's drive to dominate society in a Shakespearean perspective. The promise of the fates to gain endless riches is like the Weird Sisters' promise to Macbeth. Although it comes true, it is a lie. He was never to be master of society. Yet in one respect, "The Magic Crystal" is profoundly out of keeping with the narrative. It looks forward to the very punishment of desire that the novel argues against. By comparing Cowperwood to Macbeth, it makes him a criminal rising up against the rightful order. I don't believe that is what Dreiser was looking for in this analogy. He was seeking a non-Christian world for his comparison and a way of putting his hero's ultimate frustration in a context where there would be no punishment for breaking the Ten Commandments. Dreiser's world must always show the ultimate frustration of the desires it arouses. It is a world of radical disequilibrium, where the prolific energy that creates leaves nothing intact for long.

III

The Financier, more than any of Dreiser's novels, makes us aware of the assumptions operating in our thinking if we see man in Dreiser's writing as Richard Lehan, for example, sees him—a victim because he aspires to goals he cannot reach, a victim of his temperament, his physical needs, his time, his society, and of the natural balance Dreiser speaks of that acts as a limit on all self-assertion (153). Such a view has two main sources. One is the tradition in which man's reason and conscious will alone are properly his, and other modes of human behavior are alien. The other is a dualistic conception of society in which social forms and institutions are separate from man, who can, in some sense, stand outside them, acting independently of them, transcending them or being victimized by them. These concepts of man and his society are foreign to Dreiser's naturalist universe.

In *Hey, Rub-a-Dub-Dub* (1920), Dreiser adopts Herbert Spencer's idea that there are always opposing forces in contention that make up life. The universe avoids "ghastly extremes and disorder" because there is a "rough balance or equation" in this contention.[14] Whenever one force grows too strong it calls into existence the resistance to itself that will curb it. Whatever harmony is established is soon upset by an inherent impulse that makes for change. In the arena of human action, the moral law as it is understood by some is in conflict with our impulses that are "assuredly provided us by a Creator. . . . We do not compound ourselves" (161). We cannot always control ourselves, but "the warring, frustrating impulses of other compounds (or individuals or force, social opinion being a phase of them) do that for us. . . . Nature may wish us to be forceful in many strange ways in order that we may contest, bicker with other things equally forceful in other ways (all created by Her) so that out of the contest such as we see may come something which we can never see" (162). But the warring elements are all part of an organic whole and cannot exist without each other. Luther and his enemies are both made of the "underlying chemistry with its cell mechanism" (208–9). Saints and sinners are essential to each other and to the universe. What is most terrible and most wonderful alike came from this strife, which is "the only key to knowledge or sensation and life that we have" (177). Although he refers repeatedly to the process as "strife," he also calls it "an enticing and a fit game" that is "well enough suited to our capacities and we to it, since essentially we are of it—it, in fact" (177).

Later in his life, he expresses a somewhat darker view of the essential strife of life in a letter to Michael Gold in 1928, when he says that the human race is a "predatory organism, fighting and killing to not only save but advance and even luxuriate itself at the expense of and as against every other type of organism" (September 19, 1928, 2:

474). Games and wars both must have losers, and Dreiser is insistent that any strength is at another's expense. While he begins "Ashtoreth," an essay, with a celebration of the freshness and newness of everything, "the perennial up-welling of life," he goes on to explain what makes possible our zestful participation in the process. Identifying life and society, he says that life hides away the maimed, the blind, and the defective in institutions. Each generation in its youth and vigor forgets the older generation that once felt as it does. Seeing only the young and whole, it believes that life is not so cruel as to maim us. See how many are whole, it seems to say. But the sick, aged, and dead are hidden away: once life's "tools," now her "victims." But "while your strength is budding, that of others is failing. While your cheeks are reddening, theirs are paling" (204). Nature provides hundreds of thousands that one may think or invent or lead; "The rest may die as they will." Nature prevents us from accepting "pain, weariness and death . . . as the controlling facts they are" (200).

So Dreiser's vision is compound. He sees life from within the process and from outside it. He sees the costs and losses of the individual and the balance and creativity of the whole. When he speaks of the strong and gifted who survive and the weak who do not, we see that the process itself makes that identification. The weak never succeed and the strong never fail, because weakness and strength are defined by the outcome of the action. He rarely speaks of the laboring classes as unjustly kept down by society in the years through the writing of *The American Tragedy*. In *Hey, Rub-a-Dub-Dub,* for example, he tells of his experience working as the foreman on a railroad crew. He speaks of the men under him as fitted only for their menial tasks because of their "mental equipment" (93). In *An American Tragedy,* when Clyde walks the streets after coming to Lycurgus and seeing the shirt factory, he observes the millworkers. Dreiser says of them that they are "touched with a peculiar something—ignorance or thickness of mind or body, or with a certain lack of taste and alertness or daring, which seemed to make them one and all as of the basement world which he had seen only this afternoon. Yet in some streets and stores, particularly those nearer Wykeagy Avenue, a better type of girl and young man who might have been and no doubt were of the various office groups of the different companies over the river—neat and active."[15]

They come into life with certain gifts as Cowperwood does, and Dreiser never suggests that education or efforts to achieve greater social justice will increase their chances in the world. In *Hey, Rub-a-Dub-*

Dub, he laughs at the magazine articles that exhort Americans to raise themselves by their own bootstraps, "Napoleons all" (109–10). He sees it as a foolish American notion that character and personality are different, that we are supposed to make the one, while we come into the world with the other, and he hopes that the belief in character is waning: "Can it be that we are getting ready to admit that we are not Caesars each and all, held back by our own idleness and indifference?" (110).

No more than Dreiser has seen Cowperwood made by his experience does he see society as explicable by its history. The Civil War is an important factor in Cowperwood's career, but as a "financial opportunity" analogous to the Chicago fire and the panic of 1873. Dreiser exploits Jay Cooke in his formal design. He appears at the beginning as a man whose judgment on how much money can be made on a state loan is better than the conventional wisdom and who makes a great fortune. Cowperwood envies him, and at the end Cooke plays the role of the man whose judgment on the capitalization of the railroads is wrong, and his failure becomes Cowperwood's great financial opportunity. This design comes out of Dreiser's sense that while one's cheek is reddening, another's is fading. It is also made possible by his understanding of the way the financial markets worked in the second half of the nineteenth century. But we get no sense that there is any relation between the Civil War and the financial life of the nation that makes Cowperwood possible. He never exploits the war as James or Howells exploited it. The Civil War in *The Bostonians* and *A Hazard of New Fortunes* foreshadows, warns, promises, inspires, and offers standards for judgment of actions within each narrative. It supplies principles that make experience rational when the immediacy of personal life threatens to swamp the actors. The changes in American life that are these novels' subjects cannot be understood without the Civil War. The war, however, is of no interest to Cowperwood. It has no connection with the financial events through which Dreiser depicts the story of his will to dominate. Rather than exploiting the connections between the war and the making of large fortunes or between the war and the competing drives of North and South for political and financial hegemony, he has Cowperwood think of the war as a delay in the "true commercial and financial adjustment of the country" (78) and hope for its end.

The local political scene is as irrelevant in Dreiser's mind to making money as the national. Following Cowperwood's observations on the Civil War comes this: "A local election intervened and there was a new city treasurer, a new assessor of taxes, and a new mayor; but Edward Malia Butler continued to have apparently the same influence as before" (78). Dreiser does not relate the power of Butler to a larger political reality existing parallel to the public institutions and wielding the power they do not. The fact of Butler for Dreiser means that politics doesn't count. His power rests on personal grounds—on the energies that flow through a man from natural, sexual sources, not social networks.

Similarly, when Dreiser is arguing against morality in history, as he does in *Hey, Rub-a-Dub-Dub*, what he looks for and fails to find in history is rationality. The motives for our entrance into World War I have been sought for in our historical ties with France, he tells us. Yet when it suited us, he argues, although we were treaty bound to help France in its war with England, we failed it. Now, a hundred years later, "all the refused sympathy and gratitude of 1800 was revived and France became once more the object of our tenderest solicitude. So much for national moods and gratitudes." Wilson took us into the war by feeding us the "sweet milk" of making the world safe for democracy. Yet, continues Dreiser, he led us into repression of the opposition, conscription, propaganda, and the control of public expression. "I am not quarreling," writes Dreiser, "with the process; I am showing the thin line of difference between autocracy and democracy where necessity or passing opinion favors one course of conduct or another" (37). So neither politics nor history matters. Passing moods, the response to immediate situations, the felt need of the moment, these explain how things happen. Just so Dreiser argues that America fought Germany "very practically" in its own "future interests," though it gave "sentimental reasons" (30). History for Dreiser is inextricable from the moral ideas with which American historians up to his own period imbued it, and in rejecting its explanations for the principles of force and necessity, he appeals to nature as opposed to history. He rejects a view of the past that is used to make the American believe that "he was here only to save the world, never by any chance to further his own interests" (39), just as his inventions were supposedly for "moral purposes only." What Dreiser rejected was what James rejected in *The Princess Casamassima*, the view of history as the improvement of morals. He sees in American democratic ideals the promise that the individual who is protected against tyranny will develop better thoughts and aspirations than his oppressed forebears, but he believes this remains to be demonstrated.

History does not show it. He argues that just as nations in the past built for state or king, not for the individual, so the modern republic builds for the money baron. Our reliance on the popular historical ideals of American life stand in the way of our intelligence and our culture. He writes of Henry Ford's peace ship as the epitome of the provincial grasp of life to which these ideals doom us and laughs at the widespread support his efforts to end the war received from middle western and far western newspapers who actually thought it could be done. "Human history," he writes in one of his most bitter moments, "is a series of spectacles and has nothing to teach man except that man is a creature of attitudes. He—or the atoms, electrons, molecules, elements, and their integrations of which he is a composite—strikes various attitudes, now barbaric, now religious, now philosophical, republican, communist, tyrannical, nomadic."[16]

But in *A Hoosier Holiday* (1916), he gives another version of what it means to live without history and the satisfactions it affords. Traveling west toward his origins in Indiana, he stops in Warsaw, New York, and daydreams that he is in the Warsaw of his youth. "There was no real difference," he thought. "'What ideas have we today that we did not have then?' I was dreamily asking myself. Are the houses any better, or the clothes? Or the people in their bodies and minds? Or are their emotions any richer or keener or sweeter? Euripides wrote the Medea in 440 B.C. Shakespeare wrote 'Macbeth' in 1605 A.D. . . . The general feeling is that we are getting on, but I should like to know what we can get on to, actually. And beyond the delight of sensory response, what is there to go on to?"[17]

Dreiser believes that the changes we see in our lives are the result of our machines, but these inventions don't add to our capacity for feeling. We don't add to the immense variations of life. These, he has already argued in *Hey, Rub-A-Dub-Dub*, come from nature, in which nothing is fixed. Like Henry Adams he believes that man "uses all the forces he can conceive . . . but he does not understand them, and his individual share in the race's cursory response to them is apparently no greater than ever" (154). But unlike Adams, Dreiser is not appalled by our limitation to "sensory response." He does not imagine our use of forces and our refinement of our observation of forces as a substitute for understanding and a path to mastery as Adams does. When our sensory response arouses sufficient desire, it will impel us to conflict and mastery. When it is weaker, it leaves us in a passive state of mind that is sweetness and delight in itself. Then the objects of our desire are in our memory or our imagination, and as Warsaw, New York, melts into Warsaw, Indiana, our past melts into our present. The life of this sensory response is a life like Freud's unconscious, ruled by wish and association, with feelings aroused by one object interfused with other objects, times, and places.

The "paraphernalia of fate—ill luck, the shadowy and inscrutable pattern of things that ground effort into the dust" that Kazin, almost at the beginning of serious Dreiser criticism, puts at the center of Dreiser's sense of life is not the result of the "failure of his education to prepare him to select events and causes," as Kazin argues.[18] It is, on the one hand, the way people in Dreiser's world explain their failure to themselves, and, on the other, as Dreiser sees it, the face the strife of existence must inevitably wear to those who fail. When Dreiser says he does not understand the world or that he can see no purpose in life, he means he cannot see that there is any meaning beyond itself to this rising and falling he describes. In this lies the insurmountable barrier between his naturalism and Emerson's transcendentalism. This is not to say that he cannot discern the principles that he feels govern the world. On the contrary, his long campaign against conventional morality is grounded, as it is in *The Financier,* in his desire to make our demands on life and on ourselves consonant with the way things are.

In showing us the success of Cowperwood, he shows one of the few who "may think or invent or lead," not a superman, not someone who transcends the natural limits of humanity, but someone who embodies its natural fullness. It is true that the nature of this success foretells his inevitable frustration, and Dreiser as a naturalist cannot resist overshadowing his protagonist's brightest moment with its reminder. Cowperwood's dream of dominance through the control of material resources cannot come true. He, like all men, must always be an agent, a tool of the natural energy that urges him on. Yet the exhilaration of his story comes from its communication to us that the existence it shows us is "an enticing and fit game." The perspective that makes Cowperwood only an agent is overlaid with a perspective equally vital to the naturalist vision that makes any separation between energy and agent, game and player, a falsification. Out of this compound vision comes the challenge of the novels to the moralizing gentility of his own generation. Out of it comes also the compassion for both the winners and losers of a contest in which our relations to the power that determines its outcome can never be precisely fixed.

Cowperwood fulfills Adams's notion of the significant individual who is a type, a center of the energies of his world, not a source of energy himself. Through the strategy of placing the achievement of wisdom outside the narrative, by removing it as a function of the experience recounted and making it a function of the novel as experienced by the reader, in other words displacing it from life to art, Dreiser's use of the biographical model makes it possible to go beyond irony and paradox into empathy and pathos.

IV

An American Tragedy is a true companion piece to *The Financier*. It, too, aims at an explanation of a crime that dissolves common moral categories. But unlike Cowperwood, Clyde Griffith is not well enough equipped by nature to win the objects of his desire. No more than Cowperwood is Clyde an everyman: they are rather two archetypal possibilities. Donald Pizer uses the classic terminology associated with biographies to cast Clyde's story into the pattern of an "education": "All three books [of *An American Tragedy*] are also segments of the underlying ironic theme and form which is Clyde's life: his 'education' and his punishment by a world which 'educated' him but which has never taken responsibility for that instruction by understanding him." But the quotation marks around education suggest Pizer's uneasiness with the word and the extent to which the process of Clyde's experience is emphatically not educative. And, of course, Pizer goes on to speak of the failure of Clyde's character "to develop or deepen in the course of the novel except to a slight degree in the closing section of Book Three" (*Novels* 234–35).

Just as Cowperwood's ability to manipulate the financial markets and to locate the lines of power are gifts, not skills developed in the course of the novel, Clyde's experience serves to exemplify his capacities, not as occasions for the growth and discovery of new capacities. Dreiser says of him during the time he works at the Union Club, after the affair with Hortense and the car accident that in a different sort of novel might be thought of as teaching the protagonist something, "For to say the truth Clyde had a soul that was not destined to grow up. He lacked decidedly that mental clarity and inner directing application that in so many permits them to sort out from the facts and avenues of life the particular thing or things that make for their direct advancement" (169).

The metaphor underlying Cowperwood's experience is the struggle for survival between the lobster and the squid, and the underlying analogy for Clyde's experience is also scientific. It stems, as Ellen Moers has shown, from Dreiser's recent reading in Jacques Loeb's theory of tropism.[19] Neither of these metaphors leaves room for experience as educative. A third scientific element enters Clyde's narrative, however, and that is the Freudian emphasis on the crucial effects of early family life. Pizer's study of the first draft of *An American Tragedy* shows that in it Clyde is controlled by an early psychic wound, an idea that is much less explicit in the final version (213). Here, although Clyde is in rebellion generally against the dreariness of his early life and its moral restrictions, he specifically expresses his hatred of a way of life that "required constant appeals for aid, as well as constant prayer and thanksgiving to sustain it" (16).

The central theme of Clyde's life—whether he will ever be independent—is established through an early insight into the way he believes himself to be different from his parents and their clients when, in fact, he is not. While the ne'er-do-wells who come to the mission irritate Clyde because their testimony is about how God saved them, never how they rescued anyone else, and Clyde thinks of his Lycurgus uncle who is "different," he thinks not of how he too can be master of his life, but of what this particular uncle "might do for a person" (17). He will never surmount the forms of his life as he exhibits them in the opening pages. The more he looks for another father, the more he is his father's son. There will be no education, no recognition of the self, and no reintegration of experience and the self that we commonly call maturity.

Clyde himself is a ne'er-do-well who looks repeatedly to a father figure to save him and ultimately is lost because he cannot rescue another. The failure of the father is inseparable from the failure of experience to educate. From Hegglund, who takes him to the brothel; to his uncle, to Belknap, the lawyer; to Nicolson, his friend in the deathhouse; to the minister, McMillan; the line of fathers who promise much but fail ultimately extends to God. Each of these fathers is associated with the satisfaction of Clyde's hunger, each promises a sense of satisfaction and a place in the world, an easing of the deprivation that permeates Clyde's sense of being. A father's task is to identify the sources of power and well-being; he uncovers the principles of the world, its motive forces and thereby makes possible the mastery and satisfaction of the son. Hegglund introduces him to beauty, Dreiser tells us, though of a "gross, fleshly character" (66). Yet Hegglund's principle not only brings immediate frustration with Hortense but ultimate frustration because of Roberta.

Esta's plight during this part of the narrative is often identified by critics as a foreshadowing of Roberta's and is understood by Clyde later as a reason for not standing by Roberta. But it is also the occasion for Clyde's failure to come to terms with the morality of sex. He blames Esta's lover for what has happened to Esta, but he blames her too. He cannot feel that sex is wrong. The misfortune arises, he believes, from "not thinking or not knowing" (100). His assumption that thinking or knowing could have averted Esta's misfortune or any future tragedy of his own constitutes a failure to grasp the principle of sexuality as it operates in the world. Later in the novel, when Sondra replaces Roberta for Clyde at the height of his desire for Roberta, and Roberta conceives a child after he no longer loves her, sexuality is shown to elude reason, intention, and expectation. Moreover, social differences also make certain kinds of thinking or knowing about sex, as well as doing, impossible.

Belknap, the father figure who seems to understand Clyde's situation and seems to Clyde, even after Belknap has essentially given Clyde up, to hold out salvation, has had an experience like Clyde's. But his family had the money and a doctor for the pregnant girl, so that he could escape and return later to marry more suitably. Throughout the time that Clyde and Roberta are searching for an abortion, Dreiser makes clear that had they the money and family connections they could have been successful. Belknap seems to be a man who thinks and knows, yet he turns out to be powerless. In fact, he is wearied and confused by Clyde's experience, and the failure of the story he concocts for the jury is his failure to make sense of it. Belknap's doomed effort to make thinking and knowing the road to mastery is inseparable from Roberta's death with its multiple ironies and causes and the narrative's insistence on the clouded nature of Clyde's guilt.

Here is a trial like the one in *The Financier* in which the easy assumptions of the reader about the meaning of guilt and justice are challenged. Belknap's invented story is an attempt to deal with the critical question of intention. In *The Financier* Cowperwood's lawyer does not deny Cowperwood's intention to use the city's money. He merely argues that circumstances made this appear criminal, while it was in essence legitimate. There the argument turned on what constituted legitimacy. Belknap's story, however, seeks to deny Clyde's true intention by asserting his incapacity to enact it. Whether Clyde's claim is true or not, Belknap is certain it will not exculpate him in the jury's eyes. He wishes to convince the jury that while the evidence appears to support the idea that Clyde took Roberta to the lake with the intention of telling her he could not marry her, he had a change of heart by the time he took her out in the boat. The question of intention also causes the judge to instruct the jury: "If the jury finds that Roberta Alden accidentally or involuntarily fell out of the boat and that the defendant made no attempt to rescue her, that does not make the defendant guilty" (736). Clyde's failure to rescue Roberta, which Dreiser knows must in the reader engender the firmest belief in his guilt whatever his intention as he sat in the boat, is thus explicitly rejected by the law as a grounds for guilt.

Action then, the clearest basis for our judgments, is downplayed, and for the actual grounds of our judgments we are turned back to what we can never certainly know—what in fact Dreiser is at pains to show us Clyde himself can never know—his motives and intentions. Belknap observes to Jephson that whatever Clyde's role in the event that caused Roberta's death, if he planned her death when he took her to Great Bittern, he was, according to the law, guilty. Belknap as a sympathetic, knowledgeable, and authoritative father who neverthe-less cannot deal with real experience, seems to promise Clyde that he will make these desires and experience blameless in the eyes of the law. To that end as a father, he makes a new life and a different experience for Clyde in the story they tell the jury. In contrast, Cowperwood's testimony fails to win him acquittal but his "story" is indeed his "life." For a brief moment, his desires and experience are understood by himself and his judges.

Belknap's function as a father to give Clyde a life different from the one his real father has given him is the function of all his surrogate fathers. Hegglund early tries to give him a life of simple sensual pleasure entirely different from the life of the mission. The theme of the possibility of a different father and therefore a different nature and a different life is most centrally developed in his relationship with his uncle and his cousin Gilbert. In Clyde's eyes, the uncle is an authen-tically admirable figure "whose very great ability had erected this im-portant industry" (181). While Gilbert is only "apparently authoritative and efficient," the uncle is genuinely so. Yet Dreiser makes us see what is either not known or not significant to Clyde, that the uncle's success is built in part on money that the Griffith grandfather withheld from Asa Griffith. Guilt is part of the uncle's motivation as it is Belknap's. Dreiser gives to both older men an uneasy realization of his own view, that every success is at someone's expense.

At the very time when Clyde appears to have the chance of a new father and a new life, he walks the streets of Lycurgus observing the millworkers, and Clyde accepts in them social distinctions as reflecting personal realities, although Clyde cannot accept them so in Gilbert or in himself. Gilbert's fear of Clyde as a competitor speaks for Clyde's convertibility into a brother. The men who introduce him to work at the factory don't know whether to treat him with respect. While status depends on how he is treated by the Griffiths, father and son, it also depends on how other workers treat him. Later Dreiser identifies this uncertainty about status as contributing to the tragedy. Insofar as the uncertainty makes for mobility, it is attributed to Clyde alone. The men and women Clyde observes in the street are marked irreversibly by their own bodies and minds.

The view of environment and heredity at the heart of naturalism is not nearly as clear as it has long been assumed to be. In both *Pudd'nhead Wilson* (1894) and *A Connecticut Yankee at King Arthur's Court* (1889), Mark Twain shows the same indecision about whether our training or our natural proclivities determine our actions. If environment is potent rather than decisive, then culture can modify nature not merely express it. Twain and Stephen Crane in *The Red Badge of Courage* (1895) both emphasize how our reality is shaped by the ways others treat us. Henry Fleming, as much as Valet de Chambres and Tom in *Pudd'nhead Wilson*, receives his identify through the social nexus. It is not enough to say that Clyde's mental weakness makes him imagine that his uncle can elevate him into another class, that a change of clothes can give him the beauty and excitement he craves. The pathos of Clyde's situation comes not from how difficult it is, but how easy Dreiser makes it seem. The world he shows us is one where such things appear to be possible.

Roberta's situation is an echo of Clyde's. Although her parents are failures, ignorant but honest, upright, and God-fearing, she is fitted, Dresier writes, by "natural gifts" (244) for something better. Like Clyde, she is isolated in her work among people inferior to her. This is part of what draws Clyde and Roberta together, as well as part of what makes Roberta more demanding of our sympathy. She is someone who cannot be dismissed as unworthy of love or so inferior to Clyde as to have no moral claim on him. But neither Clyde nor Roberta have "natural gifts" enough, as Cowperwood does, to build houses for themselves, to make an environment or enter an environment consonant with their beings. Where Roberta lives constitutes an important subject in the account of their relationship. The room she moves into when she leaves Grace's house is importantly isolated from the rest of the building. Its defining relations are to the out-of-doors, not to the interior. It is "to the right of a small front porch and overlooking the street" (285). Unlike Cowperwood's affair with Aileen, which is so closely identified with significant interiors, Roberta and Clyde's affair is identified with the outside. He courts her at an amusement park, on a lake, and in an open summer dance pavilion. She admits her love for him on a dark street because they cannot meet in Grace's house.

In contrast, Clyde initially meets Sondra in her uncle's house, and, then crucially, when she mistakes him for Gilbert, she gives him a lift in her car, alienating him from Roberta. He continues to meet Sondra at other people's houses until the scene in Sondra's kitchen where she makes hot chocolate after a party, and he tells her he loves her. There, where she is playing at domestic life in the confines of her own house, he brings larger, yet unformed energies, and she is fascinated by his passion, feeling him to be "intense" and "dynamic." He is at his most masterful, and she at her most submissive. When they meet at the lake, the vacation house, with its boats and horses that so importantly define Sondra, brings together the interior and the exterior, the social and the natural. But even here, the crucial scene where she promises to run away with him in the fall if she cannot convince her mother to accept him, takes place out-of-doors on one of their horseback rides together.

The motifs of houselessness and the search for the father come together in the scene of the murder. The journey to a lake beyond a lake, deep into nature is also a journey that culminates in Clyde's feeling that he is "drifting, drifting—in endless space . . . no plots—no plans—no practical problems to be solved" (489). At the heart of nature lies the lake, a "huge, black pearl," suggesting to Clyde a serene, unprotesting death. Not merely a projection of Clyde's desire to be rid of Roberta without pain to her or to himself, it is an evocation of a natural self without definition and therefore without limit or frustration, a self that feels at last the hand of its father: "And he now felt for the first time the grip of some seemingly strong, and yet friendly sympathetic, hands laid firmly on his shoulders. The comfort of them! The warmth! The strength! For now they seemed to have a steadying effect on him and he liked them—their reassurance—their support. If only they would not be removed! If only they would remain always—

the hands of his friend! For where had he ever known this comforting and almost tender sensation before in all his life" (489). When the hands disappear he feels alone and chilled by the beauty that surrounds him.

In the period leading to the murder he cannot think of himself as the kind of person who "would want anything to happen to Roberta." When the thoughts of her death come to dominate his mind, he feels as if he is possessed by an efrit from another world he had known nothing about, "peopled by creatures otherwise than himself" (463). At the center of the complex and subtle moment of Roberta's death to which everything leads in the novel and from which everything afterward evolves is the fact that Clyde is, indeed, the kind of person who would want something to happen to Roberta but he is not the kind of person to make it happen. The death scene is clearly designed in two parts to parallel the two pieces of legal interpretation the narrative later gives to the reader. The parallel contrasts ironically the legal view of the event and the response Dreiser's handling of the event compels in the reader. Immobilized by his conflicting desires, Clyde hits Roberta truly by accident and throws her in the water by reaching out to help her and to apologize. Yet in the law's view, which seems contrary to common sense; accident or not, if Clyde brought Roberta to the place where it happened with murderous intent, then he is guilty.

Once Roberta is flailing about in the water that part of himself that he cannot acknowledge and that was held in check by his own terror and cowardice while Roberta was in the boat, speaks out successfully against his saving her from drowning. Here the reader feels Clyde's guilt powerfully, yet later the judge specifically admonishes the jury that he cannot be held responsible for not going to her aid. Much more successfully than in *The Financier,* where Dreiser also aimed at a tangle of action to which public judgment and moral and legal conventions were shown as inadequate for moral assessment, Dreiser asks questions about this action that he does not allow his narrative to answer. He makes the death happen in the undefined and unlimited space he has represented the lake to be. Just as he argued in *The Financier* that the morality of Cowperwood's actions ought to be defined by Cowperwood's nature, so too here Clyde's action cannot be seen separately from what he is. His own failure of definition is echoed in the inchoate nature of his action. Cowperwood knew his own nature and the nature of his actions. He found a social form for the natural energies he felt, understood, and valued. It might be opposed to the conventional, but it was coherent.

In this respect Dreiser's concept of moral action is entirely Emersonian. Cowperwood followed the deepest prompting of his inner being and thereby found wholeness. The unconventionality of his behavior would have been as little a sign of immorality for Emerson as it was for Dreiser. However, Dreiser's imaginative vision challenges Emerson's conviction that no evil can come from following these deepest promptings.[20] Because Emerson believed that being had goodness at its core, he could voice his revolutionary definition of moral action with scarcely a tremor. That he recognized the logical danger of his position he made clear by saying in "Self-Reliance" that if he were the devil's child, why then he must live by the devil. Because Emerson believed he knew his own father, this was a rhetorical device, not a real risk. For Dreiser's characters, more is at stake. But both Emerson and Dreiser voice the same naturalist morality: goodness is the acting out of our nature; evil is its denial, perversion, corruption, or frustration.

Unlike Cowperwood, the fatherless Clyde, although he has followed the best Emersonian advice and sought his father in deepest nature, away from society and convention, in Dreiser's vision finds only incoherence in the undefined and unlimited space of nature. He emerges from the lake thanking God that he had not killed Roberta: "And yet (stepping up on the near-by bank and shaking the water from his clothes) had he? Or had he not? For had he not refused to go to her rescue, and when he might have saved her, and when the fault for casting her in the water, however accidentally, was so truly his? And yet—and yet—" (494). He will die without conviction, either about this act or his own nature. The legal definitions of guilt that the judge and Belknap have emphasized are not useful to Clyde in his own attempt to determine his guilt. Dreiser has Clyde focus on the elements the reader feels most keenly, both of which have to do with what he was actually capable of doing in the moment of crisis, not what he had planned. Although the law might exculpate him for not rescuing Roberta, his own sense of humanity, like the reader's, will not. At the same time his and the reader's sense of what human nature is like make the reader less likely to blame him for a desire to kill that is frustrated by his own desire not to kill.

V

In the prison episode, Dreiser brings the theme of Clyde's search for a father and for self-definition to its fullest realization. Only then does

Clyde find the house that expresses him—a prison, a death house. Unlike Cowperwood's prison with its isolation, its hood, its apparent attempt to efface Cowperwood's identity but its ultimate malleability to his sense of mastery, Clyde's is always lit and has no privacy. In its glare, we will discover both what men can know about their lives and what they can never know. The prisoners live a shared terror, their lives controlled not only by the walls and bars but by constant surveillance and exposure. In this illumination, Clyde continues to seek his father and the meaning of his actions by which he will know what he is. Critics on the whole have not come to grips with the importance of this section in the thematic and narrative structure.[21] Even Donald Pizer, whose work on Dreiser is most comprehensive and insightful, seems to feel that the major work of the narrative is done once the murder occurs. He criticizes the prison section as being too long, as if it should function as an epilogue. Yet only in the prison does the narrative transcend the dreary limitation of Clyde's personal desire and reverberate with the moral ambiguity of all human desire.

The first important event in the death house narrative is the execution of the young Italian convicted of slaying his brother for attempting to seduce his wife. Driven by his terror of death and damnation, he spends his days in obsessive penance, "crawling up and down his cell on his hands and knees, kissing the floor, licking the feet of a brass Christ on a cross that had been given him" (771). His brother and sister come to him from Italy, but he is beyond human sympathy. Dreiser emphasizes the young Italian's loss of himself, both here and in Clyde's image of his execution. Clyde thinks, "they were strapping him in no doubt," while imagining they also ask him what more he has to say—"he who was no longer quite right in his mind" (773). The other inmates recognize by the dimming of the lights when the execution is accomplished and mark his death with a litatny of "Well, it's all over with him" and "Yes, he's topped off, poor devil," and "There—sure—that's the end now." Clyde feels the certainty of death in spite of the man's nights of prayer, his moaning, and self-flagellation. And he recognizes as he has not before what lies ahead of him. He imagines the empty cell and another man put in the dead prisoner's place. Others had been in his own place, he thinks, and jumps up from the bed and then from the chair, not wanting to be one with them, trying to escape from the procession to the electric chair.

Dreiser's narrative turns our attention from the crimes that brought these men to the prison, even from the question of their guilt, to the terror of apprehending one's certain death. He further enhances the symbolic, rather than the social and historical side of his narrative, by providing in Nicolson a concerned and sympathetic father for Clyde. Nicolson's own guilt is not examined. Only his behavior in the death house is important. He remains calm and in telling Clyde that another prisoner was "more animal than man," he identifies himself as someone who knows what a man is. Yet we feel how inadequate his legacy to Clyde is for the questions that he must deal with: the example of self-control, thoughtfulness for others, stoic calm, and his two books, *Robinson Crusoe* and *The Arabian Nights*. It is hard to know what Dreiser meant to imply by the Defoe. He is not likely to have sympathized with the moral implications of the book and is most probably calling attention to the isolation of man in nature. In conjunction with the *Arabian Nights, Robinson Crusoe* seems to underscore Clyde's lack of father, his lack of identity, status, and tradition. *The Arabian Nights* captures both the terror and the wonder of existence, an Aladdin's cave of riches over which the giant efrit Clyde has released so calamitously promised control. For all his attractiveness to Clyde, then, Nicolson is another father who fails him, not merely by leaving him alone in prison, but by confirming the chaos in which Clyde lives rather than leaving him any clue to order. And we remember that Nicolson was "tall and slim and decidedly superior looking—a refined, intellectual type, one you would have said was no murderer—any more than Clyde—to look at, who nonetheless was convicted of poisoning an old man of great wealth and afterwards attempting to convert his fortune to his own use" (768).

Reverened McMillan replaces Nicholson as loving father and potential guide, but McMillan is misleading also and must inevitably fail Clyde, for McMillan offers the peace of mind that comes from confession and repentance, and it is just the question of his guilt that Clyde cannot resolve. He had after all been incapable of executing his plot to kill Roberta. He was, he sees now, almost a lunatic under the fever of his obsession for Sondra. These seem to him important mitigating circumstances. Yet he cannot free himself of the feelings of responsibility for the anger that caused Roberta to fall into the water and failing to rescue her. The young Jew who chants, "I have been evil. I have been unkind. I have lied," chants Clyde's sense of guilt too. This guilt presses him to confess all, every nuance of emotion surrounding Roberta's death, to the man who promises God's peace of mind to him. And this public exploration of all the moral ambiguities of that moment seals his fate. McMillan's religion is inadequate to the questions he is asked to judge. When he summarizes the reasons he finds for Clyde's guilt: he had plotted, he had not rescued, he had wished her dead and afterward was not sorry, the blow had come partly out of anger, and the mood that had kept him from acting was also angry; these are factors that the reader also holds against Clyde. Yet they are not equal in weight. Most readers would not hold Clyde's wish and lack of sorrow or his anger as strong enough to warrant his death. The mixture of the vital—his leaving Roberta to drown—with the peripheral vitiates the case against him, and our sympathy for him is further enhanced when McMillan adds to these reasons the further ones of "fornication," "selfishness," and "unhallowed desire" (797). Here, the reader is alienated, as Dreiser wishes him to be, from a religion that cannot allow room for natural appetite, and, worse yet, allows the question of its sinfulness to cloud an issue of a vastly different order. So while Clyde's confession causes McMillan's inability to confirm his innocence, although in McMillan's mind, Clyde's guilt is compounded of many spiritual failings quite independent of murder and surely not in themselves deserving of the death penalty, the reader is ready for the intense conviction that Clyde gains from his own confession, that he was not guilty and that anyone who had lived through his emotions would realize it. Yet just as McMillan's reasons for thinking him guilty make us readier to accept his innocence, so his reasons for his innocence—the torture of Roberta's insistence that they marry and the intensity of his desire for Sondra—diminish our sympathy for Clyde and make us withhold the exoneration he hungers for.

And indeed, Clyde cannot resolve the question, nor will Dreiser, who turns away in his conclusion from the attempt to resolve it, to deal instead with the effects on McMillan of a moral reality too large for his scheme of the universe. All of McMillan's love, generosity, and compassion are rendered useless by the religious teaching that feeds these aspects of his nature and yet constrains them. That which has brought him to Clyde also delivers Clyde to a worldly justice that has been shown incapable of true judgment even as the God in whom McMillan and Clyde's mother have believed has failed him. But Dreiser does not allow us to suppose that because religion and the courts cannot resolve the moral doubts about Clyde's action, he is therefore innocent. What the prison section leaves us with is grief over the compound of innocence and guilt that human action is. In the opening essay of *Hey, Rub-a-Dub-Dub*, Dreiser argues that people don't know what "right, truth, justice, mercy" (7) are, yet they cling to ideas of moral order in the universe. And Clyde clings, too. In his last months he seeks, not exoneration, but a just view of his actions. But in *Hey, Rub-a-Dub-Dub*, Dreiser expresses the conviction that real moral dilemmas do not allow of just solutions (9–10). Pizer shows in his analysis of *An American Tragedy* that the trial and public justice reflect "a sophisticated and covert expression" of public sentiments that falsifies Clyde's situation (59, 270). Similarly, Clyde's mother's view and McMillan's also falsify it. Dreiser wrote to Jack Wilgus that he wished to give "a background and a psychology of reality which would explain, if not condone, how such murders happen" (April 20, 1927, 2:458).

The subversion of morality by necessity and conflicting claims, the explosion of conventional abstractions about life, these are the powerful effects of a mature art, but they are familiar. *An American Tragedy* has a further unsettling effect that is not so familiar. Never finding a father, Clyde does not achieve self-recognition; he is unable to discover a consistent identity. That Clyde should not change, grow, achieve insight is something recognized by most readers, yet not sufficiently appreciated. In a novel written on the model of biography, Dreiser denies the assumptions about experience that customarily underlie that model. In *The Financier*, too, as we have seen, experience is not the education of consciousness. Cowperwood acts always on the promptings of his nature. The book is the story of his triumph against all the forces that would constrict him and prevent the realization of his nature in society, yet like Clyde he fails to discover himself. The effect is obscured in *The Financier* by the rising action of Cowperwood's success and the ease of mistaking the externalization and materialization of his self as the growth of self-knowledge and self-control. Cowperwood neither knows nor controls himself. On a feeling level, he is powerful and coherent, and he acts always on those feelings. In *An American Tragedy*, however, Dreiser insists on the failure of Clyde's education through experience. He continues to ask the same questions about himself until his death, and through them and his failure to experience contrition he affirms the conflicts and weaknesses that marked him throughout the novel.

In this sense, he is a brother to Henry Fleming, who mistakenly believes he has achieved manhood, but whose claim is undercut by Crane's irony. Crane also uses the model of biography even while denying its view of experience. But Crane's irony, like Henry Adams's, provides another perspective within the narrative that makes it clear to the reader that there is a standard of rationality and manliness by which the assumptions of the actors in the narrative are to be judged and found wanting.

There is a local irony, to be sure, in *An American Tragedy*. Drieser's handling of Mrs. Griffith's and McMillan's belief that God will, in some sense, save Clyde, and Clyde's expectation that McMillan will restore him to his father in heaven is surely ironic. But Clyde's fate ultimately transcends irony. No perspective outside the novel is invoked to provide a truth against which his error can be juxtaposed. On the contrary, Clyde's moral muddle is as accurate a reflection of moral reality as Cowperwood's clarity.

The strength of Cowperwood's natural drives and gifts created the moral values by which he lived. They were real as opposed to the conventional values by which his enemies judged him. The combination of Clyde's natural weaknesses and strengths prevents him from achieving that moral clarity, but Dreiser has none to offer him and the power of the narrative prevents the reader from supposing that he has. Those readers who read the book as a criticism of American society bring to bear assumptions foreign to Dreiser's view of experience. Clyde is not the victim of America's delight in flash and glitter or of America's class system. To Dreiser, these aspects of American life are themselves expressions of human appetite and the natural distribution of personal abilities. All human achievements of order, coherence, or satisfaction are local and short-lived from an individual perspective, and there is no indication in this last of his great novels that he surmounted that perspective. He ultimately embraced communism, and this suggests that his philosophical naturalism permitted him, as it did Henry Adams, to develop a version of materialist history. His greatest novels, however, show what fiction can achieve when it is written on the model of biography by someone who worked persistently to demolish the assumptions and expectations associated with that model throughout the nineteenth century.

The Financier and *An American Tragedy* both fulfill the exemplary role that biography traditionally assigns its subjects, but their experience denies the usefulness of such exempla to the life of action. Far from nurturing the hope that we can strive to achieve the coherence of our authentic selves, Clyde's fate makes clear that, willy-nilly, we live out our authenticity. There is nothing to achieve, nothing to learn in time to do any good, and only the immense pity for the tears in things to feel.

8 Virtual History and Actual History: John Dos Passos

In spite of striking stylistic differences, John Dos Passos follows in the tradition of William Dean Howells and the Henry James of the period of *The Princess Casamassima*. Like Howells he saw social injustice as a central truth of American life that sullied the values on which it was founded. Lionel Trilling exaggerated only a little when he said of *U.S.A.* (1937), "The national, collective, social elements of his trilogy should be seen not as a bid for completeness but rather as a great setting, brilliantly delineated, for his moral interest."[1] Also, like Howells, Dos Passos tried to make biography an adequate model for his vision of experience. But *One Man's Initiation: 1917* (1920), and *Three Soldiers* (1925) share the limitations of *Annie Kilburn*. They strive to make their protagonists' identification with other people's suffering appropriate, to transcend sentimentality, and to make it believable that people pass beyond their class and personal interests to suffer others' wrongs. If this could happen, both writers agree, then social justice could be achieved with relatively little social dislocation. But just as Howells passed beyond this belief to show a world in which economic strife was the reality in which every life had its roots, so Dos Passos moved steadily toward a fiction written as what we may call virtual history. In it the partial perspectives of the earlier novels written on the model of biography give way to the multiple and all-encompassing perspective of experience understood as history, existing through the desires and actions of contending centers of consciousness. While any individual life can be understood only as part of the entire field of action, the novels transcends the inevitable limits of biography and achieves for the reader though not for any of the characters in the novel, an explanation of the way things really happen.

I

Dos Passos's changing treatment of World War I in *One Man's Initiation: 1917, Three Soldiers,* and the first two novels of *U.S.A.* shows biography giving way to history as the model for his narrative, as the merely personal sense of isolation and loss that the war embodied for him is transformed and the war becomes the symbol of social injustice and agony that he had striven to make it from the beginning. Ultimately, Dos Passos's final version of the war depended on his conviction that the sources of his own identification with the war's victims were aesthetically secondary. In *U.S.A.,* Dos Passos's view of literature goes beyond the romantic aesthetic he admired in Whitman. Whitman, and Emerson before him, was convinced that in the personal lay the universal; at the deepest level of the merely individual lay the root that connected mankind. But to live at that deep level of experience was also to negate the weight and force of the difference of social existence. In Dos Passos's first efforts, he did attempt to establish a sense of brotherhood through the obliteration of social forms, to reach beyond differences to a community of deep emotion. But the vision of *U.S.A.* depends on the surrender of the romantic notion that forms stand between us and reality. It differs as well from the naturalism of Dreiser, which seeks to assimilate social forms to the biological, thus also denying history.

It has been a commonplace of Dos Passos criticism to see the stylistic innovations of *U.S.A.* as growing out of his need to reflect structurally the fragmentation of modern society and its alienation. Yet I think it is time to recognize, as Harry Henderson has in *Versions of the Past,* the strength of the attempt to overcome the alienation of the world depicted and to save the sense of history that Henry Adams's education threatened. Henderson, too, invokes Henry Adams in speaking of Dos Passos's historical consciousness, and he finds in that consciousness not only the despair bred by Adams's sense of multiplicity but the drive to transcend it as well.[2] When the historian John P. Diggins denies a sense of history to *U.S.A.,* he does so on the basis of the characters' incapacity to understand their lives. His view is that Dos Passos cannot rise above chronicle to history because he "dissociates himself from the very characters he has created."[3] Invoking Benedetto

Croce's distinction between the historian and the chronicler as lying in the historian's attempt to relive in his own mind the experience of the past, he finds Dos Passos "unable to enter his characters' lives and experience their thoughts because they themselves are hardly conscious of the meaning of historical events" (332–34). For this reason, in his view, Dos Passos fails to resolve the disorder of events into the order of history.

But we can assent to Diggins's view only to the extent that we agree that, because Dos Passos's characters do not understand their experience and cannot rise above the random disorder of their lives, the novel cannot, and we as readers cannot. Diggins sees the "denial of a redemptive telos, of an unfolding unity behind the diversity of events . . . as one purpose of Dos Passos's brilliant stylistic innovations" (332). Yet I would argue that it is through those innovations that the underlying unity in events is communicated to us. Furthermore, to locate freedom in the past is, as Diggins says, to deny a Marxist historical consciousness, but it is not to deny historical consciousness itself. The experience of the failure of justice and the futility of political organization is a historical theme as old as Thucydides.

In fact, Dos Passos had not yet turned, at the time of the writing of the first two books of *U.S.A.*, to early American history in his attempt to understand the failures of his society. The economic struggle, whether as conceived by Marx or by Veblen, dominated his attempts to explain what he saw around him. The first two books move steadily toward an explanation of the death of the Unknown Soldier that ends *1919* (1932), and it is an explanation for which any single character's experience, including that of the Camera Eye, which is autographical, is insufficient because the explanation lies in the social ties and conflicts in which the tragicomedy is enacted and in the interplay of all the levels of discourse that make up the novel. That the characters so often do not understand events and their own suffering comes in large part from the degree to which they are ignorant of the larger struggle from which all events and the shape of the world itself arises—the economic struggle. Joe Williams, who is afraid of foreign radicals, and Eveline Hutchens, who believes reality lies in impulse and sexuality, are in their different ways cut off from a view of reality that, by enabling them to distinguish virtue from power, would give meaning if not success to their lives. But the novel does not cut the reader off from this reality. Diggins seems to feel that the absence of meaning in the events of *U.S.A.* is so patent that it does not need to be argued. Such a conviction can only come, it seems to me, from a reading of the fictional narratives in isolation from the newsreels, Camera Eyes, and biographies.

While Diggins misses historical consciousness in *U.S.A.*, he does find it in Dos Passos's efforts at formal history, *The Ground We Stand On* (1941) and *The Shackles of Power: Three Jeffersonian Decades* (1966), because in them he creates an eighteenth-century America that was meaningful and rational. Giving up the stylistic devices of *U.S.A.*, Diggins writes, he "reconstructed that America through the traditional story-telling function of the narrative historian" (336). But, as we shall see, *The Ground We Stand On* represents an important change in Dos Passos's view of history, a change signaled by the stunning contrast in narrative technique. But Dos Passos's move toward history in the period leading to *U.S.A.* entailed a surrender of the traditional narrative to which he returned when he wrote actual history.

One Man's Initiation: 1917, which is essentially traditional narrative, fails on the whole to bring the war home even to its hero; he remains only an observer, an outsider to the suffering just as he is an American in a French war. The second version of the war, *Three Soldiers*, which contains innovative divisions of consciousness, communicates genuine suffering but loses a good part of its impact because of the intellectualizing of the one figure in the book who understands his experience. Only in *U.S.A.* do we feel the war as both foreign to and yet a part of normal life: the war reflects the central meaning of society merely enacting itself on another stage. No one in the novel is capable of the perspectives that beget moral and social judgments, and yet those judgments are made by the novel and communicated to the reader.

One Man's Initiation: 1917 conveys Dos Passos's realization of the failure of his traditional technique to embody what the war meant to him. What he has seen was so at variance with his customary modes of apprehending and making sense of experience that much of the book consists of a casting about for new ways to approach experience. In *The Great War and Modern Memory*, Paul Fussell shows how central that disparity was in the impact of the war on literary culture,[4] but the irony that results from that disparity and that, indeed, enters *One Man's Initiation: 1917*, is submerged in a reaching after pathos. The pathos in turn is undercut by a misconceived effort to render the war through the senses. Dos Passos writes in his war diary that he wants to express "all the tragedy and hideous excitement" of the war and then goes on, "I must experience more of it and more—the grey crooked fingers of the dead, the dark look of dirty mangled bodies, their groans and joltings in the ambulances, the vast tomtom of the guns, the ripping tear shells make when they explode, the song of shells outgoing like vast woodcocks—their contented whirr as they near their mark—the twang of fragments like a harp broken in the air—and the rattle of stones and mud on your helmet."[5] But sights and sounds, beautifully realized as they are, are separated throughout the novel as they are in this diary fragment from the emotions he wishes to capture. The tomtom, song, whirr, twang, harp, and rattles of this bombardment are busy denying the horror of the exploding shells.

In this novel, Dos Passos is looking for a style for the war. Martin Howe admires the style of the doctor and the chaplain who maintain the civilized manners of dinner and rational discourse under heavy fire and presents for our admiration his own ability to write a novel with his friend in the midst of chaos. A scene that so impressed Dos Passos that it crops up four other times in his writings has Richard Norton, commander of the Norton-Harjes Ambulance Corps, saying goodby to his men on the occasion of the dissolution of the corps. As the United States Army officers who have come to replace the volunteers with a regular corps lose their self-possession and bolt for shelter under fire, Norton, unruffled, his monocle in his eye, speaks the words Dos Passos seemed unable to forget: "As gentlemen volunteers you enlisted in this service and as gentlemen volunteers I bid you farewell" (25). The scene seems to have epitomized for Dos Passos one of the fundamental polarities of his experience: the amateur, an outsider, with superb style; the professional, an arriviste, with none.

However, the two most effective scenes in the novel describe the breakdown of style and the inadequacy of civilization. In one, Martin Howe watches the truckloads of soldiers coming up for the offensive, drunk, terrified, tearing the truck covers, and cursing. In the other, he sees the doctor again; this time, his voice shrill, he is throwing out into the darkness soldiers who seek shelter from a gas bombardment in his hospital dugout. The book ends with the futility of civilized discourse, as we hear of the death of all the men who have taken part in an extended political dialogue.

There are several reminders that the French, suffering though they are, are inflicting a similar suffering on the Germans, and the climax of Dos Passos's appeal to common humanity comes when Martin Howe tries to help a wounded German prisoner: "Sweat dripped from Martin's face on the man's face, and he felt the arm-muscles and ribs pressed against his body as he clutched the wounded man tightly to him in the effort of carrying him towards the dugout. The effort gave Martin a strange contentment. It was as if his body were taking part in the agony of this man's body. At last they were washed out, all the hatreds, all the lies, in blood and sweat. Nothing was left but the quiet friendliness of beings alike in every part, eternally alike" (148).

Here, Dos Passos tries not only to underline the common humanity under the crumbling forms of a polarized and self-destructive society but also to make the suffering of that torn humanity Martin's. Because Martin assumes the suffering in this key passage, divisions between men, if only momentarily, are healed. But we feel this to be altogether too easy. Martin never hated the Germans, nor did he believe the propaganda about them. He has no bitterness to be eased. Yet the scene proposes that his anguish over the war is removed and he is made content by thus taking part in the soldier's agony. In fact, nothing in the war seems really to touch him aside from the gassing, where he, too, sweats behind his mask. But, pain? We don't believe he feels it, and we cannot assent to the claim this scene makes. The young Dos Passos has gone to the war, and he has admired the coolness of the gentleman volunteer, but he has been moved by the vision of the passive and helpless driven to slaughter, the dying betrayed, intelligent energy wasted. Yet Martin Howe, with his sights and sounds, stands between this vision and the reader.

II

In calling his second novel *Three Soldiers*, Don Passos shifts his interest from exploring the effect of the war on a single sensitive observer to a sense of the war as a subject beyond the comprehension of any single awareness. Although he wants to distinguish his soldiers and make them representative of certain elements in American life, he also wants to show them losing their individuality in a shared experience larger than any of them. As the consciousness on which the realization of the war in *One Man's Initiation: 1917* depends, Martin Howe remains equal to his surroundings. It is never implied that Howe does not register all the elements of his reality. In the opening scene of *Three Soldiers*, however, Dos Passos is at pains to show that no one man at attention there is aware of all the aspects of his world.

This second version of the war is based on another aspect of Dos Passos's war experience. No longer a gentleman volunteer after the entry of the United States into the war, he served with the American Red Cross Ambulance Corps in Italy. His letters were so critical of the bureaucracy that he was forced to resign and returned to the United States to enlist in the army. Various complications landed him for a time as a private in a medical corps casuals company in Pennsylvania. He felt it to be the "trash can" of the corps. Too awkward to drill, the men were put to sweeping and washing windows, and Dos Passos with them. "My luck as always," he wrote to a friend, "is with the unclassified. . . . I'm glad I'm here even if I seem to grumble. I've always wanted to divest myself of class and the moneyed background—the army seemed the best way. From the bottom, thought I, one can see clear."[6]

The casuals company, then, quite accidentally, gave Dos Passos an opportunity he embraced to surrender his background. His use of the word *unclassified* is revealing. It speaks, of course, of his sense of individuality, a strong counterforce to his sense of fraternity and community, as Andrew Hook, [7] among others, has noted. But *unclassified* is an ambivalent word. It may signify rarity and originality or only singularity, a less clearly blessed condition, or more unhappily, it may suggest someone who is unrecognized, even without identity. Similarly, looking back on the war from his seventies in *The Best Times* (1966), Dos Passos wondered if he had been a gentleman volunteer or an amateur proletarian. Both conditions escape social hierarchy and they are both expressions of his sense of his own condition. Was he part of his father's world, the father, a man dedicated to the law who did not legitimize his son for sixteen years? Harvard was the first school to enroll him under the Dos Passos name. Yet his relationship with his father was very close. At least one thing he learned through it was that real belonging and attachment could flourish outside the law and social arrangements, that real claims and affection might have nothing to do with public status. At the same time he was closed off from the power that went with status; he was in a fundamental sense, déclassé.

So the division of consciousness of *Three Soldiers* also permits him to exploit that part of him which feels, as he says, unclassified and to bring into prominence his feelings of fraternity with the true victims of war. The sense of an overriding social organization is fundamental to *Three Soldiers*. We are meant to feel its weight on these men at the bottom. Representing different aspects of American life, the men deal with its pressures differently. Fuselli, an urban man, ignorant, ill-educated, eager, is prepared, apparently by city life, to suppress his impulses, to take orders, to "get in right" with the officers and rise in the ranks. He feels, as the others do, the alienation and helplessness of his position, and ambition is his response to it. He is not sentimentalized; he doesn't want to be seen with "a kike" or "a frog," as he calls them, talking revolution: that would be getting in wrong. His mind is stocked with the vulgarities of the movies. We feel the foolishness of his belief that the army functions rationally and that his behavior make a difference. But we feel also the pressure of his anxiety and isolation. He lives in a waking nightmare, as if some "gigantic figure were driving him forward through the darkness, holding a fist over his head, ready to crush him."[8] His girl and his belief in promotion keep him going. When the army takes both away, he feels at last the reality of his life, and his heart dies out of him.

From the first, Chrisfield is contrasted with Fuselli: an Indiana farm boy, he is open, independent, eager, not to rise but to fight. His anger is close to the surface, and he has no ambition to keep him in line. Balancing Chrisfield's impulsiveness and angry individuality are his affectionate response to Andrews and his need for the group. Dos Passos is very good at giving a sense of the way the group sustains its members in spite of their enslavement. The instability of Chrisfield's character and the negative aspect of his dependence on his mates are revealed best when he kills his enemy, Sergeant Anderson. Alone in the woods, hurrying to keep ahead of his own army's artillery barrage, anxious in separation from his buddies, and angry at his own hunger, he comes across Anderson, wounded and promoted yet again, now a lieutenant. He wonders at the promotion and walking away finds that he has pressed the spring of his grenade. When, without apparent decision or control, he finds he has thrown it, he is warm with joy. He finds a terrified German, kicks him, gives him up without thought to be shot with other prisoners, eats, rejoins his outfit, and his loneliness gone, marches in the ranks. The sinister possibilities of Chrisfield's impulsive behavior are clear. John H. Wrenn is right to remark on Andrews's admiration of Chrisfield, but he is surely mistaken in seeing Chrisfield as Dos Passos's suggested model for the more inhibited Andrews.[9] Andrews is also shown in enraged reaction to authority, but when he finds himself reacting with aggression, with the belief that he should impose his will on others, he rejects that response. "More of the psychology of slavery," he calls it (342). Fuselli and Chrisfield, different as they are, are both enslaved.

However, Fuselli and Chrisfield are the triumphs of the novel, and Andrews is its problem. Alfred Kazin and Blanche Gelfant, among others, comment on Andrews's weakness as a character, but they do not fully explore its significance.[10] Andrews goes to war as an escape from a self that he feels not to be real in the way the slavery of the army is real and the scorn and comradeship it generates are. The music Andrews hopes to write is a way of both expressing and transcending the slavery. But he is ambivalent about transcendence. The music is part of the self he has gone to war to repudiate. Music also has erotic associations, for he sees himself as another Anthony tempted in the desert. The music is about the temptation, and the desire to create music is itself a temptation. In addition, art presents the chance to avoid degradation, but in some way art is not real, and it is reality he has gone to war to find. However, at the same time, his submission to authority disgusts him, and he admires Chrisfield's rebellion.

The fighting ends with Andrews still in the hospital and a third of the book to go. In this way, Dos Passos emphasizes the extent to which army life is not simply an organized response to an acute crisis in society but is society itself. Andrews thinks of his life as "industralized slaughter" (269). It is a representative condition, not a special case of industrial society, and he vacillates between submerging himself in its reality and transcending it through art. We might see this vacillation, as Andrew Hook does, as simply the necessary polarity of an artist's life, except for the conclusion of Andrews's story.

Ultimately music, love, natural beauty, social pleasures, all prove insufficient to balance his anger at authority. He cannot bear to be ordered about by people just like him but "who've had the luck to get in right with the system" (400). He gets to Paris by exploiting the system, being obsequious to YMCA officers, and trading on his Harvard credentials. But he cannot endure his success and he invites destruction. His sense of life allows only for slave and master. If he is not the latter, he must be the former, and his shame and self-disgust are unbearable. But we don't know why he feels this way, and the book is not about how he came to feel it. It presents him as feeling it and supposes that what the book shows us about Fuselli, Chrisfield, and the army is enough to justify those feelings. But they are not. Once he is in the labor battalion, we can understand his going AWOL, but we don't believe he needed to be there. We do not feel the inevitability of Andrews's desertion and self-destruction in the way we believe Fuselli's loss of heart and Chrisfield's rebellion. The real reasons for his identification with the forlorn and hopeless are hidden from us. He claims to be powerless, though we see that he has power and is able to use it when he chooses. Why does he choose not to?

Andrews is developed as an extension of the Martin Howe who is made strangely happy by sharing in the agony of the soldier he holds close to him. War is the occasion for the discovery of brotherhood in suffering, for initiation into the fundamental reality of loss and dispossession, of impotence. If it is only that way for the ignorant, the ill-educated, the naive, the Fusellis and Chrisfields, that is not good enough. Because what Martin Howe and Andrews feel, as opposed to what the novels succeed in showing about them, is that it is true for the intelligent, the talented, and the favored too and that there can be no understanding of experience and therefore no peace until this is realized.

III

When Dos Passos treats the war for the third time, two important changes appear. One is that, even more than in *Three Soldiers*, the war is seen as an extension of American social behavior. The other is the revolution in narrative technique. Diggins and many others with him have seen the fragmentation of style only as a reflection of the alienation of industrial society. However, it is more importantly the means by which solidarity is maintained and is, like the war itself, the means by which society can be shown as oppressive and yet be revealed as yielding in its oppression the occasion for brotherhood.

War breaks out in *U.S.A.* in a newsreel of *The 42nd Parallel* (1930). Surrounded by the trivia of popular songs, glimpses of the amusements of society and its silly attempts at serious social thinking, the pompous failures of officialdom shine out in the headlines. Mockery and scorn usher the war in, not the adventurism of *One Man's Initiation: 1917* or the naïveté of the rookies in *Three Soldiers*. Through the mind of Janey Williams, we are shown the response to anti-German propaganda of an unreflective and gullible general public. Opposed to her conforming mentality is the gruff refusal of her brother, Joe, to be taken in. He verbalizes one of the major themes of this treatment of the war: "The whole damn war's crooked from start to finish."[11]

The growing estrangement between Janey and Joe is a measure of her increasing absorption into the fraudulent elements of American life, which profit from the war at the expense of the men at the bottom of society who do the fighting, sail the boats, and get torpedoed. Joe encompasses the emotions of the fighting men Martin Howe watched going drunk to the front as well as the warring impulses of Fuselli and Chrisfield, on the one hand to "make it" and, on the other, to tolerate no insults. He manifests also Andrews's drive to drop out of society, although for him it is not from choice but from lack of it. As a member of the merchant marine, his helplessness under fire and his passive suffering, together with his ignorance of the issues underlying the war and his inability to articulate his experience, carry a major part of the war's impact in *1919*. Although Joe is shown to suffer, as America as a whole suffers in the novel's view at the hands of the British, the victims in this version of the war are Americans and chiefly noncombatants, while the enemies are almost all Americans. Those who resist, evade, or repudiate the war are its heroes; those who support and take part in it willingly, its villains. The innocents who do not understand the war's true nature, which is to say that they do not understand the way society works, are dupes and are destroyed.

Dos Passos divides his experience in interesting ways in *1919*. In *Three Soldiers*, he gave his own humanitarian impulse and his desire to deal with private woes by going to war to Andrews and attempted to endow them with heroic stature. Here he clearly finds them worth only the sympathy we give to weakness, because he gives them to Daughter, who is admirable but naive. His experience in the ambulance corps, both Red Cross and regular army, he gives to Dick Savage, whose history begins promisingly and mirrors much of Don Passos's own. But Savage becomes increasingly unappealing, and his selfishness and careerism come to a climax in the war, although he retains enough virtue to feel self-disgust.

When the novel follows the troops to Europe, it concentrates on the life behind the lines, the self-indulgence and empty sensuality of the officer and his contempt for the men in the ranks. The sort of well-bred superiority to sordid circumstance Dos Passos held up for our admiration in Martin Howe and which he made Andrews self-consciously cultivate and then, in disgust, repudiate, here appears as the object of impersonal mockery.

Joe Williams survives the wreckage of his ships only to be killed in a fight in a bar on Armistice Day. His death follows his surrender to Janey's importunities to take advantage of the war: he decides to buy Liberty Bonds. Three paragraphs after his reflections on the war as an opportunity for a guy who doesn't get in wrong, his own disorderly life, the only real option society offers him, kills him. Society's ultimate rejection is a meaningless death, a precursor of the futility of the great summary figure of the Unknown Soldier who ends *1919*. Joe's death bitterly repeats the theme of which every successful character provides a variation. Some kind of death, spiritual or emotional, awaits all those Americans who go to war and benefit from it: Dick Savage, Eveline Hutchins, Eleanor Stoddard, and, of course, the epitome of them all, Ward Moorehouse. Society's virtue dies with them, as it does with the Unknown Soldier. But for all these characters, the war merely brings to a culmination or enhances tendencies and qualities evident in their prewar lives. The war initiates nothing; it allows us to see the true nature and relations of things.

As the war defeats Joe, it brings Moorehouse to greater prominence. It consolidates his position as an intermediary between authority, whether business or government and the public, and makes possible the identification of war propaganda and capitalist propaganda so central to Dos Passos's version of the significance of the war. This is supported by the biographies of Carnegie, La Follette, Randolph Bourne, Paxton Hibben, Wilson, and the House of Morgan. The biographies are, of course, both true and slanted. They are a rhetoric aimed at reinforcing and lending the credence of fact, the inevitability of history, to the fictional elements. The fictional narratives share with the real biographies that summary style and sense of closed options Jean-Paul Sartre was so taken with, lending them, as he saw, the effect of destiny.[12] In the newsreels, with the help of Dos Passos's masterly juxtapositions, society's most impersonal voice speaks its own fatuity. Furthermore, Dos Passos reaches through the real figures' part in the war to their social commitments, to the strife between labor and business that he sees as the fundamental reality of which the war is one form. The victimization of the talented La Follette, Bourne, and Hibben merges with the suffering of Joe Williams to create that sense of brotherhood in defeat for which Dos Passos had created Martin Howe and John Andrews.

Even more important for the impact of this version of the war is the reduction of its immediate appeal to emotion. As if Dos Passos recognized his earlier failures to bring alive his personal anguish over what he saw, he finally found stratagems to avoid direct expression. One is the use of the nonfictional elements. A second is the restriction of his own memories and feelings to the Camera Eye, where, cut off from the action of the fictional narratives, they have the self-validation of lyric, and the reader does not ask if they are commensurate with the

action because they are not ostensibly generated by it. Yet, at the same
time, the Camera Eye is related to the events that surround it. For
example, *1919* opens with a newsreel about the war that concludes with
a snatch of song in which soldiers make obscenely clear they will not
reenlist. Then Joe Williams drops his uniform in the water, as Andrews
does at the end of *Three Soldiers*. But none of Andrews's feelings are
here, none of his striving for the larger meaning of his desertion, only
the grubbiness of the Buenos Aires waterfront, the matter-of-fact statement of how Joe knocked out his petty officer, and the smell of the
hallway where he buys a false A.B. certificate. Then we read a Camera
Eye in which the deaths of father and mother and the experience of the
war are brought together. For the first time in his fiction, Dos Passos
allows the inference that his feelings of loss and victimization have to
do with feelings about his own family, that they are engendered by
private as well as social events. But he can afford to do this because the
newsreels and the events of Joe's life come together with those feelings
and convince the reader that they are appropriate responses to the
public events as well. They are the responses of pain and anger to
which Joe's social experience, like that of Fuselli and Chrisfield, entitle
him but which he cannot articulate even to himself because that same
social experience has denied him the means.

A further stratagem Dos Passos finds to avoid and yet express
feeling is to shift from the pathos or melodrama that dominate the first
versions of the war, to comedy. The dispersion of sympathy that results
from the absence of subjectivity in the characters, from the multiplicity
of characters, and from the mixture of real and fictional, is further
maintained by the dominant notes of irony and comic scorn. Arthur
Mizener was the first to do justice to this aspect of Dos Passos's art by
putting him in the perspectives of Swift, Ben Jonson, and the eighteenth-century novel.[13] The United States entry into the war is treated
in a scene in which Eleanor Stoddard and Moorehouse walk in Man-
hattan. She is excited by the French flag and the song "Tipperary." She
is also worrying about paying for the fur coat she has on and the bills
for the Sutton Place apartment she is remodeling:

> They'd been talking about the air raids and poison gas and the effect
> of the war news downtown and the Bowmen of Mons and the Maid of
> Orleans and she said she believed in the supernatural and J. W. was
> hinting something about reverses on the street and his face looked
> drawn and worried; but they were crossing Times Square through the

eight o'clock crowds and the skysigns flashing on and off. The fine lit-tle triangular men were doing exercises on the Wrigley sign and sud-denly a grind-organ began to play The Marseillaise *and it was too beautiful; she burst into tears and they talked about Sacrifice and Dedication and J. W. held her arm tight through the fur coat and gave the organ-grinder man a dollar. When they got to the theater El-eanor hurried down to the ladies' room to see if her eyes had got red. But when she looked in the mirror they weren't red at all and there was a flash of heartfelt feeling in her eyes, so she just freshened up her face and went back up to the lobby where J. W. was waiting for her with the tickets in his hand; her gray eyes were flashing and had tears in them. (1:353)*

Here are so many finely controlled comic rhythms and effects it is difficult to do brief justice to them. Simply to point to a few: the way the first sentence moves from war to business to sentimental history and religiosity and back again with a thud to the real worry of losing money; the way Eleanor takes emotional flight again on the unlikely wings of neon signs and a street organ's patriotism to be brought back again by J. W. to money; the climactic "flash of heartfelt feeling" Eleanor theatrically leaves in her eyes to impress the lover who, indeed, holds the tickets to the false drama the war is to Eleanor at this moment and will be throughout *1919*. Nor is the authority of this passage unusual; it is the stamp of Dos Passos's mature style and is, in fact, the voice by which we might easily recognize him.[14] It is certainly very different from the mannered lyricism of Hemingway or the baroque intensity of Fitzgerald, but to see it as anonymous or as machinelike must strike us as the inattention of a generation of critics who, not finding the familiar, came away with nothing.

The biographies, which show Dos Passos's sympathies and moral judgments more directly, often turn to bitter comedy to avoid obvious appeals to emotion. In the portrait of Paxton Hibben, a journalist whose background and experience are very like Dos Passos's own, the disorder of the war is the precursor of Hibben's vision of order, work, and hope in the Russian Revolution. For this vision and for the act of laying a wreath on Jack Reed's grave, America punishes him but in ridiculous ways: "They tried to throw him out of the O.R.C.," writes Dos Passos. At a Princeton twentieth reunion, his drunken classmates offer to lynch him. The focus is on the absurdity of the response, not on Hibben's suffering. Similarly, Randolph Bourne, another talented victim of the war, survives his own defeat; his "unscared ghost" cries out in a "soundless giggle . . . 'War is the health of the state.'"

The point of view of the narrative is fundamentally that of comedy: it highlights the absurdity of events. The pain and suffering they evoke come because, in this dark version of comedy, wounds can be fatal and there are no eleventh-hour escapes. Most importantly, the absurdities are not accidental, nor are they the very nature of experience that we must accept, nor are they consequences of isolated fools or knaves. They are social. They spring from the highest powers in the land, from what we as a people admire as well as what we are accustomed to deplore. They are unnecessary. For most painful of all for the reader is the fact that although we are shown no alternatives to the cruel absurdities of the narrative, the combination of the pervasively social contexts of the action and the unremitting anger and condemnation that underlie the comedy, causes us to feel that it can be different. We do not so savagely judge what cannot be otherwise.

The device of the Camera Eye also contributes to the sense that events can be different. It supplies a sensibility and intelligence apart from the inevitability of the events in the stories, the biographies, and the newsreels. Though the lives in those three aspects of narrative are closed, life in the Camera Eye is still open. And not least is the impact of all the technical innovations together. Through these repeated shifts of perspective, voice, and level of reality, we are being reminded of the author's hand. This world that so resembles life, we are never permitted to forget, is made, not natural. Even the fictional narratives do not strive to approximate the ongoing experience in which we are immersed but have the summary quality of an epitaph. Although the language of each narrative suits the character, the words are not so much what he actually says but, as Sartre has acutely commented, what he would like to have said for him. One of the most impressive aspects of the Stoddard, Moorehouse, and Savage narratives is that they never say anything these characters would not be willing to say about themselves, yet, like the voice of the public in the newsreels, they convict themselves out of their own mouths.

Through all these techniques, Dos Passos is finally able to achieve the sense of shared experience that he dimly struggled for in the image of Martin Howe holding the wounded German. When *1919* concludes with a biography of the Unknown Soldier, the details of army life and the realities of wounds and death are all the more striking because they make us realize how little of this part of the war there was in this broad and complex picture. This mud and torn flesh are what lay behind the posturing of Moorehouse and Savage. But more than that, it makes the soldier's wounds metaphors for what the body of America suffered and continues to suffer in the awful piety of the public response to the war dead. The image of the soldier echoes Dos Passos's accomplishment throughout this version of the war. He has converted the war into a metaphor for the battles and losses of American life. Through its power he commands our assent at last to the authenticity and strength of the suffering his war experience engendered in him, and moral judgment is at last lodged in a commensurate subject, justified at last by a wide-ranging vision of experience. The whole technical panoply, the fragmentation, the impersonality, the mixture of real and fictional, take the reader into the shared suffering that is history. Not actual history, of course, but the virtual history Dos Passos creates to convince us that, whatever our talents and energies, perceptive readers and powerful writers alike, we take part in that fundamental reality of loss and dispossession.

Yet at the same time, because this is fiction, not history, we have transcended that reality, for through the historical perspective Dos Passos has expressed the unity and significance of experience that any of these lives, in itself, real or fictional, must be denied. The history that failed to teach Henry Adams anything was modeled on biography. His account of its failure contains the unexamined expectation that individual consciousness would be equal to experience, if not at first, then at least ultimately. In his theory of the acceleration of force he surrenders his demands for an understanding of causation and settles for measurement as the furthest reach of his intellectual domination of experience. But it was a bitter diminution of his morning wishes, and his rage and hurt pervade the *Education*. The historical sense that informs the rendering of the war in *U.S.A.*, however, has already discounted the education of consciousness and relegated it to the Camera Eye to be a mere fraction of the experience rendered. Blanche Gelfant [15] and Richard Chase place more value on that part of the novels than did Dos Passos himself because they have in mind a biographical model for the novel, with its important themes of individual identity, growth, and the "quest for selfhood and reality" (180), as Chase puts it. But Dreiser had already shown how outworn such a model was for understanding twentieth-century American reality. Dos

Passos turned to history as a model for fiction because he saw people as essentially incorrigible and as necessarily leaving to others the meaning of their own actions. As early as 1942, Albert Camus articulated in *The Myth of Sisyphus* the consequences of using biography as a model for fiction after the view of experience that supports it is surrendered: the result is the absurd—in his version heroic but heartbreaking. And like the final lesson of Henry Adams's failed education, the absurd was dominated by what Camus called "Don Juanism,"[16] the multiplication of experience without the growth of understanding or moral force, mathematics not meaning. Dos Passos's turn to history as model was both to admit to the failure of individual consciousness and yet to save meaning and value by locating them outside that failed consciousness in a community that both shared and transcended individual failures.

As in *An American Tragedy,* where Dreiser's use of the model of biographical narrative explicitly denies Clyde the achievement of coherence and insight into the significance of his actions, so Dos Passos gives us biographical naratives, both true and fictional, that do not culminate in self-knowledge or mastery of circumstance. Whether the biography is a worldly triumph as in Woodrow Wilson or defeat as in Paxton Hibben, the meaning of the life cannot be understood outside the historical narrative in which it is embedded. This is as true for the fictional biographies as for the real, which "resonate" with each other as Cushing Strout has observed.[17] The actions of all these lives are significant, that is, they become actions instead of happenings, they receive shape and point by being part of historical action. The powerful no more than the impotent understands what he does or what happens to him. Whatever his claim to knowledge, submerged in ongoing life, he cannot know. Knowledge is reserved for the historical perspective.

Dos Passos's narrative is a fascinating version of the interplay between the biographical and the historical models. Initially it may appear that the biographical model dominates the work. And Dos Passos has been read as the heir of Dreiser. But he is more truly the heir of Henry Adams here as elsewhere. As in the *History of the United States of America during the Administrations of Jefferson and Madison,* the individual is seen as the locus of historical forces and the type of national character. The individual, then, is truly explained only by what transcends individuality, and the biographical is rescued from the catastrophic alternatives of the absurd and the mute by its incorporation into history.

IV

U.S.A. makes clear that Dos Passos's goals as a writer extended beyond the clarification of values in his culture. For all his admiration of technology, he could not follow Henry Adams's glorification of the engineer of force who would put an end to politics as Western culture understood it; for him, fully human action was political, and he hoped his novels would make such action possible as it was not in the world of *U.S.A.* In the years between the Spanish Civil War and World War II, Dos Passos turned from virtual history to the actual history of America's founding, hoping to embody in his narrative the conditions that made the victory of republican principles possible and that might renovate the political life of his own time. His growing disillusion with Russian communism came to a climax with the execution of his anarchist friend José Robles by the Communists in Spain in 1937. Spain had always been for him the embodiment of an anarchist ideal closer to his vision of the political life than the communism he saw developing in Russia in the twenties and thirties, and with Robles's death Spanish anarchism seemed as futile as Big Bill Heywood's IWW.[18] The novels after *U.S.A.* are obsessed with the moral futility of contemporary political life, while the history that he writes during the same period envisions an alternative in our own past.

The Ground We Stand On is the first step in the recovery of a political creed. His use of an epigraph from Joel Barlow's *Columbiad* (1807) and the role Barlow plays in the book itself shows how short the way was in his mind from the work he had been doing to the work he now took up. Barlow had written: "My object is altogether of a moral and political nature. I wish to encourage and strengthen in the rising generation, a sense of the importance of republican institutions, as being the great foundation of public and private happiness, the necessary aliment of future and permanent ameliorations in the condition of human nature."[19] Dos Passos's fiction, like Barlow's epigraph, had always taken it for granted that there was no separation between "public and private happiness" and also supposed that human nature was inextricable from the social matrix that nourished it.

In *The Best Times,* Dos Passos says he thought of himself as being shaped by the revolutions in modern art and in politics that came from Europe during his Harvard and war years (23, 45–46). Yet Dos Passos's admiration for La Follette and the Wobblies that he expressed so well in *U.S.A.,* his lifelong support of the individual against powerful combinations of business or government, his distrust of the business establishment and his belief that government was in the hands of "the interest," all reflect the homegrown populism and progressivism of the late nineteenth and early twentieth centuries. These are domestic political movements, the one expressing the inland fear of eastern money and industry and what they do to the average man and the other full of the moral fervor and the sense of civic responsibility of educated Easterners. Dos Passos's history comes out of a self-conscious sense that the past can be used to solve the problems of the present. In the Preface to the *Columbiad* that Dos Passos quotes, Barlow refers to the "false and destructive" ideas of glory that "have degraded the species in other countries" and hopes to secure for the new generation a belief in the virtues of the American Revolution to protect them against the disappointment of republican hopes after the French Revolution. Like Barlow, Dos Passos turns to that past as a reaction to the failed promise of the Russian Revolution that he saw exhibited in Communist party policy during the Spanish Civil War. Dos Passos rejects the "debunking" of the past typical of his own time, as well as what he calls the "provincial tone" Americans take towards Europe (4). At the same time that *The Ground We Stand On* repeatedly evokes the special quality of America that enables political virtues to thrive, this history is at pains to remind us that England was the source of those virtues. English-speaking people, he asserts, have "habits" of politics, and by politics he means the "contest between the self-governing habits of the mass and various special groups that have sought to dominate it for their own purposes" (9). Continental Europe lacks it. England is persistently contrasted with France, whose political experience vis-à-vis England is analogous to that of Russia compared to the United States. France is a country where Richelieu can build a police state, while in England William Laud's attempt to do so fails. However there are times, as when England fails to support the ideals of the Commonwealth, that it figures with France in contrast to the special conditions of America. Then, asserts Dos Passos, the Anglo-Saxon political tradition, which arose in England, was overwhelmed there at the very time it prospered in America. Writing in 1940, Dos Passos feared that industrialization and the "diverse habits" of European immigrants may have destroyed the political tradition or damaged it beyond help, but he doesn't really believe this. His faith is that the study of history, in revealing the roots of our political tradition will restore us.

To those readers who saw in *U.S.A.* only the individual's defeat in a battle whose determinants are beyond his grasp, Dos Passos's history may seem merely an exercise in wishful thinking. It may appear to be a well-intentioned but intellectually weak-minded search for the life of reason and self-determination. But two factors should preclude such a hasty judgment. One is the high place accorded to history in *U.S.A.*, a place that contrasts it with personal experience and promises transcendence of the chaos of mere contemporaneity. The other is Dos Passos's affinity with historians like Frederick Jackson Turner and Charles Beard to whom contemporary political struggle wore a blank face and made rational life impossible until it was given feature and intent by historical study. What his work shows more clearly, perhaps just because it is less successful as history than theirs, is the conflict between their belief in the special coherence historical vision allows and any view of the individual as a force rather than a center in the historical process. As clearly as in their work the individual functions as the representative of a group, never as a force in himself. In a narrative in which individuals nevertheless figure so importantly, the contradiction between the special coherence historical vision allows and the popular American mythology that makes individual will so powerful is especially sharp.

Dos Passos begins by writing history on the model of biography, not biography as Emerson understood it, revealing a man representative of the possibilities of essential selfhood, free of the accidents of place and time, but as Adams conceived of it in his biographies of Gallatin and Randolph: the account of those moments in men's lives when they were historically significant, when they embodied what the author has already identified as the significant social and political changes he wishes to describe and explain. In a recent study Linda Wagner calls Dos Passos "character oriented," finding his reporting, fiction, and history alike in this respect. "Even the books," she writes, "that might well have become treatises in political science . . . are built on portraits of individual people."[20]

In Dos Passos's first history, *The Ground We Stand On,* Jefferson and Roger Williams represent the two ways back to the antecedents of the American republic in English society. Jefferson leads back to the country gentleman republicanism of the seventeenth century, and Williams to the Roundhead townspeople and Protestant sects. They are the ancestors of the "liberal mind" that supported the struggle of people aspiring to equality, justice, and brotherhood against privilege and power. That struggle Dos Passos identifies as the cause of all the events of modern history. For Dos Passos the religious conversion Williams experienced was a social and political conversion too, for Protestant politics and religion alike are marked by the "conviction of the sublime importance of any one man's thoughts and feelings at every separate moment of his life" ever since "the day of Luther's cry of 'Ich kann nichts anders' "(27). In order to strengthen the identification of Williams and his defense of religious freedom with political equality, Dos Passos persistently links him to the English jurist Sir Edward Coke. He calls him Coke's protégé to enhance the role of law in our view of Williams's contribution to the American republic. Similarly he links *The Bloody Tenet* with the *Areopagitica* as fueling the Independents' effort to make a republic in England. So Williams is made to represent the "Commonwealth generation," as Dos Passos calls it, that is obliterated at home but thrives abroad, as Williams and his ideas flourish in America, while Algernon Sidney, a counterpart in England, is executed by Lord Jeffries.

Benjamin Franklin epitomizes the eighteenth century as Williams does the seventeenth. He has an English counterpart in Daniel Defoe, who sums up "the practical aspirations of English men of business" and "foreshadowed in the cast of their minds the century of invention and industrial growth that was to come" (197). But Dos Passos sees Defoe as ruined by stratified English society, while Franklin blossoms in casteless America. As Dos Passos moves from Franklin to Samuel Adams and the events surrounding the Stamp Act, we are made to feel the possibilities of social disintegration in the impending violence. But Adams is shown to be a man who, in organizing the Sons of Liberty, organizes all the law-keeping functions of the community so that the aggressive energies that might tear the Revolution apart can instead be mobilized in its service. His own random, disorganized life takes form at the same time. He marries a "strongminded woman" and prospers in society after his victory in the Stamp Act Affair. As he rises and stabilizes, he sees Thomas Hutchinson, who had been at the summit of anglophile society, thoroughly ruined, both materially and in reputation.

This reversal of fortune is as close as the narrative comes to the Revolution itself, which is never recounted. With Jefferson's appearance, the Republic is already in place. His life is represented as inseparable from the public drama he figures in. At the age of forty, he is said to be at an age "when all the blank checks of youth have been cashed and a man has to face himself as an adult, the way he's going to be until he dies; that is the point from which a man of ability either goes on to mature and to take his place for better or worse in the world, or else drops back into the great army of might-have-beens" (236). It is, ultimately, the Republic that must take its place or fall back into the might-have-beens. Similarly Dos Passos's narrative affirms Jefferson's importance as lying in his membership in the Virginia gentry, who lived like the gentry of seventeenth-century England. In America their great estates avoided bankruptcy long enough to give the men formed by that way of life the "leeway they needed to put all their energies into public service" (243).

The threats to the Republic are enacted first through Joel Barlow's experience and then through Hugh Brackenridge's. Barlow saw the French Revolution firsthand. Dos Passos's descriptions of the details of Barlow's life are like his accounts of his own life abroad, and the emotion of the time is like the emotion of his own early years. He describes Barlow at a dinner with friends in France: "The excitement of hope that the world might shake off the groveling and the subservience of fearsoaked centuries and become suddenly all open and free like America, the hope that was soon to begin to be expressed in the toast to which Barlow's political friends lifted their wineglasses after dinner: 'To the Revolution of the World'" (303). But from the first this emotion is tempered by Barlow's doubt, shared by Jefferson, that the French are capable of a free constitution. Around Robespierre cluster the feelings Dos Passos had about the Russian Communists by the end of the 1930s: "Establishing a republic was to them [the English and Americans] a day-to-day business of adjustments of men's rights; the means were allimportant. For the French who followed Robespierre, the means didn't matter: the Republic was a mystic and bloody ritual; the end was unity" (318). Barlow backs away from what he sees as Dos Passos tells us John Reed did from what he saw in Russia. And of course as Dos Passos did. Dos Passos makes the analogy even more explicit when he says that even in 1798 with his knowledge of French politics, Barlow couldn't foresee the rise of a new tyrant any more than sympathetic observers in Russia in the 1920s could.

In other significant ways Barlow is a version of Dos Passos. In calling him repeatedly "the man who never turned down a trip," Dos Passos summons up the almost compulsive traveling of his own early years. Like the reviews of *U.S.A.*, the reviews of Barlow's epic, the *Columbiad*, divide along political lines. Barlow's political sympathies, misunderstood by his friends, bring him a letter from an old friend, Noah Webster, telling him that their friendship is destroyed by his irreligion. Dos Passos, who suffered Hemingway's rejection of him and who was childless until later in life, remarks on the painfulness of breaks with friends on whom, as a man without children, Barlow was more dependent than most. Through this identification with Barlow Dos Passos makes himself historically significant. Just as Barlow defines the ground we stand on and takes possession of it for America, so Dos Passos as a writer can be a potent political force in recovering that ground for America in circumstances he finds similar to its early perilous years.

The last episode in this account of the founding of the Republic, the Whiskey Rebellion, is also, on the one hand, compared with European experience, and on the other, seen from the perspective of a representative figure. The rebellion is put in the context of William Pitt's repression of reformers and republicans after Edmund Burke's outcry against the French Revolution. George Washington and Alexander Hamilton both figure as dangers to the Republic because Washington sees this local event as a result of the Jacobin incitement "to burn the landlords out of their mansions," and Hamilton sees it as an occasion for glory (386). Here Brackenridge is the Dos Passos figure, caught between two political extremes, who exacerbates his position by writing a book that "made fun of everything and everybody." He is blameless of incitement to arms and had actually been trying to restore order. Hamilton never fulfills the threat of Pitt's mindless repression because he sees the truth of the situation when he comes to Pittsburgh and his honesty prevails over his ambition. In his exoneration of Brackenridge, he shows the superiority of the early training of the Anglo-Saxons as well as of their tradition, which gave them the self-restraint needed for a self-governing society.

What is remarkable about *The Ground We Stand On* is that while it is an account of a revolutionary period, the burden of its narrative is restraint. No one in America is defeated, the political battle that rages through *U.S.A.,* in which men can be either exploiters or exploited, in this book goes on only in Europe. There, we are made to see, whether the Revolution is unsuccessful as it was in England or successful as it was in France, freedom and justice lose. The struggle that Dos Passos early in the book defines as political, between the mass with its instincts for self-government and self-interested groups, which seek to dominate it, does not appear in America. The Anglo-Saxon tradition, a combination of training and heredity, subsumes conflict. On the one hand, it is marked by an inclusiveness that allows the integration of men as different as Roger Williams, Ben Franklin, and Alexander Hamilton. On the other hand, it is distinguished by a ruling class that refrains from domination. The single example of domestic repression of dissent suggests, in the way it is dealt with through Brackenridge, that no repression occurred.

Barlow and Jefferson are shown to suffer from politics, but not because of fidelity to one or the other of the competing elements. Barlow, like Brackenridge, is caught between extremes: he is not the godless Jacobin that Noah Webster believes him to be, but the American dialectic between the Federalists and the Republicans is never developed; nor does any conflict over the Constitution arise. Similarly, Jefferson is shown to have been made a scapegoat during the Revolution for Virginia's suffering. Disillusion overtakes him because of the resistance of the people to his innovations: "The process of getting people to accept political changes or novelties, even those from which they will immediately benefit, has broken the hearts of innovators since history began," comments Dos Passos (254). Jefferson tried to keep *Notes on Virginia* (1787) from American publication for fear his views on slavery would "do more harm than good." In the account of the failure of the Commonwealth, Dos Passos gave a similar explanation for the failure of democratic innovations. Just as he says in writing of Jefferson, that it is "a part of the nature of consciousness . . . that free reason is only a very occasional function of people" (253), so he says apropos of the Commonwealth that the monarchy returned because people "were sick of sermons, of the strain of trying to lift themselves by their own bootstraps into a rational life according to scriptures." They needed "pageantry . . . bootlicking . . . the old hogwallow" (152). So much for the self-governing instincts of the mass!

At the same time Dos Passos claims for the very survival of the race the importance of the emergence of a type of mind that has qualities he groups under "the parental bent" (254). Men of this type were able to bring others to effective action and yet were "unwilling to use their ascendancy for their own selfish ends." Virginia produced these men in numbers, but even Franklin, the Adamses, and Hamilton were of that sort.

For all Dos Passos's declarations of a political dialectic between the self-governing mass and the powerful few seeking to dominate, his narrative tells a different story. In England and France, he shows the victory of the minority, not a continuing conflict, and a victory that owes as much to the moral failures of the masses as to those of the dominant few. In America he shows an escape from the dialectic, caused, on the one hand, by the foresight and self-restraint of the few and, on the other, by an Anglo-Saxon tradition that supposedly sustains this political dialectic through its respect for individual freedom.

V

Dos Passos's second book about the founding fathers, *The Men Who Made the Nation* (1957), also projects a view of American political life as determined by compromise rather than contention. He begins by representing Hamilton, Madison, and Jefferson agreeing on the need for a strong continental government. Jefferson's plan for Virginia's cession of western lands to Congress is said to reflect this, as does Morris's plan for the assumption and funding of state and continental debts, which is to be the sugar for the pill of the surrender of western claims. Men with interests in land companies, including Washington and George Mason, are said to forget their private interest for the benefit of the nation of western lands, and the dispute of New York and New Hampshire over Green Mountain territory is arbitrated.

The split at the Constitutional Convention is not seen as having to do with the issue of more or less self-government but with the issue of having a central government at all. Yet he does advance as decisive James Wilson's argument that the people were "shut out of the federal government"[21] under the Continental Congress but were made the supreme authority under the new system. Dos Passos asserts that grassroots support for the new constitution won over the old Revolutionary leaders like Sam Adams and John Hancock, who were not initially supporters. Emphasizing discussion and compromise, he does not recount what was discussed and what compromised. He quotes (144) a letter from the committee that wrote out the Constitution that speaks of the sacrifice of interests to the greatest interest, the "creation of a nation." The man who saw money as the dominant force in his own society, who observed in *The Ground We Stand On* that after a revolution "a set of rules nobody had foreseen" appeared and that "King Status" was replaced by "Citizen Money," not "Citizen Man," writes about the Convention as if Charles Beard had never raised the question of the economic interpretation of the Constitution.

Only when Hamilton's policies begin to shape a government modeled on the British system does Dos Passos develop the clash of policies represented by Hamilton and Jefferson. Unlike Beard's account that shows the material benefits particular groups pursue, Dos Passos's narrative develops a vision of the people versus a special group that is much like the version of politics he advances but does not depict in *The Ground We Stand On*. For example, when the cabinet discusses Genet's recall, Washington is in favor because Robert Morris assures him that businessmen will support it. Jefferson sees Morris's rationale as a failure to trust in the "virtue and good sense of mankind" and a turn to other props.

One of the reasons Washington's and Hamilton's views are identified as special interests and Jefferson's as the people's is that Dos Passos sees events primarily through Jefferson's notes and letters. He never applies other material that casts doubts on Jefferson's identification of his interests with the people's. Hamilton is never taken at face value or on his own representation, while Jefferson always is. Dos Passos reinforces this effect by quoting from Brackenridge's *Incidents of the Insurrection in the Western Parts of Pennsylvania* (1795): "I knew well that secretary Hamilton would have a disposition against me. He would rather find the opposition to the law to have originated in the plan of some leading individuals, than with the mass of the people: for the excise law being a result of the finding system . . . it would save the pride of judgment to have it thought opposed by the seditious acts of one, or a few, rather than by the feeling of common sense of many" (290).

Dos Passos's handling of the tax treaty is also illuminating in this regard. Dos Passos blames Hamilton for the bad treaty Jay makes because Hamilton assured the British envoy that America would not take part in armed neutrality with Denmark and Sweden. To do so would have been a logical extension of Jefferson's policy of insistence on freedom of the seas. Without this threat, Jay can bring no pressure to bear on England. However, Hamilton's fiscal system depended on import taxes. In Hamilton's mind, anything that threatened Anglo-American trade threatened American credit and the Federalist party and, Dos Passos is careful to emphasize, America. Yet Dos Passos does not explain the Federalists' demand for ratification of the Jay treaty, which he describes as amounting to a return to colonial status on the ocean, as material self-interest. "It seemed to them," Dos Passos says, "that only Jay's treaty stood between them and bloody revolution." Washington felt "as Hamilton pretended to," that opposition to his administration was "opposition to law and order itself" (301).

The effect of all this is to reduce Hamilton as a representative of particular interests in America whose support is the true source of his power and enhance Hamilton as a Machiavellian trafficker in power. Dos Passos emphasizes Hamilton's power by portraying Washington as a man of easy emotion, subject to "towering rages" (310), unable to take criticism, and entirely under Hamilton's influence. To this Dos Passos adds Talleyrand's admiration of Hamilton as ranking with Pitt and Napoleon, while Hamilton is quoted as calling Talleyrand "the greatest of modern statesmen because he had so well known both to suffer wrong to be done and to do it" (310). In summary, Dos Passos quotes John Adams's thought that Hamilton was "the most restless, impatient, artful, indefatigable and unprincipled intriguer in the United States if not in the world" (374). The special group in this history, then, seems not so much to achieve particular material benefits but to achieve domination.

While the Hamilton that emerges from Dos Passos's narrative is not very different from the able, ambitious aristocrat familiar in school texts by the end of World War II, the figure of John Marshall might have surprised the reader of Adams and Beard, let alone Henry Steele Commager and Allan Nevins. Compared to Jefferson's "scholarly aloofness" stands Marshall's "gladhanding philistinism of the man of the people" (372). A man who works on the prejudices of the ill-educated although he doesn't believe in popular rule, he plays cards, drinks, pokes fun at booklearning and philosophy. When he runs for Congress, he is seen dancing with his supporters around a bonfire while they destroy opposition votes. He marries into a family that never forgives Jefferson for the repeal of the laws of entail and his criticism of slavery. His wife is the daughter of a woman Jefferson courted and fell out with during his student days. He takes a mission to France for the money he will get out of it and makes $19,000. His brothers lay claim to a large tract of land; if made good, the claim will dispossess small landowners, and it depends on carrying out in the courts the terms of the Jay treaty with which Jefferson was so unhappy.

Like Marshall and Hamilton, Robert Morris represents the dangerous forces inherent in Washington's view of government and in his administration. Washington, who is shown to be a man without good judgment and the self-discipline that Dos Passos admires everywhere in his histories as the necessary brake to power, loves the speculative financier Robert Morris, and he defers to him both in matters of taste in home furnishings and matters of political principle. In the context of Washington's long admiration of Morris, the scene where Washington visits Morris in jail becomes a cautionary tale.²² Dos Passos contrasts the asparagus, strawberries, plums, pears, and grapes of three seasons from The Hills, Morris's fine estate, and the Prime Street Jail of his winter of bankruptcy and says, "the man whose financial judgment and whose taste in worldly things Washington had always deferred to had managed to keep in the air, by endless juggling of paper and kiting of promissory notes, an unbelievable structure of interlocking partnerships, land options, loans, mortgages, speculations in everything from ships' timbers to snuff boxes. With the tightening of credit that followed the failure of the Bank of England the whole thing crashed; ingenious men figured that Morris and John Nicolson, his latest partner in dishonor, were in default when the bailiffs at last seized hold of them, of something like thirty-four millions of dollars" (382).

While Morris's failure reveals the greed and dishonesty that was inextricable from Federalist ideals of political organization, Washington's death removes the veil from Hamilton's ambition. As long as Washington lived, Dos Passos argues, his beneficence obscured Hamilton's true purposes. He shows Hamilton's emotion at Washington's death to be bitterness at the recognition of his own indebtedness to the man who was in Hamilton's words "an *Aegis very essential to me*" (390). As Hamilton emerges from behind Washington's protection he appears more nakedly as a threat to the nation rather than its maker. John Adams's administration is less central to the narrative than the downward curve of Hamilton's career. The reasons for Adams's political failure remain unexplored. He figures largely as a man who could have removed the obstructive Hamiltonians from government long before he did, so that he appears there, as well as in the making of peace with France, in the weak role of a man who came to good actions too late to forestall the harm already done. Hamilton looms as the dark figure, seemingly responsible for the split that was to destroy the Federalists. Dos Passos never makes it clear whether Adams cannot get good men to serve because he is a bad judge of men or because of the political disintegration of his party. When his presidency comes to an end, again it is Hamilton who dominates Dos Passos's account of the political stalemate of the 1800 election. He is shown to be obsessed with keeping Aaron Burr out of the presidency, but while the narrative recounts the political argument for excluding Burr that he gave Jefferson, we are not invited to believe them. Rather, Burr is made to seem bad for the country in the same way Hamilton was bad: they were both men of imperial ambition. Hamilton has already been linked with James Wilkinson in a scheme to take Spanish lands. Hamilton and Burr figure as men who recognize in each other the Napoleonic urge and as a result ultimately destroy each other.

Jefferson, in contrast, figures as a man who does not reach out for power. In Adams's view, which Dos Passos is careful to give us, Jefferson could have secured his election by agreeing to the Federalists' four points, but he does not, and he is shown to be relatively passive throughout the crisis. Yet Dos Passos seems to imply that it is the lack of the drive to power rather than the lack of a spirit of compromise that causes his inaction, for the concluding chapter, which opens with his inaugural, emphasizes Jefferson's theme of conciliation, the theme with which the book opened. The period of an antagonistic political life, of suppression of opposition to the government, of fear of the principles of equality and fraternity is over. Jefferson, not Hamilton, lays "open a path of empire to American settlement" (449). Dos Passos points to the purchase of Louisiana at the moment when Hamilton is demanding a new army and war measures. Hamilton's opposition to the Essex Junto is made to lie, not in any rejection of the principle of nullification, but in his distress over its plan to have Burr lead a new confederacy.

The portraits of these men in *The Men Who Made the Nation*, more than the biographical elements in *The Ground We Stand On*, show how personal and public interest merge to create a sense of history as a process in which there is no dichotomy between private action and public. While *U.S.A.* emphasized how people are locked into the larger communal actions from which there is no escape and underscored the lack of individual freedom, Dos Passos' histories emphasize that history is not a matter of forces acting upon people but a process by which they secure their material lives and establish their place in a common way of life. The essence of such a history is not a conflict with repeated revolution and rebellion, as in Charles Beard's very popular *The Rise of American Civilization* (1927), but ongoing compromise. Men like Hamilton threaten not only the young republic but Dos Passos's vision of the process, and his fate is revealing not only of Dos Passos's view of the significance of early American politics but of political action itself.

The Men Who Made the Nation moves toward Hamilton's death and with it the death of the opposition "to republican and attachment to monarchical government" (457) that Gouverneur Morris identified Hamilton with in his funeral oration. Hamilton represents the forces of aggressive egoism that threaten the compromise that made the nation possible. He also represents the claims to superior status that is the social form of that egoism. Dos Passos illustrates this by referring his expression of religious emotion, a feature of his life during Jefferson's administration, to his desire to combine "hightoned religion with hightoned politics" and throw the "atheistic Republicans out of office" (452). Yet Dos Passos quotes Hamilton's letter to his wife that allows us to conclude that his religious scruples prevent him from shooting at Burr and cost him his life. And he also quotes from Morris's oration the telling line: "You have seen him contending against you, and saving your dearest interests as it were in spite of yourselves" (456).

The narrative moves from the funeral oration to Aaron Burr's flight from the city after the duel. Dos Passos quotes from correspondence that describes Burr as "that little devil" and shows him practicing with his pistol the morning after the duel, while the last sentence brings Jefferson and Hamilton together in a final reconciliation. As if in answer to the request Morris made in his funeral oration—"And now you feel the benefits resulting from the firm Energy of his Conduct. Bear this testimony to the Memory of my departed Friend. I charge you to protect his fame"—Jefferson places Hamilton's bust in his university "collection of great men." Hamilton cannot be allowed to remain the illegitimate stranger Morris's oration has called him. His Napoleonic ambitions are reduced in Morris's rhetoric to vanity and "indiscretion." He has fought the people, but he has defended their interests. Nor is his death on republican consciences. The true outsider is Burr. He has enacted the terrible possibilities only potential in Hamilton and will carry as a fugitive the guilt of aggression and the pursuit of power beyond the community, which now may safely install Hamilton in its pantheon.

In *The Ground We Stand On*, as John Diggins argues, Dos Passos found in his early American figures "legitimate moral authority that could be entrusted with power" (95). Their moral authority comes from inner restraints on their exercise of power. The stated dialectic that is supposed to maintain a healthy balance between the masses and the few does not play that part in the narrative. America is conceived of as a middle ground where the autocracy of England and the post-revolutionary tyranny of France cannot prosper. In that middle ground, the grasp on power is weak. Just as Sam Adams defuses the anarchic desires of the masses and integrates their energy into the Revolution, so Washington and Hamilton set limits through their inner decency to the ambitions of the favored. In *The Men Who Made the Nation,* the pattern of the narrative is just as clear, yet the book moves toward an equivocal conclusion. The compromise of the Constitution with which it opens is endangered by Federalist excess, by an exaggeration of the power of the few. The monarchy declined by Washington in *The Ground We Stand On* remains a threat, as his party seems to crave a return to the forms and exercise of power of the English system. While Jefferson's inauguration seems to argue a return to the balance of the opening, in fact only the death of Hamilton, which is like the assassination of Caesar (a similarity enforced by Dos Passos's quotation from Gouverneur Morris's oration, so obviously imitative of Antony's speech over Caesar's body in *Julius Caesar*), really makes the nation safe.

VI

The Shackles of Power represents a retreat from an investment in the American government achieved through the compromise and self-restraint of the founding fathers. Through the diary of a Federalist senator, William Plumer, who finds himself moving toward the Republicans, Dos Passos further develops the portrait of Jefferson as a "safe" president. He is distinguished in Plumer's eyes by "more honesty and integrity" than most in "higher ranks."[23] Not a man of the world, impractical, credulous, with defects of the head not the heart, Jefferson continues to figure in Dos Passos' vision of justice and power as an essentially private person, not comfortable with institutionalized authority, easily misunderstood by the public. In this book's version of the tie with Burr, Dos Passos makes Burr, through his own greater interest in money and status, surrender his chances at the presidency, so that Jefferson can appear to accept rather than grasp at it. The drama in the House, with Gallatin mustering Jefferson's supporters, goes unreported here.

The failure of the government to prosecute Burr successfully in Henry Adams's account was in part Jefferson's failure, in part the failure of talent in the government, and in part the result of the care the framers of the Constitution took to prevent the abuse of power by government. In Dos Passos's narrative, Marshall appears to express great animus toward Jefferson in his decisions and is reported to attend a dinner for Burr. Furthermore, his interpretations of the meaning of treason during the trial, which Adams construes as safeguarding individual rights, appear capricious. His portrait of Jefferson makes clear that Dos Passos cannot remain at ease with the government whose establishment he has praised. Because in Don Passos's history there can be no "private" life apart from the public, we must expect that Jefferson's life in this narrative which he dominates will constitute a criticism of the existing government and a suggestion of possibilities not yet realized.

Federalist figures against whom Republican ideals can be effectively juxtaposed recede. Dos Passos does not shape, as Adams did, the account of the War of 1812 in terms of Federalist-Republican conflict or in terms of the growth, either sought for or ironically achieved, of a strong nationalist government. As the egalitarian ideals Jefferson espoused seemed to become more safely ensconced in a government dominated by Republicans, Dos Passos emphasizes the ways in which Jefferson moved away from that accomplishment of earlier compromises. He stresses Jefferson's Bill for the More General Diffusion of Learning in which wards would have the responsibility not only for schools but for the care of the poor, roads, police, elections, jurors, and the administration of justice. The wards are seen as better units of administration for these matters than the states or the Republic. Meeting on a particular issue simultaneously, they would enable the state to act on the sense of the people. So through Jefferson, Dos Passos returns to his own earliest ideals of village communities, essentially anarchist, ruling themselves by self-restraint and consensus. For the same reason, he highlights the importance of John Taylor's *Enquiry into the Principles and Policies of the Governments of the United States* for Jefferson's thinking about a new constitution for Virginia. Dos Passos ascribes to Jefferson his own admiration of New England townships as the best units for self-government.

Jefferson's plan for education, especially his efforts to establish the University of Virginia, are followed in greater detail than any of his political activities. In this volume, for the first time in Dos Passos' histories, he becomes central; earlier he was peripheral, rarely the dominant actor effecting his will. Hamilton, Washington, Burr, and Marshall were more figures of conflict than Jefferson. His victories, like the Louisiana Purchase, come as the avoidance of conflict. Otherwise, in Virginia politics he is a scapegoat and in international affairs his policy of coercion short of war is seen as falling to accidents of time and distance; he cannot publish because he is misunderstood and cannot endure public controversy. This is the Jefferson Dos Passos gives us, a Jefferson who sees his most important gift to the nation the university he labors indefatigably to bring into existence.

Dos Passos uses Tocqueville's visit to America and his comments on it to underscore what he sees as central in Jefferson's final response to American politics. Tocqueville admires, as Jefferson would, "the idea of the state being a union of small republics" (391) suggested to him by Josiah Quincy, the president of Harvard. He begins to see, as Dos Passos implied Jefferson saw, "the New England town as the key to American democracy." The significance of the title of the history, *The Shackles of Power,* becomes clear only in this last section, as we realize that Jefferson is the president in Dos Passos's pantheon who shrinks from the wielding of power and the exploitation and aggression that Dos Passos sees as inextricable from it. The only sort of power Dos Passos can assent to as legitimate is the power of knowledge. Every other sort is to him merely force. So, like Henry Adams, he admires Gallatin who turns down the job of secretary of the treasury in favor of a diplomatic post. Adams sees it as a refusal of power, the act of a true statesman. Dos Passos sees it as the choice of power: "In Europe as 'a private gentlemen' he was courted and admired for his achievements. His native language was French, the language of scholarship and diplomacy. As plain Albert Gallatin he was a power in the world" (270). We are reminded of the repeated appearance in Dos Passos's fiction about World War I of the figure of the gentleman volunteer, courageous and debonair, free both of the lust for power and the mean-mindedness of the bureaucrat. The power of government itself is always problematic for Dos Passos. The reader senses that, unlike Henry Adams, Dos Passos is not sorry to see Jefferson fail in exercising it.

Dos Passos makes a distinction between the power of government and true service to the nation. Through Tocqueville's reaction to democracy in America, Dos Passos expresses his own distaste for a government he recognizes as mild and paternal but controlling every aspect of life. Tocqueville sees the future American citizen enmeshed and inhibited by rules, "complicated, minute and uniform." Even worse he imagines men "alike and equal, endlessly turning in on themselves to procure small and vulgar pleasures." A stranger to all but his family and friends, the American, thought Tocqueville and Dos Passos with him, "has no country" (403–4). The patriotic ideal for Dos Passos is to live a public life but outside the sphere of politics. The political life that he celebrated in *The Ground We Stand On* as the particular talent and gift of the Anglo-Saxon strain in America in this last of his important histories is one to be avoided. Its heritage is alienation.

In *The Ground We Stand On*, Dos Passos saw the nineteenth century as regression from the eighteenth, as breaking the promises of the late eighteenth-century revolutions. He appeared there to be characterizing the French experience and specifically isolating the American political life as distinct from either English or French. In *The Men Who Made the Nation*, the tension between the few who sought power and the many who resisted is resolved at the beginning in the consensus that created the Constitution and at the end in Hamilton's death and transfiguration as the man who served the people's interests though he was their antagonist. But the dialectic of the few and the many was weakened from the beginning by Dos Passos's insistence that in America at least, the Anglo-Saxon political heritage included internal decencies that drew the teeth of the most aggressive seekers of power. His vision of the conflict at the heart of American political life was always muted. Yet this was never the case in *U.S.A.* There the conflict was unlimited, and events in Europe, instead of being the means of distinguishing American political experience from the rest of the failed world, became in World War I the extension and embodiment of the conflict that was American reality. In the histories, Dos Passos's celebration of the high point of Anglo-Saxon political life is inseparable from its nadir and betrayal in Tocqueville's vision of the citizen who has no country. The very quality that Dos Passos singles out as vital for the success of government in *The Ground We Stand On*—the parenting instinct—is identified with the enslavement of the American of the future through its mild paternalism. The muting of the tension between the few and the many that is creative in the first two histories is destructive in the third, and it is destructive for Dos Passos as a writer as well. That tension was the organizing principle in the first two books. With its disappearance, Dos Passos is unable to find an alternative structure for *The Shackles of Power*, which remains diffuse and shapeless, its progress dictated by mere chronology and the accidents of research.

Yet, through the aging Jefferson and the young Tocqueville, Dos Passos seeks to maintain the tension. The legacy of the founding fathers has turned, in this third view of it, into the bonds from which they would now free us. What was once liberation is now constraint. Against the tyranny of France, on the one hand, and England, on the other, this legacy was the ground to be won. Threatened by Hamilton, it was to be defended. Once out of danger, the new government itself becomes the condition against which the autonomous self must struggle if it is to feel itself free. The vision of the ward and the New England town meeting opposed to the state and federal governments tries without success to reestablish the tension Dos Passos feels to be creative in history.

In *The Big Money* (1936), which closes the virtual history of *U.S.A.*, the central historical event is the Sacco and Vanzetti affair. The failure to prevent their execution results in Camera Eye 50 which asserts that "we are two nations" (462). The government appears as the front for "strangers" who have appropriated the language, laws, and resources of America and defeated the country. Yet the language, "the old American speech," representing the true America, remains alive in immigrant mouths and in the writing of the men who were executed. The immigrant nation and the stranger nation form the dialectic that Dos Passos would posit in *The Ground We Stand On* as the process that made America possible. But in the virtual history of *U.S.A.*, that dialectic is embodied in bloody conflict and death. The end of the novel is a powerful vision of a defeated America, and while the promise of the Camera Eye is that the language of democracy lives on, *The Big Money* makes no suggestion how the battle can be resumed. The two nations are as far apart as the affluent plane passenger and the starving Vag who sees the plane in the sky above him. The absence of conflict in *The Ground We Stand On*, the powerful impulse toward conciliation in *The Men Who Made the Nation*, and the weak attempt at restoration of a dialectic in *The Shackles of Power* suggest that Dos Passos could not imagine its resumption and hoped to find other principles to explain experience. Yet the authorial voice of these histories, as we have seen, shows no sign of awareness that its insistence on the importance of conflict between the many and the few is contradicted by the narrative itself. The disparity between his virtual history and his actual historical writings and the contradictions in the histories themselves point to the failure of the imaginative impulse that made Dos Passos's major works possible. The histories show that the most powerful effort in realist literature to overcome the inadequacy of individual consciousness to experience by using the historical model had come to an end. He continued to use the technical innovations he had devised for *U.S.A.* in his later novels but the vision that informed them disappeared. The fragmented and baffled but richly particularized lives of the powerful and the vulnerable alike, the world without a moral center where every action is worthy of the moral scourging Dos Passos's mordant humor administers, the promise of transcendence for the reader, though not for the characters who cannot rise above their individual consciousness, all this eludes Dos Passos's grasp for the remainder of a long career.

Dos Passos thus marks the end of a period when historical writing in America was in great ferment, richly alive with questions about the sources of power in the historical process and in American history particularly. Like Adams he imagined the writing of history not only as the revelation of hidden reality but as a weapon in the struggle to assimilate, not be assimilated by, the swirling patterns of social change. While Adams projected a very limited role for the individual, an exertion over the lines of power through comprehension and prediction, Dos Passos hoped that the individual could recover his lost power not only through historical knowledge but in group action. The threat to individual autonomy and the rational life that Adams exposed for his culture brought James, Howells, and Dos Passos all to history as a way of surmounting individual powerlessness. Only Dreiser worked out the implications of Adams's fears while denying the significance or importance of history.

As part of an intellectual milieu that seems entirely absorbed by the single perception so well exemplified in Hayden White's study of history, that we can never experience what really happened directly, that we never know the past but only texts, we ought to be energized by the work of these men. Edward Said reminds us now of what these novelists and historians knew well and acted on, that "texts are worldly, to some degree they are events and . . . a part of the social world, human life, and of course the historical moment in which they are located."[24] These writers shared the perception of the gap between justice and power, between reason and society. Whether or not they believed these gaps could be narrowed, they hoped that by replacing social myths and comfortable fables with historical explanations they could arrive at a solid foundation for a more rational and humane existence.

Notes

Index

Notes

Introduction

1. Ralph Waldo Emerson, "History" (1841), in *The Selected Writings of Ralph Waldo Emerson* (New York: Random House, Modern Library, 1940), p. 126.

2. Henry Adams, *The Education of Henry Adams* (New York: Random House, Modern Library, 1931), p. 439.

3. Erich Auerbach, *Mimesis: The Representation of Reality in Western Literature*, trans. Willard R. Trask (Princeton, N.J.: Princeton University Press, 1968), p. 491.

4. Leopold von Ranke, Preface to *Histories of the Latin and Germanic Nations from 1494–1514,* in *Varieties of History,* ed. Fritz Stern (New York: Meridien, 1956), p. 57.

5. R. G. Collingwood, *The Idea of History* (Oxford: Clarendon Press, 1946), pp. 233–34. Collingwood's lectures were originally delivered in 1936, but their publication was delayed by the war.

6. Wilhelm Dilthey, "The Dream," in *The Philosophy of History in Our Time,* ed. Hans Meyeroff (New York: Doubleday, 1959), p. 43.

7. Georg Lukács, *The Theory of the Novel,* trans. Anna Bostock (Cambridge, Mass.: MIT Press, 1971), p. 81.

8. See Hayden White, *Metahistory: The Historical Imagination in Nineteenth-Century Europe* (Baltimore: Johns Hopkins University Press, 1973), pp. 170–71.

9. Thomas Carlyle, "Biography," in *Critical and Miscellaneous Essays,* (1832; reprint, London, 1866), 3: 38.

10. See, for example, John A. Garraty, *The Nature of Biography* (New York: Knopf, 1957), p. 3. This historical survey has not been very much improved upon by later work, although the student of biography must consult Paul Murray Kendall, *The Art of Biography* (New York: Norton, 1965); Alan Shelton, *Biography* (London: Methuen, 1977); James L. Clifford, ed., *Biogra-*

phy as an Art (New York: Oxford University Press, 1962); Daniel Aaron, ed., *Studies in Biography* (Cambridge, Mass.: Harvard University Press, 1978); Anthony M. Friedson, ed., *New Directions in Biography* (Honolulu: University Press of Hawaii, 1981); and Marc Pachter, *Telling Lies* (Philadelphia: University of Pennsylvania Press, 1981).

11. Kendall, *The Art of Biography*, p. 14.

12. James Clifford, "Hanging Up Looking Glasses at Odd Corners: Ethnobiographical Prospects," in Aaron, *Studies in Biography*, p. 44.

13. See Sacvan Bercovitch, *The Puritan Origins of the American Self* (New Haven: Yale University Press, 1975), especially chaps. 1 and 2. See also an early view, Dana K. Merrill, *The Development of American Biography* (Portland, Maine: Southworth Press, 1932), pp. 17 ff.

14. Cushing Strout, "Ego Psychology and the Historian," in *The Veracious Imagination: Essays on American History, Literature, and Biography* (Middletown, Conn.: Wesleyan University Press, 1981), p. 237.

15. James posed his question in "Great Men and Their Environment" (1880). Fiske replied in "An Evolutionist's Reply to Dr. James," quoted in Garraty, *The Nature of Biography*, p. 110.

16. Peter Gay interestingly argues in *The Bourgeois Experience: Victoria to Freud* (New York: Oxford University Press, 1984) that the idea of respectability in the Victorian age cannot be separated from the emergence of a sphere of privacy in which intimacy and expression were indulged.

17 For the same reason Collingwood regarded biography as distinct from history. However, his idea that the framework of biography is natural process while the framework of history is thought is the kind of opposition that Adams, the first figure in this study, and Dos Passos, the last, would both disagree with for quite different reasons. *The Idea of History*, p. 304.

1

1. George Levine argues persuasively that in English fiction of the mid-nineteenth century, realism was already self-conscious about the necessary failure of its claims to an unmediated vision of a coherent reality. See *The Realist Imagination: English Fiction from Frankenstein to Lady Chatterly* (Chicago: University of Chicago Press, 1981).

2. Henry Adams, *History of the United States of America during the Administration of Thomas Jefferson*, 2 vols., intro. Henry Steele Commager (New York: Albert and Charles Boni, 1930), 1:xii.

3. Henry Adams, *History of the United States of America during the Administrations of Jefferson and Madison*, 9 vols. (New York: Scribner's, 1889–91), 9:224–25.

4. See Richard C. Vitzthium, *The American Compromise: Theme and Method in the Histories of Bancroft, Parkman, and Adams* (Norman: University of Oklahoma Press, 1974) for a different perspective on Adams's relation to Parkman and Bancroft. He sees Adams as the culmination of a tradition that includes the other two.

5. John Higham's survey of American historiography from the nine-

teenth to the twentieth century gives an excellent account of the emergence and fate of scientific history. He characterizes scientific history as resisting large theories, while Jordy identifies August Comte's call for generalizations that hold for more than one sequence of events as its touchstone. I think Higham and Jordy disagree because they emphasize different periods and downplay contradictions integral to the movement as a whole. Adams's own debt to Comte is clearer in his work after the *History,* but as early as his biography of John Randolph (1882), he was making a distinction between the narrative of the historian and the theory of the political scientist. Yet when Higham describes the way social scientists increasingly distinguished themselves in the twentieth century from historians because they saw historians as surrendering their earlier emphasis on comparative analysis and their interest in the model of evolutionary change, then he implies the coexistence of a search for generalizations and a resistance to large theories early in scientific history, a contradiction that may be partially explained by a third belief, that the "facts" themselves in proper sequence would reveal their explanation. In the *History,* there is no hint of difficulty in establishing sequence, only the disappointment of the historian in what the sequence reveals. Adams's later career is marked by an agonizing search for other kinds of sequence and a continued belief that once sequence was properly established, historical meanings would emerge. See John Higham et al., *History* (Englewood Cliffs, N.J.: Prentice-Hall, 1965), pp. 107 ff.; and William Jordy, *Henry Adams: Scientific Historian* (New Haven: Yale University Press, 1952), pp. 1–23.

6. William Dusinberre, *Henry Adams: The Myth of Failure* (Charlottesville: University Press of Virginia, 1980), pp. 116–22.

7. Alexis de Tocqueville, *Democracy in America,* vol. 2, bk. 1, chap. 20, quoted in J. C. Levenson, *The Mind and Art of Henry Adams* (Boston: Houghton Mifflin, 1957), p. 126.

8. George Hochfield, *Henry Adams, an Introduction and Interpretation* (New York: Barnes and Noble, 1962), p. 55.

9. Melvin Lyon, *Symbol and Idea in Henry Adams* (Lincoln: University of Nebraska Press, 1970), p. 71.

10. Henry Adams, *John Randolph* (Greenwich, Conn.: Fawcett, 1961), p. 26.

2

1. Henry Adams, *The Life of Albert Gallatin* (New York: Peter Smith, 1943), p. 67; and *John Randolph* (Greenwich, Conn.: Fawcett, 1961), p. 23.

2. Melvin Lyon, *Symbol and Idea in Henry Adams* (Lincoln: University of Nebraska Press, 1970), p. 19.

3. J. C. Levenson, *The Mind and Art of Henry Adams* (Boston: Houghton Mifflin, 1957), pp. 20–23.

4. Adams to Henry Cabot Lodge, 6 Oct. 1879, *Letters of Henry Adams, 1858–1918,* 2 vols. ed. Worthington Chauncey Ford (Boston: Houghton Mifflin, 1930, 1938), 1:314.

5. See William Dusinberre, *Henry Adams: The Myth of Failure* (Charlottesville: University Press of Virginia, 1980).

3

1. For the most recent example of this point of view, see John Carlos Rowe, *Henry Adams and Henry James: The Emergence of a Modern Consciousness* (Ithaca, N.Y.: Cornell University Press, 1976). Following in a long tradition, Rowe sees the book moving toward the exaltation of art as the means of organizing experience when reason fails. Adams, in this view, is a protomodernist who surrenders truth for design. Charles R. Anderson also agrees that Adams's purpose was to "grasp unity through the vision of the anarchist, the historian's view being inadequate." See "Henry Adams, 1838–1918," in *Critical Essays on Henry Adams,* ed. Earl N. Harbert (Boston: G. K. Hall, 1981), pp. 115–39.

2. For the first, see Melvin Lyon, *Symbol and Idea in Henry Adams* (Lincoln: University of Nebraska Press, 1970). For the second, see J. C. Levenson, *The Mind and Art of Henry Adams* (Boston: Houghton Mifflin, 1957). For the third, see William Dusinberre, *Henry Adams: The Myth of Failure* (Charlottesville: University Press of Virginia, 1980). R. P. Blackmur's view of *Mont-Saint-Michel and Chartres* as organized by its three conceptions of God also makes unavoidable an essentially ahistorical view of *Chartres* and makes it impossible for him to integrate the chapters on philosophy into his structure. See *Henry Adams,* ed. Veronica A. Makowsky (New York: Harcourt Brace Jovanovich, 1980), p. 178.

3. Henry Adams, *Mont-Saint-Michel and Chartres* (Boston: Houghton Mifflin, 1963), p. 1.

4. See, for example, vol. 1, chap. 2 of Henry Adams, *History of the United States of America,* 9 vols. (New York: Scribner's, 1889–91). Also pp. 10–16 and 71–74.

5. See for example, Adams's reflections on Jefferson's foreign policy, ibid., 4:74, 136.

6. See also Henry Adams, *The Life of Albert Gallatin* (New York: Peter Smith, 1943).

7. Indeed, Rowe sees the architects of Chartres as coping with the inaccessibility of God's justice. See *Henry Adams and Henry James,* p. 73.

8. Although in speaking of Adams's rejection of history for art, Rowe also remarks the extent to which *Chartres* shows the "successive breakdown of old systems of order and the quest for new forms and original symbols." See ibid., p. 73.

9. Here I diverge from Anderson's view that love of the Virgin led to the synthesis of St. Thomas. See "Henry Adams, 1838–1918," pp. 128–29.

10. Adams to Brooks Adams, 4 March 1900, quoted in Levenson, *The Mind and Art,* p. 296.

11. *Henry Adams and His Friends: A Collection of His Unpublished Letters,* ed. Harold Dean Cater (Boston: Houghton Mifflin, 1947), p. 134.

4

1. John Carlos Rowe, *Henry Adams and Henry James: The Emergence of a Modern Consciousness* (Ithaca, N.Y.: Cornell University Press, 1976), p. 97.

2. Henry Adams, "The Rule of Phase Applied to History," in *The Degra-*

dation of the Democratic Dogma, intro. Brooks Adams (New York: Peter Smith, 1948), pp. 308–10 ff.

3. Henry Adams, *The Education of Henry Adams* (New York: Random House, Modern Library, 1931), p. 273.

4. Especially William Jordy, *Henry Adams: Scientific Historian* (New Haven: Yale University Press, 1952).

5. William Dusinberre, *Henry Adams: The Myth of Failure* (Charlottesville: University Press of Virginia, 1980).

6. Adams to William James, 27 July 1882, *Henry Adams and His Friends: A Collection of His Unpublished Letters,* ed. Harold Dean Cater (Boston: Houghton Mifflin, 1947), p. 122.

7. "Letter to American Teachers of History," in *The Degradation of the Democratic Dogma,* pp. 112–13.

8. James to Henry Adams, 17 June 1910 and 26 June 1910, *Letters of William James,* ed. Henry James 2 vols. (Boston: Atlantic Monthly Press, 1920), 2:346–47.

5

1. Sergio Perosa, *James and the Experimental Novel* (Charlottesville: University Press of Virginia, 1978), p. 19.

2. Henry James, *The Bostonians* (New York: Random House, Modern Library, 1956), p. 407.

3. David C. Stineback, *The Shifting World: Social Change and Nostalgia in the American Novel* (Lewisburg, Pa.: Bucknell University Press, 1976), p. 75.

4. Peter Buitenhuis sees a "lack of emotional commitment" in James to his characters. See *The Grasping Imagination: The American Writings of Henry James* (Toronto: University of Toronto Press, 1970), p. 159. C. T. Samuels finds *The Bostonians* "an unusually amoral novel" for James. See *The Ambiguity of Henry James* (Champaign: University of Illinois Press, 1971), p. 98.

5. Stineback agrees with Irving Howe that Basil wins because his ideology merely exploits the rhythms of life while Olive's violates them. In this perspective, Verena's choice does illuminate the historical themes, but that is to suppose that James sees the woman's right movement as Basil sees it. See Irving Howe, Introduction, James, *The Bostonians,* and David Stineback, *The Shifting World.*

6. Frederick J. Hoffman relates this to the function of the novel of manners. See "The Princess Casamassima: Violence and Decorum," in *Henry James's Major Novels: Essays in Criticism,* ed. Lyall Powers (East Lansing: Michigan State University Press, 1973), p. 142.

7. Charles R. Anderson, *Person, Place, and Thing in Henry James's Novels* (Durham, N.C.: Duke University Press, 1977), p. 126.

8. Henry James, *The Princess Casamassima* (New York: Harper and Row, 1959), p. 241.

9. J. M. Leuche, "The Princess Casamassima: Hyacinth's Fallible Consciousness," in *Henry James: Modern Judgements,* ed. Tony Tanner (New York: Macmillan, 1968).

10. Lionel Trilling, "The Princess Casamassima," in *Henry James's Major Novels*, ed. Powers, p. 124.

11. James to Charles Eliot Norton, Dec. 6, 1886, *Henry James Letters, 1883–1895*, ed. Leon Edel (Cambridge, Mass.: Harvard University Press, 1980), p. 146.

12. Henry James, *A Little Tour of France*, quoted in Oscar Cargill, *The Novels of Henry James* (New York: Macmillan, 1961), p. 151.

13. For example, Trilling claims that Hyacinth's suicide is heroic in its acceptance of both parents. Leuche argues that it constitutes irresolution or weakness. See Trilling, "The Princess Casamassima," p. 125, and Leuche, "The Princess Casamassima," p. 188.

14. Henry James, *The Tragic Muse*, 2 vols. (New York: Scribner's, 1908), 1:xv.

15. Cargill, *The Novels of Henry James*, p. 189.

16. Quentin Anderson, *The American Henry James* (New Brunswick, N.J.: Rutgers University Press, 1957), p. 161.

6

1. William Dean Howells, *A Hazard of New Fortunes* (New York: New American Library, 1965), p. 265.

2. Kenneth S. Lynn, *William Dean Howells: An American Life* (New York: Harcourt Brace Jovanovich, 1970), p. 300.

3. Kermit Vanderbilt, *The Achievement of William Dean Howells: An Interpretation* (Princeton, N.J.: Princeton University Press, 1968), p. 146; George N. Bennett, *The Realism of William Dean Howells* (Nashville: Vanderbilt University Press, 1973), p. 36.

4. William Dean Howells, "On Ibsen," in *W. D. Howells as Critic*, ed. Edwin H. Cady (London: Routledge and Kegan Paul, 1973), p. 229.

5. Howells to Henry James, 10 Oct. 1888, *Life in Letters of William Dean Howells*, ed. Mildred Howells (Garden City, N.Y.: Doubleday, Doran, 1928), 1:417.

6. William Dean Howells, *Annie Kilburn* (New York: Harper and Bro., 1889), p. 49.

7. Kenneth Lynn thinks Peck's end "associates self-destruction with schemes for introducing middle class intellectuals to poverty," but Peck's scheme was for workers; he explicitly discouraged Annie. See *An American Life*, p. 292.

8. Hayden White, *Metahistory: The Historical Imagination in Nineteenth-Century Europe* (Baltimore: Johns Hopkins University Press, 1973), pp. 188–89.

9. Edwin Cady rightly sees this narrative mode as integral with his realism. "Howells' realist believed in persons in defiance of monism, whether monism lost men and women in soaring abstraction, the minuet of bloodless categories; or whether it lost men in vortices of blind force and chance." See *Howells as Critic*, p. 4.

10. William Dean Howells, *A Boy's Town* (New York: Harper Brothers, 1890), p. 185.

11. See, for example, Bennett, *Realism of Howells*, pp. 56, 59.

12. William Dean Howells, *The World of Chance* (New York: Harper Brothers, 1893), p. 88.

13. For these reasons I cannot follow Bennett when he argues that their love affair is not "a function of anything but their instinctive emotional responses." See *Realism of Howells*, p. 59.

7

1. Theodore Dreiser, *The Financier* (New York: New American Library, 1967), p. 126.

2. Ralph Waldo Emerson, *Representative Men, English Traits, and Other Essays* (London: Ward Loeb, 1912), p. 7.

3. Dreiser to William C. Lengel, 15 Oct. 1911, *Letters of Theodore Dreiser: A Selection*, 3 vols., ed. Robert H. Elias (Philadelphia: University of Pennsylvania Press, 1959), 1:121.

4. See, for example, Charles Walcutt, *American Literary Naturalism: A Divided Stream* (Minneapolis: University of Minnesota Press, 1956), p. 199, and Richard Lehan, *Theodore Dreiser: His World and His Ideas* (Carbondale: Southern Illinois University Press, 1969), p. 50.

5. H. L. Mencken, "The Dreiser Bugaboo," in *Critical Essays on Theodore Dreiser,* ed. Donald Pizer (Boston: G. K. Hall, 1981), p. 19. See also Walcutt, *American Literary Naturalism*, pp. 203–5, and Eliseo Vivas, "Dreiser: An Inconsistent Mechanist," in *Critical Essays,* ed. Pizer, pp. 35–37.

6. Donald Pizer, *The Novels of Theodore Dreiser: A Critical Study* (Minneapolis: University of Minnesota Press, 1976), pp. 170–71.

7. Donald Pizer, "Introduction," *Critical Essays,* pp. xi–xii. As Pizer notes, critics who have considered Dreiser's naturalism tend to see it not so much as a source of his power but as inconsistent with it. To extend Pizer's argument: Santayana, a philosphical naturalist also in revolt against the genteel tradition, saw the naturalist as one with Virgil in pity for the tears in things.

8. Alfred Kazin, Introduction, *The Stature of Theodore Dreiser: A Critical Survey of the Man and His Work,* ed. Alfred Kazin and Charles Shapiro (Bloomington: Indiana University Press, 1955), p. 10.

9. See also Roger Asselineau, "Theodore Dreiser's Transcendentalism," in *Critical Essays,* ed. Pizer, pp. 92–102. See especially p. 102.

10. Walcott believes that later in Dreiser's career he changed his mind; I see no evidence of this through the writing of *An American Tragedy.* See *American Literary Naturalism*, p. 120.

11. John J. McAleer, *Theodore Dreiser: An Introduction and Interpretation* (New York: Holt, Rinehart, Winston, 1968), p. 106.

12. See Warwick Wadlington, "Pathos and Dreiser," in *Critical Essays,* ed. Pizer. Wadlington also sees the pattern of submission and dominance as central to Dreiser and discusses it in the context of the basic mode of his writing, which he terms pathos in contradistinction to tragedy.

13. Larzer Ziff, Afterword, Dreiser, *The Financier*, p. 488.

14. Theodore Dreiser, *Hey Rub-a-Dub-Dub: A Book of the Mystery and Wonder and Terror of Life* (New York: Boni and Liveright, 1920), p. 158.

15. Theodore Dreiser, *An American Tragedy* (New York: New American Library, 1964), p. 190.

16. Theodore Dreiser, *Notes on Life*, ed. Marguerite Tjader and John J. McAleer (University Park: University of Alabama Press, 1972), p. 16.

17. Theodore Dreiser, *A Hoosier Holiday* (New York: John Lane, 1916), pp. 153–54.

18. Alfred Kazin, *On Native Grounds* (New York: Doubleday, 1956), pp. 62–63.

19. See chapter 3 of Ellen Moers, *The Two Dreisers* (New York: Viking, 1969).

20. Because David Weimer sees Dreiser's characters as innocents and Dreiser as aware of disaster, not evil, he links him with transcendentalism. Since goodness, not innocence, lies at the heart of the transcendentalist universe, Weimer seems instead to put his finger on the difference between naturalism and transcendentalism. See "Heathen Catacombs: The City as Metaphor," in *Critical Essays*, ed. Pizer, p. 133.

21. Only such a failure could lead acute critics like Charles Thomas Samuels to read this section as an account of Clyde's "essential innocence" or "his comparative virtue" or to suppose that Clyde accepts "an essentially Christian view of his guilt" from McMillan. See "Mr. Trilling, Mr. Warren, and *An American Tragedy*," in *Dreiser: A Collection of Critical Essays*. ed. John Lydenberg (Englewood Cliffs, N.J.: Prentice-Hall, 1971). See also Lehan, *Theodore Dreiser*, pp. 168–69.

8

1. Lionel Trilling, "The America of John Dos Passos," in *Dos Passos: A Collection of Critical Essays*, ed. Andrew Hook (Englewood Cliffs, N.J.: Prentice-Hall, 1974), p. 97.

2. Harry B. Henderson, *Versions of the Past: The Historical Imagination in American Fiction* (New York: Oxford University Press, 1974), pp. 243–45.

3. John P. Diggins, "Visions of Chaos and Visions of Order: Dos Passos as Historian," *American Literature* 46 (Nov. 1974): 334.

4. Paul Fussell, *The Great War and Modern Memory* (New York: Oxford University Press, 1975).

5. John Dos Passos, Introduction, *One Man's Initiation: 1917* (Ithaca, N.Y.: Cornell University Press, 1969), p. 22.

6. John Dos Passos, *The Best Times: An Informal Memoir* (New York: New American Library, 1966), p. 23.

7. See his excellent Introduction to *Dos Passos: Critical Essays*, pp. 1–12.

8. John Dos Passos, *Three Soldiers* (Boston: Houghton Mifflin, n.d.), p. 9.

9. John H. Wrenn, *John Dos Passos* (New York: Twayne, 1961), p. 112.

10. See Blanche Gelfant, *The American City Novel* (Norman: University of

Oklahoma Press, 1954), p. 139, and Kazin, *On Native Grounds* (New York: Doubleday, 1956), pp. 271–72.

11. John Dos Passos, *U.S.A.* (New York: Random House, 1939), 1:344.

12. See Jean-Paul Sartre, "John Dos Passos and *1919*," in *Dos Passos: Critical Essays,* ed. Hook, pp. 64–65.

13. See Arthur Mizener, "The Gullivers of Dos Passos," ibid., p. 164 ff.

14. Richard Chase did not find a recognizable voice in Dos Passos. See "The Chronicles of Dos Passos," ibid., p. 177.

15. See Blanche Gelfant, "The Search for Identity in the Novels of John Dos Passos," *PMLA* 74 (March 1961): 133–49.

16. Albert Camus, *The Myth of Sisyphus* (New York: Random House, 1955), a representative cultural essay throughout. See pp. 51–56 for Don Juanism.

17. Cushing Strout, "The Antihistorical Novel," in *The Veracious Imagination: Essays on American History, Literature, and Biography* (Middletown, Conn.: Wesleyan University Press, 1981), p. 184.

18. See David Sanders, "The Anarchism of John Dos Passos," *South Atlantic Quarterly* 60 (Winter 1961): 45–55.

19. John Dos Passos, *The Ground We Stand On: Some Examples from the History of a Political Creed* (New York: Harcourt, Brace, 1941).

20. Linda Wagner, *Dos Passos: Artist as American* (Austin: University of Texas Press, 1979), p. 145.

21. John Dos Passos, *The Men Who Made the Nation* (Garden City, N.Y.: Doubleday, 1957), p. 151.

22. John P. Diggins, *Up from Communism: Conservative Odysseys in American Intellectual History* (New York: Harper & Row, 1975), p. 95. Diggins thinks Dos Passos's treatment of Morris is uncritical, unlike the treatment of the speculators in *U.S.A.,* and an instance of the distance between the history and the fiction. I would argue that this episode with its implicit mockery of Washington, its cold-eyed view of Morris, and its withholding of explicit judgment might have come from a biography in *U.S.A.*

23. John Dos Passos, *The Shackles of Power: Three Jeffersonian Decades* (Garden City, N.Y.: Doubleday, 1966), p. 12 ff.

24. Edward W. Said, *The World, the Text, and the Critic* (Cambridge, Mass.: Harvard University Press, 1983), p. 4.

Index